POWER IN THE SOUTHERN CONE BORDERLANDS

An Anthropology of Development Practice

CARMEN A. FERRADÁS

BERGIN & GARVEY
Westport, Connecticut • London

Library of Congress Cataloging-in-Publication Data

Ferradás, Carmen A.
    Power in the Southern Cone borderlands : an anthropology of
development practice / Carmen A. Ferradás.
        p.   cm.
    Includes bibliographical references and index.
    ISBN 0–89789–560–6 (alk. paper)
    1. Entidad Binacional Yacyretá.   2. Hydroelectric power plants—
Social aspects—Argentina.   3. Hydroelectric power plants—Social
aspects—Brazil.   4. Hydroelectric power plants—Social aspects—
Paraguay.   I. Title.
HD9685.A74E584   1998
333.91'4'098—dc21   97–40997

British Library Cataloguing in Publication Data is available.

Library of Congress Catalog Card Number: 97–40997
ISBN: 0–89789–560–6

First published in 1998

Bergin & Garvey, 88 Post Road West, Westport, CT 06881
An imprint of Greenwood Publishing Group, Inc.

Printed in the United States of America

The paper used in this book complies with the
Permanent Paper Standard issued by the National
Information Standards Organization (Z39.48–1984).

10 9 8 7 6 5 4 3 2 1

For my mother,

Yvonne Larrieu–Let de Ferradás

Contents

Illustrations

Preface

Like thousands of other men and women, my grandparents came to Argentina dreaming of progress and committed to "hacer la América." They died without having made it but still hopeful of the prospects of the country. The generation of my parents shared these dreams and was somewhat luckier. My generation was not. We have been raised with a nostalgia for a grandiose past in which Argentina was one of the wealthiest nations on earth. In my childhood, development discourses promised a golden future in part based on the recovery of this idyllic past. We have witnessed economic depression, unemployment, and authoritarian brutality. Like my contemporaries, I have been puzzled with the resilience of the development chimera and I have been deeply concerned with the furthering of social inequalities. To ask questions about development is to ask questions about who we are and who we would like to be. This book explores such questions through following the long history of a development project, the Yacyretá hydroelectric dam.

Clearly, the ambitions of this book could not have been approached without the help of many. I owe much of my thinking to the inspiration provided by colleagues, friends, students, and, most of all, to the people of Posadas, Argentina, and Encarnación, Paraguay. Any inaccuracies and misinterpretations are my sole responsibility.

This book is the culmination to date of various metamorphoses in my theoretical interests and in the dynamics of the process under study. The content of a few chapters developed directly out of *Communication Processes in a Development Project. The Yacyretá Hydroelectric Dam* for which the Northeastern Council for Latin American Studies granted the best dissertation award.

In the early stages of this research I obtained invaluable help from the Universidad Nacional de Misiones. I will always be grateful to the encouragement from authorities and colleagues. I am particularly indebted to the faculty and students of the anthropology department.

Dionisio Baranger and Gabriela Schiavoni have generously shared their data on Misiones and offered me their friendship and intellectual support during my various visits to Posadas. Leopoldo Bartolomé, the major specialist in social impact of hydroelectric projects in Argentina, and a distinguished scholar in anthropology, encouraged me to study the case of Yacyretá. He shared his knowledge and expertise and was always a model of academic excellence and professional responsibility. I also thank him for his warm hospitality on my many visits to Misiones.

Many people at the Graduate School and University Center at the City University of New York helped me mature intellectually and discussed my work extensively. I will always be grateful to the invaluable guidance of June Nash. I was extremely lucky to have her as my mentor and my friend. She has taught me cherished lessons about the craft of anthropology, and, more importantly, about life, social commitment, and human integrity. Eric Wolf and Vincent Crapanzano guided me in my theoretical journeys and pushed me to think creatively and independently. I profited greatly from discussions with both of them.

In different stages of my research I obtained generous financial support from various institutions. The Organization of American States and the Wenner-Gren Foundation for Anthropological Research provided economic help for the first years of this study. The Consejo Nacional de Investigaciones Científicas y Técnicas (CONICET), granted me awards to cover field work and writing expenses. While teaching at Binghamton University, SUNY, I was awarded a Summer Research Grant and a Research semester award. With this help, I completed the last stages of my research and wrote the final version of this book.

Friends and intellectual companions came to my rescue in difficult times, and for this, I would always remember them. Some of them patiently listened to my dilemmas and made important suggestions to improve my ideas. In Posadas, Elena Krautstofl, Maria Rosa Fogel, Rosario Mottola, and Alicia Locket have joined me in my queries as professionals and friends. My assistants Susana Moniec, Gustavo Azar, and Nancy Albohaires contributed to important phases of field work and data analysis. At the GSUC at CUNY, I discussed my work with Cristiana Bastos, Bea Vidacs, Leyla Neyzi, Gustavo Ribeiro, Carmen Medeiros, Lygia Simonian, Maureen O'Dougherty, Aisha Khan, Alfredo González, Patricia Tovar, Robin Sheriff, and Tom Burgess. At Binghamton University, William Isbell, the former chair of the Department of Anthropology, and my colleagues Safia Mohsen, Richard Antoun, Richard Moench, Michael Horowitz, Neville Dyson-Hudson, and Randall McGuire mentored my work and encouraged me to finish this book. Many of the ideas explored in this book have been reworked after inspiring discussions with graduate students. María Lugones, the Director of the Latin American and Caribbean Program (LACAS) took special interest in this project and has made stimulating comments on my thoughts. Colleagues in the LACAS program and in sociology have followed my achievements and helped me survive in the difficult environment of academic life. I also thank the editorial staff at Greenwood Publishing Group for their assistance and patience through the production of this book.

My debts to the people of Posadas and Encarnación are enormous. Yacyretá staff from Paraguay and Argentina have volunteered important information. Municipal authorities and personnel from Posadas and Encarnación participated in interviews and generously gave me data on their cities and the Yacyretá dam. I cannot mention many of them by name because I want to preserve their anonymity. In Asunción,

Paraguay, I spent days studying the documents compiled by Base ECTA. I wish all members of institutions where we work were as helpful and friendly as those I found at Base ECTA.

Throughout these long years, my mother and my sisters Susana and Silvia have offered the emotional support to endure the hardships and joys of writing. At home, Tom Mellers helped me with the secrets of English writing and spent long hours reviewing my manuscript and making precious suggestions. During long stretches of my research and writing he fathered and mothered our dear daughter Ivana, whom, I hope one day would understand why her mother could not always play with her.

CHAPTER 1

Introduction

In 1996, the people of the Argentine province of Misiones overwhelmingly voted against the construction of the Corpus hydroelectric dam on the Paraná River. The vote sent a strong message to national authorities regarding energy policies that affect the environment and well-being of local populations. At the polls, the Misioneros expressed their anger and frustration with the failure of previously constructed gigantic hydroelectric dams to deliver on promises of regional development. By then, everybody in the region was well aware of the negative consequences of such projects. Their protracted experience with the Yacyretá dam, also built on the Paraná River, taught them valuable lessons. They had lost land and homes and increased their exposure to health risks in the name of "progress," yet the benefits of this process did not accrue to them. The energy from the hydrolectric project did not stay in the region.[1] It was sent to the most industrialized and developed areas of the country. Likewise, even though Paraguay is losing even more agricultural land than Argentina, and sacrificing the most bustling commercial part of the city of Encarnación, the current situation of four out of ten of Paraguayans will not improve: They will continue without electricity in their own homes. Despite the strong regional concern conveyed by the vote and massive popular demonstrations in the two countries to protest against dam projects, the president of Argentina, Carlos Saúl Menem, seemed quite untouched: He defiantly announced that he would go ahead with the Corpus project, which basically will produce energy for the industrial needs of Brazil, Argentina's new business partner in MERCOSUR, the Common Market of the Southern Cone.

The plebiscite vote highlights a saga that began more than twenty years ago, when the governments of Paraguay and Argentina signed an agreement to jointly construct the Yacyretá hydroelectric dam on the Paraná River. At the time negotiations started, Argentina was anxious to build this project to respond to what it believed was a threat to the geopolitical balance of power in the Río de la Plata Basin: The Itaipú dam, to be built by Brazil and Paraguay, also on the Paraná River (cf. Ribeiro 1994; *El Diario*, November 16, 1995).[2] Today, far from being concerned about the defense of the territorial integrity of a country endangered by

Brazilian expansionist appetites, the Argentine state seems quite eager to please its former geopolitical enemy.

What has happened in these last twenty years to foster such a radical change in the power dynamics of the Latin American Southern Cone region? Why have nation-states transformed their development rhetoric from representing hydroelectric projects as privileged vehicles for the promotion of national and regional economic growth and social well-being, to constructing them as "monuments of corruption," as President Carlos Menem did in 1989, and back to seeing them as "monuments of regional development" (*ABC Color*, November 15, 1995), as key resources for the industrial needs of the MERCOSUR? How did the local populations of the areas affected by dam construction respond to the changing messages of development and to the disruption of their everyday lives and the "manufactured uncertainty" [3] generated by the construction of a gigantic high dam? This book seeks to provide some answers to these questions.

To address these complex questions, I will analyze the case of the Yacyretá hydroelectric dam. I will do this by showing how and why the initial dream of development turned into the current, unfinished drama. I will present the history of this dam as an illustration of the transformation of development discourse and practice in recent decades—a process intimately linked to the new forms of accumulation of capital which are also profoundly altering the traditional role played by nation-states. I will provide some clues to understanding how local political cultures react under the increased influence of multiple global economic, social, and cultural forces. Because the events, negotiations, and struggles into which this book delves took shape in the borderlands of two Latin American Southern Cone countries, I will be able to show how territorial identities (national and regional) become imagined, manipulated, and transformed by virtue of *remapping* (Johnston, Taylor, and Watts 1995) and global attempts of "deterritorialization"—the sort of "phenomena in which the actual dynamics of a given location rely on and are shaped by forces that are decidedly nonlocal" (Deleuze and Guattari 1977 as cited in Pred and Watts 1992:11).[4] The issue here is to see how processes of regional integration, such as the creation of common market blocks and the construction of binational hydroelectric projects—which supposedly challenge the boundedness of nation-states—impinge upon spaces traditionally identified with the assertion of national sovereignty, such as frontiers. How do local people strategically organize to make claims and resist undesired socio-economic changes? Do they mobilize political, class, local, regional, or national identities when they participate in collective action against the planned interventions affecting their lives? As we will see, the residents of Posadas and Encarnación made use of various identities, depending on the time frame and location of the social interaction.

To tackle some of these issues, this study concentrates on different forms of power, mainly the power of people and the power of dams—insofar as they express the power of the "development apparatus" (Ferguson 1990). On the one hand, it unveils how dams have become powerful icons representing the power of technology and development planning. In analyzing the "power of dams," I will show the role played by hydroelectric projects in the modernization programs pursued by the Brazilian, Argentine, and Paraguayan governments. I will also discuss how these projects are now jeopardized under the conditions of the ironically dubbed "new world disorder" (Johnston, Taylor, and Watts 1995; Beck 1991, 1996). On the other hand, I am particularly interested in unraveling experts' and common people's power in affecting development outcomes (cf. Moran 1996). To achieve this goal, I focus on the particular relationship established between social planners and the population to be relocated with the construction of the dam. As we shall see, at different times during the long history of the project, different groups and individuals participated as promoters and mediators in the struggles of the population with national authorities and various regional and transnational development agencies. These strategic alliances, established to make particular demands regarding people's rights, will be discussed in the last chapters of this work.

Power, as we know by virtue of Foucault's (1980, 1988) explorations on this topic, is manifested, produced, and reproduced—although not exclusively —through discourses. By discourses, I understand those dynamic forms of knowledge and representation, themselves the result of creative recreations of past dialogues and struggles, which shape practices and condition the emergence of specific kinds of subjectivity.[5] We should be warned, as Harvey rightly suggests, against "discursive determinism"—the tendency to see us forever imprisoned by the discourses available to us—which Harvey argues was not the intention of Foucault but seems to have become the sole purpose of some of his followers (1996:95). Our purpose is to explore the dialectical relationships between material practices and discourses. Because power is asserted through the capacity to create identities by naming—the use of labels such as "beneficiaries" or "intruders" in this project (see Chapter Five) and through the control of the context where interaction occurs and the ability to determine who speaks and what is said and not said, the analysis of communication among project participants occupies a center stage in this book. This sense of power corresponds to Wolf's notion of tactical or organizational power (Wolf 1990:586). It also follows Foucault's dictum that the analysis of power should not be seen simply in terms of prohibition, but also in terms of production: "it induces pleasure, forms of knowledge, produces discourse" (1980:119). My aim here goes well beyond the disentangling of power present in social interaction. I am seeking to show how Wolf's "structural power"—how the forces of the world that impinge upon the people we study—operated throughout the history of the Yacyretá project. The questions here are why, how, and when global interests imposed their will and constrained the action of nation-states and also how, by the same token, nation-states limited the action of regional and local actors. As power does not exist without resistance, the goal will also be to explore the forms of contestation. My interest and commitment to this topic stems from my particular relationship to the project.

ON PERSONAL GOALS AND POSITIONING

In keeping with the developing custom in anthropological writings, I would like to clarify my orientation in writing this text. In significant part, my position derives from Bourdieu:

The objectification is always bound to remain partial, and therefore, false, so long as it fails to include the point of view from which it speaks and so fails to construct the game as a whole. Only at the level of the field of positions is it possible to grasp both the generic interests associated with the fact of taking part in the game and the specific interests attached to the different positions, and, through this, the form and content of the self-positionings through which these interests are expressed. (1984a:12)

Hence, I consider my particular positioning within this story as influencing my research questions, the answers I obtained, and the way I interpreted my data and organized my book. Although by disclosing my relationship to the hydroelectric project at the opening of this work I might predispose the reader toward a particular evaluation of the situation and interpretation of my own work, I opted to do so. I agree with Giddens that in doing this, I am exerting a form of social control (1984:89).

I am an Argentine anthropologist, a porteña (born in Buenos Aires, the capital city of Argentina) and therefore, a "parachutist," the term used by the local population of Misiones to refer to outsiders such as myself. I "landed" in this Argentine province in 1980 to work as a professor at the National University of Misiones (UNaM). Both while living in the United States as a graduate student in the mid -1980s and during the first years of my work in Misiones, I changed homes constantly, and in various ways my situation resembled that of the displaced I am analyzing here. Surely, my identity/ies bear the traces of all the places where I had lived. Among all of them, Misiones occupies a privileged site in my memories: I long for its people and its bright red soil and warm and flower-scented days, especially during the long and cold winters of my current home in upstate New York.

During a great part of the research, I owned a home just a few blocks away from one of the research sites. From my windows , I could observe how daily life went by. For example, I could see the *paseras*, women involved in petty smuggling, coming and going to the port, only four blocks away. They carried huge baskets on their heads and stopped at every door to offer fruit, vegetables, and other goods such as cigarettes, whisky, and whatever happened to be in demand in the local market. Right at the corner, there was a grocery store which played a key role in the social life of the neighborhood. The owners knew nearly everything that went on in the nearby areas and were very influential in community life. The *paseras* stopped there to eat, to chat, and to leave their merchandise overnight. Doña Itatí, the grocer, was very active in the neighborhood commission and in the chapel on Bajada Vieja street. She was also very well connected to the ruling *Justicialista* party, a position which enabled her to act as a broker. Moreover, as she sold her goods on credit, many of her poor clients, who resided on the slope stretching down to the river, counted on her as a patron who supplied valuable services, not the least of which was a guarantee of their subsistance.

Besides living next to one of the areas to be relocated, and therefore being a participant of the reality under study, I had also been connected to Yacyretá in various other ways ever since I arrived in Misiones. First, I was involved vicariously through colleagues and students at the university, who worked at the relocation agency. Second, I did research , at the Relocation Agency's request, on a contract to survey "the means of subsistence and capacity for repayment of the people to be relocated" (UNaM 1982). Third, I lived in the city that as a whole was affected by the hydroelectric project. Thus, I have been a participant observer and, occasionally, another actor in the processes here described, long before I formally began field work for this study in 1987. For reasons that will become apparent as this story unfolds, I initially limited myself to the analysis of the development process as it occurred in Argentina. After moving to the United States in 1991, I returned to the research area in the summers of 1993 and 1995 and twice in 1996. In these last visits, I included research on the Paraguayan side, in part because I was interested in the emergence of a social movement that transcended national boundaries, and in part because I suspected that the democratization process initiated in this country after the end of the Stroessner dictatorship would allow for a friendlier research environment. As we will see, some of my suspicious proved wrong. I was too optimistic about the political events—and maybe somewhat misguided by our academic assumptions about the effects of globalization processes. I oversaw the power of historical Paraguayan-Argentine rivalries in shaping relations in this binational project. In fact, the Yacyretá case will show the resilience of nationalist ideologies despite hegemonic discourses that envisage an integrated and borderless world with nation-states on the retreat. This resilience is expressed more blatantly in the borderlands. It is precisely in these places, which traditionally stood as symbols of national sovereignty, where nation-states are becoming corroded and threatened.

Such is my background and such are my assumptions. Such is the nature of my involvement. With this in mind, I ask readers, first, to draw their own conclusions and, second, to skirt that extreme paralyzing hyper-relativism that can only reduce chances for positive social change[6] (cf. D'Andrade and Scheper-Hughes 1995).

Three students at the *Universidad Nacional de Misiones* contributed important insights to this study through their participation as field assistants in the early stages of my research. They obtained data from Yacyretá's files, classified materials from the newspapers, and interviewed some of the people to be resettled. Two, Nancy Albohaires and Gustavo Azar, were students of anthropology, and another, Susana Moniec, was a student of social work. There were significant differences among the three: one came from Buenos Aires and two were from Misiones, one was born in Posadas and another in the interior of the province. They shared neither the same theoretical background nor the same information about the purpose of the research project. Although I did not select my assistants on the basis of their different training or origins, in the long run these distinctions proved to be relevant, helping me to detect regularities of themes, irrespective of the various dialogical contexts in which we elicited information on the project. Thus, I could identify collective concerns and the recurrence of responses that develop in processes of relocation. This does not mean that I negate the role played by the ethnographic encounter, with its corresponding negotiation of the reality to be depicted. Somewhat to the contrary, I want to stress the need for setting a balance between approaches that pose the limitations of social-science knowledge by emphasizing the influence of the observer on that which is observed and approaches that claim it is possible to grasp the social mesh through using appropriate tools. I concur with Eric Wolf when he asserted that "I think that the world is real, that these realities affect what humans do and that what humans do affect the world, and that we can come to understand the whys and wherefores of this relationship" (Wolf:1990:587). Similarly, June Nash (1997) warns us to be wary of the interpretive approaches that question the very reality of our subjects (cf. also Friedman 1996). This reality needs to be understood, as Harvey reminds us, in a dialectical sense, by which he means a view that allows "for an understanding of 'things' and systems as if they are real and stable as a special case of the proposition that processes are always at work creating and sustaining 'things' and systems" (Harvey 1996:62). We cannot reduce everything to flux and flows and must acknowledge that there are "permanences" such as institutions, organizations, and structures in the world we inhabit. Our task as analysts is to come as close as possible in the recreation of such reality in order to "open up a terrain of political possibilities"(Harvey 1996:46). My explorations into an anthropology of development seek to grasp some of the ambiguities and complexities of processes of social change and planned intervention.

ANTHROPOLOGISTS AND DEVELOPMENT

Anthropologists can approach development in two ways. We involve ourselves in the design, assessment, implementation, and/or evaluation of projects. In doing so, we are engaged in what is generally called *development anthropology* (see, for example, Partridge 1984; Cochrane 1971; Hoben 1982, 1984; Peattie 1981; Curtis 1985; Cernea 1996; Horowitz 1996). Or we can observe development with the same methods and techniques our colleagues use to look at other social processes and institutional arrangements. In this latter case we are doing an *anthropology of development.*[7] The first approach involves the application of anthropological knowledge to planned change; the second consists of a study of what others do in development.[8] This second alternative constitutes a critique of the practice of development, of the power relations embedded in such practice, and of the multiple meanings constructed to legitimize and/or contest development. This distinction of our different ways of dealing with development is quite arbitrary and only useful for analytical purposes because, in fact, most anthropologists are often involved in both.

Here, I follow some lines of inquiry suggested for the anthropology of development—albeit very rarely pursued—namely, concentrating on the development project as "project ethnographics" (Rew 1985) by focusing on the development bureaucracy (Charsley 1982; Conlin 1985; Hinshaw 1980; Ferguson 1990), as well as on the local interpretations and responses to development, including compliance and various forms of collective resistance (Dahl and Rabo 1992; Long and Long 1992). Considering that the Binational Yacyretá Entity (EBY) hired social scientists (anthropologists, sociologists, and social workers) to work in the relocation program, the study will also become a critique of social sciences as policy sciences. As such, it will call into question the basis of each discipline, goals, methods, techniques and theoretical frameworks.[9]

Roger Bastide (1973) was probably one of the first proponents of an anthropology of applied practice. His work was followed by studies such as Belshaw's *The Sorcerer's Apprentice: An Anthropology of Public Policy* (1976) and Robertson's *People and the State* (1984). More recently, a myriad of works inspired by cultural studies, as well as postmodern, feminist, and poststructural critiques, led to a renewed critical examination of anthropology and development, which, not surprisingly, has generated intense and heated debates (see, for example, Escobar 1991, 1995; Ferguson 1990; Kothari 1989; Long and Long 1992; Hobart 1993; Apffel Marglin and Marglin 1990; Rahnema 1992; Nandy 1994; Marchand and Parpart 1995). Most of these current works call into question a dominant view that presents development as "the fate of all societies" (Nandy 1994), as a synonym for progress, rationality, efficiency, emancipation, modernity, and well-being. Moreover, the majority of the critiques coincide in portraying development as a "label for plunder and violence, as a mechanism of triage" (Alvares 1992), a means of destruction of local environments and cultures. These debates awakened and challenged a group of academics and a cadre of experts who increasingly advocated and endorsed an uncritical anthropology put to the service of state agencies and private interests largely responsible for the economic impoverishment and cultural slaughter of oppressed minorities.

This much needed discussion on the role of social sciences in planned change is not new. The late 1960s witnessed anthropologists' very radical assessments of the unfortunate role our discipline played in Vietnam or in the Camelot project in Latin America.[10] We also made key contributions to the analysis of colonialism, imperialism, dependency, and development, which are not always acknowledged in current postcolonial and postdevelopment critiques. Moreover, because of the critical stand and commitment to social causes, a large number of social scientists from the South suffered exile, political persecutions, imprisonment, physical disappearance, torture, and death. Regrettably, in the postmodern arena there is often little recognition of the courage and agony of this generation of scholars. Ironically, it was precisely their uprooting and exile in the "core" countries that contributed to the discovery of dependency debates in "Western" academic circles.

Many of the current thought-provoking and welcome contributions should, however, push the critiques even further by including a reflexive analysis of some of the authors' populist and romanticized imaginings of the everyday realities and desires of the Third World common people, generally depicted as the challengers and heroic resistors of unwelcome socio-economic interventions and as jealous guardians of nature. These representations of the oppressed sometimes reflect more a feeling of guilt and/or the nostalgic longing for pastoral landscapes and untouched environments inhabited by pristine and innocent others, so common among disenchanted urban Westerners and transplanted Third World intellectuals—myself included— than an honest and realistic appraisal of people's struggles based on genuine dialogue and careful field-work observations.[11] A similar point is made by Little and Painter in evaluating Escobar's critique of the development encounter: "The voices that seek expression in Escobar's new approach (1991:678) are not those of colleagues in the South or of the grass-roots movements. Instead, they arise from a Northern intellectual agenda that has little to do with grass-roots movements in the Third World" (1995:606). Although aware of Said's discussion of Orientalism, most of the contemporary critics of development fail to see that they themselves are responsible for a similar essentialization of the West—and of the agents of the postdevelopment era (see for example, Nandy 1994, Escobar 1995). The West is not as monolithic as some of these works seem to suggest (cf. Carrier 1995). It should be remembered that the West is the cradle not only of positivism and rationalism, but also of of romanticism, anarchism, critical theory, phenomenology, nihilism, and deconstructionism, all of them intellectual sources of inspiration for contemporary writers. The West produced discourses that glorify universalism and discourses that glorify difference; it provided sources of destruction and also inspiration for reconstruction and resistance. Similar processes had been at work in the rest of the globe: different agents with diverse world views selectively chose among the available discourses and social practices—both of their own and of others—and redefined them in novel ways. I do not want to minimize the destructive power of certain hegemonic discourses and practices of development undoubtedly centered in the West. I wish to show that influences do not exclusively move in one direction, that the world is more complex than many of these constructions would admit, more like a maze that might or might not lead to one or many exits.

Rather than assuming that the grass roots necessarily resist development, democratize society, and promote ecologically sound relationships with the environment—which are very often the goals of analysts and activists—this work will show that people's struggles sometimes have outcomes that do not completely correspond to what academic debates make of them but which nevertheless challenge well-entrenched powerful groups. The so-called alternative development strategies—the praise of participation, communication, and empowerment, the emphasis on ecological awareness, local culture and knowledge—and the alternatives to development exemplified by the "new social movements" (Melucci 1996; Escobar and Alvarez 1992) generally fail to examine the way power affects and operates among the subaltern. They also work under the assumption that communities are homogeneous and fairly autonomous from the otherwise omnipresent development discourse. Internal competition and rivalries at the local level, cooptation, and factionalism are generally ignored or underestimated. In reconstructing the often contradictory collective action of the people of Posadas and Encarnación, I will try to overcome some of the common shortcomings in our studies of the grass roots. The movements formed to respond to the Yacyretá relocation policies will illustrate how popular struggles do not always meet the analysts' expectations and yet constitute serious challenges to planned development.

THE METAMORPHOSES OF DEVELOPMENT

Expert knowledge systems have a long history that predates the institutionalization of development practice by nearly two centuries. Surely, long before modernization became the driving force behind development interventions in what came to be known as the Third World, there was already a well-established machinery for regulating the "underdeveloped from within" and the chaotic and uncivilized from without, the non-Western peoples. Two related developments, the formation of the domain of the "social" (Donzelot 1979) and the "cultural vision" (Bauman 1992) allowed for the emergence of practices that came to characterize modernity: the policing and educating of those regarded as inferior. The demarcation of the "social" was linked to one of the major concerns of modernity: how to maintain order. Order became a problem once industrialization and scientific progress disrupted community life and traditional means of keeping everybody in place, and as a consequence of this, a mass of vagrants, orphans, and other downtrodden shook the stability of bourgeois society. Mechanisms for surveillance arose to control these undesirable products of modern society. Thinking in terms of culture in the sense of "cultivated and civilized" justified the ruling of those "others" at home and abroad regarded as wild and untamed (Bauman 1987, 1992). Specific forms of knowledge, possessed by the "cultured" (who happened to live in the West) became desirable and superior, while the knowledge of the rest was silenced, suppressed, and devalued. Multiple knowledge systems and corresponding coteries of experts such as teachers, social workers, doctors, and psychiatrists were created to domesticate and regulate others.

For decades, certainty in the power of reason and Western scientific knowledge to master nature and people remained unchallenged. By the end of the Second World War, fate in the Western model as measurement of progress became articulated in modernization theory which encompassed a combination of economic, political, educational, and moral goals. Most of the initial efforts to achieve economic growth, one of the major purposes of modernization, were heavily biased toward urbanization and industrialization; Great Britain and the United States were generally envisaged as paradigmatic cases to be emulated by the Third World "traditional and backward" societies. In the 1950s and 1960s development strategies pursuing modernization entailed the active involvement of nation-states to ensure the transformation of their societies. Most governments set up structures to guarantee rational development planning by creating powerful ministeries or departments in charge of studying and recommending policies to achieve the necessary take-off (Rostow 1960). This is precisely what the Argentine and Brazilian governments did, and as I will show, agencies of these two countries were instrumental in the decision to build hydroelectric dams within the prevailing developmentalist ideology of the times.

Initially, most of the planning was in the hands of economists and statisticians. Social scientists were rarely summoned and, if they were, their intervention was limited to social engineering or to "autopsies" (Grillo and Rew 1985) of projects. Either these social scientists assessed social and cultural barriers without taking any active role in decision-making, or they were called to diagnose what went wrong. After some years, however, it became apparent that the carefully designed development plans and programs were not very effective in ameliorating poverty or eradicating hunger; the "trickle-down" effect of economic growth did not occur as predicted. Social expertise was gradually incorporated into the development machinery to imbue planned change with a more humane face and to combat poverty more aggressively (as a war-like language attests: targets, attacks, combats against, elimination). Multiple examples, coming from both urban and rural experiences, showed that technological innovations, rather than reducing inequalities, were very often reinforcing or generating them. Calls for "basic needs" approaches attempted to face the shortcomings of the early development projects. By the late 1960s and early 1970s, modernization lost its appeal, as it was attacked both by development practitioners and by Marxists and Neo-Marxists. As many of the criticisms have been addressed in detailed and excellent studies elsewhere,[12] I will limit myself to providing a very sketchy summary of the major trends and transformations in development discourses and strategies and to situating my study within these processes.

As disenchantment with the dominant development discourse seemed to gain momentum, a series of alternatives were proposed to redirect it. Development in the hand of experts imposed from above without consulting community members was dismissed as a "top-down" style of intervention. "Putting people first" (Cernea 1991; see also Chambers 1983), bringing the people as active participants in planned change reflected academic concerns with rational actors and human agency; Third World peoples were no longer seen as backward dupes constrained by structures. Although for many analysts of development the perspectives which advocated the involvement of civil society in designing its own future constituted a radical departure from earlier development models, I would argue that some of the variants of communication, participation, and empowerment through which civil society was doomed to engage were indeed very welcome by a development establishment that increasingly embraced neoliberalism in the 1980s. Indeed ideas that encourage autonomy and individual responsibility for one's own destiny fit very nicely in the market-oriented global world of the 1990s, which despises the social welfare state.

Neoliberalism, the "second wave of development doctrine" (Slater 1995) was imposed without major opposition from the weakened nation-states debilitated by an unpayable foreign debt. With the collapse of the Soviet Union and the end of the Cold War, the hegemony of the West has been reasserted. Privatization, decentralization, structural adjustment, and deregulation of the economy are now the new Draconian measures to which every impoverished country in the South and in the former Second World should submit. Argentina, one of the major Latin American debtors, fell victim of all these pressures, and the current President Menem's administration gladly complied with most conditions, which entailed the privatization of every state-owned business, including the Yacyretá project.

Nation-states are no longer the dears of development, on the contrary, they are held responsible for earlier failures. With the retreat of the states from any involvement with social engineering, most departments and or ministeries of planning and social welfare have been eliminated. Reflecting the dominant discourses of the end of the millennium, they have been replaced by ministries of ecology to "scientifically manage" a crisis for which modern science is now being held responsible. Experts of all sorts, who used to be instrumental in providing mechanisms of legitimation to state policies, have become superfluous in a market-oriented economy and have been forced to seek refuge in civil society, many of them ended up joining forces with the new social actors—social movements and nongovernmental organizations (NGOs). The Yacyretá experience allows us to explore the nature of the participation of these displaced specific intellectuals among other displaced peoples, the relocated men and women of Posadas and Encarnación. It also gives us some clues for understanding the "ecologization" of social movements.

OVERVIEW OF THE BOOK

The final section of this chapter is a structural summary of the chapters. In Chapter Two, I review concepts relevant to the study of development practice, and I discuss the logic underlying the organization of the book. I define two models usually followed by social scientists in development projects: a neopopulist and an authoritarian model of social intervention. I briefly summarize how anthropologists have studied large-scale projects and development bureaucracies. The chapter highlights the shortcomings of the concepts of rationality and efficiency as used in the development literature. I emphasize the need to look at time and space as strategic power resources employed to shape social encounters. Development projects generate crises—uncertainty, unpredictability, loss of meanings, identity disorientation—with long-lasting implications for all participants in the process (professional groups and the local population). By seeing the connection of these specific crises with the crisis of modernity, we can discern the role played by various experts in the development process. Do they speak from a position of power, or are many of the professions as suspect as the men and women to be relocated? Development experts and diverse regional actors participate in positioning processes either to assert their identity/ies or to construct new ones through employing linguistic strategies (speech genres, forms of address), body gestures, presentation of selves. The relationship between communication, knowledge, and power is examined to provide the reader with a conceptual framework to understand the following chapters. Finally, this chapter defines the communicative practices of professional groups, politicians, and the local population.

Chapter Three outlines the history of the Río de la Plata Basin Region, focusing on the relationship among Brazil, Argentina, and Paraguay. It looks at how contemporary borders were formed after the defeat of Paraguay in the War of the Triple Alliance in the nineteenth century. The chapter examines the political economy of the region and places the decision to build Yacyretá in this context. It focuses on the interconnections of local, national, and global levels. The chapter is also concerned with the connections and conflicts between the national state and the region and among cities within the region. It aims to show how different representations of the region and its inhabitants evolved. The understanding of this historical context provides clues to interpreting legitimating discourses, power struggles, and peoples's responses in the Yacyretá project. Until recently, most of the history books dealing with the region or Misiones Province had been written by travelers or local amateur historians. These studies generally reflect the local "invented traditions" from which the scarce scholarly sources are not necessarily exempt. To write this chapter, I have used old chronicles and local histories and organized the material according to the way I interpret these past events. Therefore, this chapter sums up my own construction of the region's history. I intentionally make visible some historical events and actors that are generally negated. I assume this role of a transgressor—I confront the official version of history—with the deliberate purpose of linking the present dwellers of the areas to be flooded with a past most of them and the dominant social groups ignore. In following chapters, I show that devaluation of the history and culture of some social groups has an effect on the way they organized, on the way they responded to being organized, on how they were defined in the project, and on the social policies designed for them.

Together with the previous chapter, Chapter Four portrays the context of population resettlement dramas. The chapter shows how time and place matter. It traces the vicissitudes of the project, including the various political and economic factors causing serious delays. It reviews the various interest sectors arguing about the construction of the dam, justifying it to the general public, and considering the issue of population relocation. It includes a discussion of the impact of global changes in the organizational structure and the role of the relocation agency. This chapter addresses the issue of regional participation in decision-making and the sharing of benefits in energy production. Changes in planning styles and development rhetoric are also explored (from state-sponsored development to privatization, from authoritarian models of social intervention to more participatory ones).

Until the modern state fell in disgrace, development entailed an encounter between the nation-state and the people (Robertson 1984, Escobar 1995). More recently, the nature of the encounter has changed as it came to include other social actors such as NGOs which are now either sharing or taking over completely the responsibilities of social welfare. Chapter Five describes the encounter between the people and members of the relocation agency as it is recalled by participants. The text reflects the drama of this encounter; it shows how actors interpreted both actions and messages and organized them into their own frame of reference. Within the multiplicity of voices representing this drama, we can discern regularities in the construction of past events. The encounter marks the beginning of a very critical period in the lives of both the Yacyretá's staff and the people to be relocated, an encounter characterized by anxiety, uncertainty, and a rather resigned anticipation. The chapter explores events identified as key markers of the critical situation which signal the transformation and/or creation of settings of interaction, social relations, symbols, and meanings, as well as the acquisition of new identities—such as those of development experts and project beneficiaries.

Once the critical encounter occurred, the population and the relocation agency's experts constituted a very particular dialogical set. Chapter Six examines how the affected population represents the agency and its staff members. This allows the reader to understand specific responses to the project. In the first part, I examine how the Yacyretá Agency becomes reified and constructed as an omnipotent actor. In the second part, I show how planners diverge in their constructions of the population to be resettled—the poor of Posadas. The chapter illustrates how existing systems of social relations and the positioning of the participants conditions communication exchanges and individuals' participation in the project.

In Chapter Seven, I describe how Yacyretá's professionals and technicians became positioned not only through their interaction with the displaced population, but also through their daily encounters with other staff members. Previous experiences in the larger society shaped the experts' ability to influence decision-making. The organization's staff did not share the same goals regarding relocation; neither did they enjoy the same power within the agency. Differences among members stemmed from their professional/technical training, their class ascription, their political affiliation, and their identity with the region. The chapter gives examples of the numerous positioning devices employed by development experts in their struggles for power within the agency. Principal among these devices are knowledge, space-time, linguistic resources, and networks.

Many development practitioners generally argue that projects do not succeed because planners fail to guarantee communication flows among participants. In these formulations, communication is assumed to be transparent and unequivocal. In Chapter Eight I deal with Yacyretá's attempt to face communication and participation throughout the years and show how these concepts are differently understood by various experts. I describe the emergence and transformation of communicative practices and include a case study—the story of Doña Azucena and some of her neighbors—to illustrate communication problems which arose in the long process of relocation. The case shows the conflicting interpretations of relocation rights and how the different professional constructions of the urban poor negatively affected the relocation process.

As dam construction took much longer than initially planned, numerous problems emerged which were not originally anticipated. Chapter Nine discusses the national, binational, and global changes that compelled the population to adopt new strategies to cope with new situations. Choice of mediators had been influenced by the recognition that in specific conjunctures certain positions might be useful in the negotiation process with Yacyretá. During the years of the military dictatorship, most forms of dialogue and negotiation were banned. With the advent of democratic politics, spaces of negotiation multiplied. The chapter summarizes the role played by various mediators in different political conjunctures. The last part of this chapter anticipates the discussion of the next one: the incorporation of NGOs and transnational actors.

Chapter Ten analyzes the development of popular movements in Paraguay and Argentina to make claims regarding relocation. It examines the social base of the movements, the nature of their grievances, their action strategies, and their relationship to key actors in the regional political life and in the Yacyretá relocation process (Yacyretá's staff and decision-makers, political parties, local authorities, NGOs, global agencies). It examines why the recent organization of the *oleros* (brickmakers) has been relatively successful. It emphasizes the role played by a multiplicity of agents (NGOs, academics, political activists) in mediating popular demands, in providing discursive strategies (mainly human rights and ecological discourses), and in connecting the local groups to a broad network of global supporters.

The concluding chapter evaluates the implications of this study for reconsidering the role of social planners, the state, NGOs, and social movements in development. It also examines how the MERCOSUR (the South American version of NAFTA) is now replacing in the collective imaginary (Zizek 1989, 1994) the once tremendous transformative power attributed to Yacyretá. The chapter also includes some reflections on the highly contested role of anthropologists in development projects.

To re-create the drama of this particular development struggle, to show how actors interpreted both actions and messages and organized them into their own frameworks of reference, I constructed the following text with their own, multiple voices. But unlike many of the recent experimental ethnographies, I do not make here any patronizing claim to grant a voice to the voiceless. The people of Posadas and Encarnación have courageously demonstrated that they know how and when to be heard. They graciously told me their story because they wanted it to be known by as many people as possible. They saw me as a potential resource. I hope I have not deceived them.

NOTES

1. In 1996, the federal government finally agreed to build a line to connect Misiones with the national interconnected energy system. After bitter confrontations between the central state and the provincial government on this issue, there were still disagreements regarding who would pay for the cost of the works.

2. In the newspaper article "*De los ríos de la discordia a la conexión fluvial*," Luis Ocampos Alonso comments that in the 1970s the "Escola Superior de Guerra" in Brazil sustained a thesis that suggested the opposition of the Amazon and La Plata River basins, and which regarded the Paraná River region as of highest tension in the South American arena. Both Argentina and Brazil developed a geopolitical strategy based on the likelihood of an armed confrontation in the Southern Cone (*ABC color*, November 16, 1995). A similar discussion is also addressed in Schilling's (1978) *El Expansionismo Brasileño*. For an intriguing discussion of the German influence on geopolitical thinking in Argentina (and also in Brazil and Chile) see Dijkink 1996.

3. I take this concept from Giddens. It refers to the changes and the scope of risk that is seen as "a result of human intervention into the conditions of social life and into nature." He emphasizes the new forms developed to cope with this kind of risk are more about "damage control and repair" than about mastering the world through more knowledge (1994:4).

4. Specialists on globalization have recently stressed how anthropology should change the way it traditionally identified specific cultures with particular places. With the increase of migration processes, we are now witnessing the spread of deterritorialized communities over the globe (see Basch, Glick Schiller and Szanton Blanc 1994; Appadurai 1996b; Latouche 1989, 1993; Kearney 1995).

5. This working definition is inspired by the work of Foucault (1988) and also of Bakhtin (1996[1981]). For a thorough and provocative analysis of the discourse of development see Escobar (1991, 1995). While Escobar attempts to subvert the discourse from outside development practice, Gardner and Lewis have recently proposed to challenge such discourse from within (1996:78). For a balanced and illuminating analysis of the dialectics of discourse, see Harvey (1996).

6. What I am doing here is addressing my multiple positions and, therefore, subjectivities that inform this text. Moore adheres to a "post-post-structuralist" view of the the subject as the site "of multiple and potentially contradictory subjectivities." This internally differentiated subject is constituted in and through discourse (1994:55, 58). Although it is important to signal our— and the peoples we study—different subject positions, we must be careful not to fall into denying any possibility of agency and radical transformation.

7. Charsley (1982), for example, defines such an approach as an "anthropological study of development which is entirely separate from application and logically prior to it" (quoted in Grillo and Rew 1985:29). See also Scholte 1974[1969]; Bastide 1973; Gardner and Lewis 1996.

8. For a thorough comparison of the two approaches, see Grillo (1985). Lomnitz (1979) also provides an overview on how anthropologists relate to development in Latin America

9. Numerous works examine the role of anthropology in policy making. See, for example, Weaver (1985), Van Willigen (1984), Hinshaw (1980), Chambers (1977), and Cochrane (1980).

10. The volume edited by Dell Hymes (1974[1969]) is a representative example of the critical assessments of the role of our discipline in the late 1960s and 1970s. Numerous articles published at that time reflect the political concerns and commitments of many of our colleagues (see, for example, Asad 1973). The most radical critics advocated a militant and even subversive social science (Stavenhagen 1971, Fals Borda 1969, Frank 1975).

11. In assessing contemporary postmodern anthropological writing, June Nash stresses that those following this orientation "are imposing Euro- and U.S.-centric definitions of global processes that can better be understood from areas once marginalized by the West where we once concentrated our field research." She strongly argues for an ethnographically informed anthropology and regrets that this professional activity is now being disparaged (1997:12).

12. The bibliography on critiques of development is so extensive that I will limit myself to suggesting further readings. Bjorn Hettne's 1982 book provides a comprehensive discusion of theories and critiques of development. See also Knippers Black 1991, Banuri 1990.

CHAPTER 2

Practicing Development

The nature of the response of the relocated population will depend, to a large degree, upon the establishment of good mechanisms of communication and upon the periodic consultation of the affected population and their organizations (community-based groups, non-governmental associations, etc.) as well as upon the encouragement of participation to look for solutions and definitions of the complex problems that emerge from the planning and implementation of relocation. (Cernea 1989)

Decision processes are . . . processes of eliminating other possibilities. They produce more "nays" than "yeas," and the more rationally they proceed, the more extensively they test other possibilities, the greater becomes their rate of negation. To demand an intensive, engaged participation of all in them would be to make a principle of frustration. Anyone who understands democracy in this way has, in fact, to come to the conclusion that it is incompatible with rationality. (Luhman, quoted in Habermas 1975:133)

It is very unlikely that Yacyretá's experts ever heard that during the 1970s two major European social thinkers had been debating the appropriateness of citizen participation in technocratic advanced societies. While one of them, Luhman, maintained that complex systems should respond to their own logic, irrespective of individual actors; the other, Habermas, argued that we should recover and encourage the active involvement of all members of society by proposing a model of communicative action (see Habermas 1979). Nor, I suspect, were the majority of Yacyretá's experts cognizant that efforts to rescue the emancipatory project of the Enlightment, supposedly threatened by the devastating effects of a modernity gone amock, were and are behind much of the rhetoric involving participation and communication to which they are exposed in their daily practice.

Most contemporary debates—concerned with the fate of modernity in a globalized world, increasingly conscious of the destructiveness of the until-now omnipotent science and technology—might seem quite abstract and removed from the everyday practices of the majority of the members of the technical staff at EBY. The experience of the Yacyretá project will show, however, that many of the tensions among professional groups are intertwined with the displacements and discontinuities of the *episteme* (Foucault 1991a) of the end of the century, regardless of the obscurity of many of these intellectual preoccupations for the development experts of this project. Surely, when development experts in Posadas were either reluctant to accept or overtly opposed any input from the population regarding relocation policies, they rarely—if ever—stopped to reflexively analyze how this refusal related to events and practices, discursive and nondiscursive, occurring elsewhere. I doubt very much that any of them would frame their dilemmas in terms of a defense of an instrumental reason. As the discussions in the following chapters will illustrate, their reasons for avoiding a dialogue with the Posadeños were framed in terms of the superiority of their various scientific knowledges, supposedly necessary to make rational decisions which would save two valuable resources: time and money. These views justifying decision-making processes solely on the basis of experts' assessments generally clashed with another perspective also held by some of the members of the technical staff but for years predominantly minoritarian. This perspective favored a greater involvement of the population affected by dam construction. The Cernea and Luhman quotes that opened this chapter represent two processes at work in projects of socio-economic change, two opposing views on how to "rationally" achieve development goals. This study challenges both those perspectives. One perspective sees communication and participation as privileged vehicles to ensure development goals; the other looks at communication and participation as inherent sources of conflict. In other words, what some planners see as a means, others see as an obstacle. I will show that both approaches are misleading because they oversimplify the functioning of development projects and rely on questionable assumptions about the nature of communication.

I will demonstrate that ideals of participation and communication can never be fully achieved because, no matter how good the intentions of planners are, communication exchanges in these kinds of undertakings always occur in asymmetrical power contexts. Participants do not have the same access to decision-making; they do not hold positions of equivalent power, and they often belong to different cultural and historical traditions. Such constraints are hard to overcome. At the same time, to think that to achieve development goals we should do away with individual actors and rely on technocratic expertise as the sole guarantor of a successful project would also be a mistake. Technocrats, like the professional staff of the Yacyretá relocation agency, may often be exposed and conditioned by political forces which are at work throughout the totality of a process of change. The "politicization of technical practice," by which expertise is a sort of social engineering subordinated to the will of power or political legitimation, is a common occurrence in Latin America. Planners are expected to orchestrate citizenship loyalty to a political party or government (see Hopenhayn 1994). It would be wrong, however, to think that because experts face similar institutional pressures and are exposed to dominant development world views, they operate in a monolithic way and share the same goals regarding social change. What the Yacyretá experience will show is that the bureaucratic agency set to deal with resettlement is far from resembling the anti-politics machine described by Ferguson (1990) or the bureaucratic type envisaged by Weber (1968). On the contrary, the study on this agency may serve as a counterexample: Most of the relations among members are personalized; recruitment of staff members is done on the basis of personal recommendations and/or political influence and very rarely are project policies oriented by technical knowledge, even though it might be extensively used to justify decisions.

EXPLORING DEVELOPMENT BUREAUCRACIES

Although this book deals with the specific case of a hydroelectric project, most of the analysis gives us insight into general problems of development. When nearly thirty years ago Colson and Scudder started their pioneering anthropological research on population resettlement caused by hydroelectric dams, they focused on the effects of relocation on local peoples. Similarly, most studies on hydroelectric dams concentrated on the impact of these large-scale projects mainly on peasants and indigenous peoples.[1]

Until recently, the most common role for anthropologists in these projects, as it has also been the case with most development projects, was either that of a social engineer who assesses possible outcomes but does not have a say in the design of policies, or that of a post-facto evaluator who tries to discern what went wrong. Few anthropologists have been active participants in the relocation programs and even fewer have been involved in all phases of a project. The Yacyretá experience is unique in this respect. Anthropologists, sociologists, and social workers took part in the design and implementation of the relocation process.

Most colleagues working in hydroelectric projects are hired as development anthropologists to undertake what is known as social-impact assessment. This kind of study is done to assess the positive and negative effects of development projects on a given population. Researchers involved in analysis of the impact of resource development complain that their studies are rarely considered by decision-makers. Furthermore, they all agree that development agencies regard the social aspects of projects as something marginal, as a residual category, only included among the costs of projects (Bartolomé 1984a; Rofman et al.1987; Suárez, Franco, and Cohen 1983).

Initially, anthropologists involved in assessing relocation projects have used mechanistic models, such as Scudder and Colson's (1982) *multidimensional stress model*, which characterizes the stages a given population goes through when affected by the construction of a hydroelectric dam. On following studies, the same authors have employed more dynamic models, which consider tensions within systems and stress strategies and choices (Colson 1976; Colson and Scudder 1988).[2] Although many authors are starting to acknowledge the importance of the larger context and no longer see the systems in isolation, very few include an analysis of the broader socio-historical contexts in their studies. Ribeiro's (1994) engaging analysis of the macroprocesses affecting the negotiation of the Yacyretá dam is probably one of the few studies attempting to fill this gap.

These recent academic concerns with broader processes and power structures stem from profound changes in the world at large. After the post-World War II triumphalism, a combination of events such as the American defeat in Vietnam, declines in economic growth in First World countries, ecological disasters such as Bhopal and Chernobyl that shook the certainties of scientific models, and the impoverishment of most of a Third World haunted by an unpayable foreign debt generated a loss of confidence in the Western path to progress. These developments opened up a space for critical thinking and reflexivity which inspired diverse theoretical discourses in political economy, feminism, deconstructionism, critical theory, and postmodernism. Issues of power, authority, domination, hegemony, and positionality became crucial for understanding a world in which metanarratives and the authority of scientific knowledge no longer held true. Not all these trends coincided in approach or priority. Here, we are mainly concerned with those who called for an analysis of power understood in terms of broad structural constraints and in those who raised issues of agency and positionality in trying to understand how power operates in specific social relations. The first proposed to "study up"; the latter insisted on actor-oriented approaches. As I will later discuss, this book tries to integrate both approaches.

In order to gain a better understanding of the functioning of structural power (both through practices and discourses), analysts have suggested the study of the state, elites, bureaucracies, and global actors (Moran 1996; Smith 1996). But until now, although there has been an increasing awareness of the relevance and desirability of such studies, not too much has been accomplished, particularly within development studies. For example, anthropologists specializing in the social aspects of dam projects, and of other development projects as well, have stressed the need for studying power holders and planning agencies (Pitt 1976; Partridge 1984; Bartolomé 1984a, 1988; Marcus and Fischer 1986; Escobar 1995). Until recently, however, few researchers have followed this advice. Current studies however, seem to indicate a welcome reversion of this trend (see, for example, Ferguson 1990, Hobart 1993, Arce and Long 1992, Quarles van Ufford and Downing 1988, Gow 1993, Ribeiro 1994).

The study of planning agencies is not a totally new field of anthropological enquiry. Our predecessors were already interested in analyzing complex organizations in industries and in public administration as early as the 1930s. As years passed, this line of inquiry was partially abandoned and became quite invisible for mainstream anthropologists. However, although interest in these topics was never totally dismissed, specialists from other disciplines, rather than anthropologists, made the major contributions to the understanding of bureaucracies.

Undoubtedly, Weber's (1968) work is the most influential in this field which encompasses diverse approaches. His ideal type conceives of bureaucracies as organizations characterized by a high degree of specialization, impersonal relations among its members, recruitment of officials on the basis of technical knowledge and capabilities, a hierarchical structure of authority, and a differentiation between private wealth and official income. This system functions on the basis of rational rules oriented by technical knowledge, with the aim of achieving maximum efficiency.

Most of the succeeding studies have attempted to challenge Weber's perspective in some way or another. The majority of Weber's critics failed to see that his aim was not to describe a concrete, specific case but an ideal type. Empirical sociological studies from the 1950s (such as Gouldner 1954, Blau 1973[1955], and Selznick 1966[1949]) analyzed bureaucracies as complex social systems and demonstrated the importance of looking at power dimensions. Such pioneering systematic observations in the field led opened the way for studies of: dynamism of organizations, conflict among interest groups, decision-making processes, unintended consequences of actions, and the role of uncertainty. Although systemic orientations diverged and changed their emphasis as they were influenced by findings in other fields of knowledge, such as cybernetics in the 1960s and 1970s, they continued to neglect the role played by the contexts in which the organizations evolved. Space and time, if ever considered, were included in the overall category of the environment, taken either as the source of "noise" or "disturbances" to the system or as something to which the "integrated whole" adapted. With the exception of the interactionist approaches, which emphasize the role of individuals in organizations, the majority of the studies solely concentrate on structures and do not look at the role of historical social actors. In my analysis of the Yacyretá relocation agency, I attempt to balance the description of key structural institutional aspects with a careful appraisal of the participation of specific professional groups and certain individual actors.

In looking at the work of the development bureaucracy, I will examine the two models of social intervention I briefly discussed at the beginning of this chapter. I will call a *neopopulist model of social intervention* in development projects any attempt to empower the "people" by promoting communication and participation in a restricted manner with the purpose of achieving predetermined goals.[3] Such a model relies on theoretical assumptions that maintain that actors freely make rational choices. In a development project with this kind of model, the role of social scientists would often be that of mediator/facilitator who helps to achieve goals already established on the basis of engineering and economic needs. In other words, social scientists are expected to manipulate the population to ensure the successful achievement of somebody else's goals. Mediation, as Greenhouse (1985) noted, is central to the maintenance of social control. As it is always performed in a context where disputants—and the third party, the mediator—have conflicting interests and occupy different positions in the social structure, agreements are reached on the basis of persuasion and on the conviction that if disputes are not settled, the partners to the dispute might encounter some sort of social censure and sanctions.

That dialogue, communication, and participation of the population must be ensured in order to have a successful relocation program, is now widely accepted among social scientists working in development agencies. Scarlett Epstein and

Akbar Ahmed (1984), for example, have asserted that efficacy of development projects is a function of communication among the different participants. Similarly, Bamberger (1986) stresses that beneficiary participation in project design and management contributes positively to cost recovery and sustainability of projects. Moreover, in a view that now reflects some of the postmodern critique, Chambers (1993) proposes a participatory methodology based on a scientific method "holistic and post-positivist," and which assumes multiple realities that are socially constructed. The rhetoric of these planners masks what happens in many of these types of projects. First, people must become accomplices in something that is already decided upon from above. Second, such statements present a unidirectional reality, where the agency generating the situation remains unmentioned, and action must be encouraged only on the part of the relational set that is created once these projects are under way. Third, planners' ultimate concern is with reducing costs of the project and not with social issues, which are regarded as problems to be reckoned with.[4]

An *authoritarian model of social intervention*, on the other hand, emphasizes expert knowledge in decision-making and favors the autonomous functioning of planning bureaucracies, free from political constraints. Models of this kind, either in their structural or evolutionary version, generally reify the functioning of systems as if they had an independent, orderly and rational dynamics. Instability and perturbations of the "normal and natural" state of the system are blamed on politics, which in the view of these theoreticians is the realm of the unpredictable and the irrational. In this position, there is no room for the subject, seen as the source of disorder and chaos.

The neopopulist model minimizes the role of the development agency, responsible for setting the rules of the game, the policies, and goals for which consensus must be attained through the instrumentation of the social base. The other model highlights the importance of the planning bureaucracy and attempts to avoid inputs from the population.

Both prevailing approaches rely on assumptions that must be questioned:

- They see certain actors as given and unproblematic. They concentrate on a particular kind of actor—be it the population or the organization—without analyzing the complex web of social relations characteristic of these units of projects.
- They regard actions in development projects as the exercise of rationality, the fundamental expression of modern, purposive, technical action.
- They oversimplify the functioning of development projects, assuming a homogeneity of motives and practices which does not occur in actuality.
- Both the development project and its side effect, in this case relocation, are presented as givens, something that is part of the natural order of things.
- Technology is also seen as something predetermined, as a "force to which communities and beliefs are obliged to adapt" (Pfaffenberger 1988: 236). Technology, as Marx (1987), however, noted, is a social product which reveals how men organize themselves to control nature and how they make sense of the relations thus resulting.[5]

However limited the first model may seem, it is rarely enforced by development agencies—especially in those dealing with large-scale projects such as dams— and the desire to implement it does not go beyond the rhetoric of projects. I would argue that this is so because this perspective entails a politically subversive potential. Indeed, encouragement of collective discussion of the best way to achieve any development goal may easily lead to question about: (1) who made the decision in the first place and for what purpose, (2) who needs the innovation, and (3) who will benefit. The unraveling of some issues may lead to collective opposition to the change itself or to demands which the agency is not willing to meet.

On the few occasions that social scientists involved in planning promote communication and participation, they do so on a limited basis and sometimes with the concealed purpose of exerting social control over the population through co-opting leadership, neutralizing trouble-makers, and controlling information. It must be stressed that these effects are not always intentionally pursued but they are a logical outcome of the practice of social scientists. This is a function partly of the agency representatives and partly of the asymmetrical relationship established between the agency and the people.

Unlike critics of authoritarian models of intervention, I would argue that, far from threatening the efficiency of projects, tight controls of communication and participation, which inevitably generate misunderstandings and communication distortions, may often facilitate the successful achievement of development goals. Surely, I am here speaking of the goals of those in power who seek to introduce a technological innovation as quickly and as cheaply as possible. Furthermore, we cannot look at restrictions in communication and their consequences as aberrant phenomena, but rather as an integral, structurally determined part of projects.

As already noted, the two models of social intervention are defended in the name of rationality and efficiency. But what meanings do these words mobilize to make opposition so unlikely?

RATIONALITY AND EFFICIENCY

The concepts of "efficiency" and "rationality" are generally used interchangeably. Neither is a neutral word; neither has a univocal meaning. Speakers often employ the words to refer to the least costly way of achieving goals. This meaning, with a clear economic overtone, is the most widely used in development projects. Thus, to find the most rational/effective solution is a question of technique: One undertakes a cost/benefit analysis in which every action is assessed in terms of its cash value. Once one has ascertained costs and benefits, one chooses the best alternative to maximize outcomes. This represents an instrumental view of rationality which finds theoretical expression in the works of Weber: Mastery of the world in response to human interest, consisting of an adjustment of means to ends.

Another sense of the "rational," in use since the times of Enlightenment thinkers, sees in reason the means to depart from a world controlled by superstition and irrationality and to reach one governed by science and knowledge. It mainly refers to the way speaking subjects acquire and use knowledge in accordance with logically defined procedures. This linear, evolutionary perspective views reason as the possibility of overcoming ideology. This is the type of rationality envisaged by Habermas (1979:198), who poses the possibility of a communicative action to counterbalance the Weberian purposive, rational action. He defines it as the interaction of free actors mutually—intersubjectively—making validity claims to reach a common understanding of something in the objective world. Habermas's utopian model of communication derives from a critique of planning in the social welfare state in advanced capitalist societies and is concerned with recovering a moral, ethical dimension of human action.

At a practical level, these two ways of looking at rationality roughly correspond to the two models of social intervention stated earlier in this chapter. The neopopulist model presupposes rational actors making choices on the basis of intersubjectively agreed courses of action. The authoritarian model assumes there is one ideal, given "rational" order to which actions must conform.

Both senses of rationality share the notion that actions are predictable. These deterministic notions rooted in classical physics, are no longer sustained by contemporary physicists who are now more concerned with coping with uncertainty and chaos.[6] Paradoxically, many development planners (especially—but not exclusively—those with training in social sciences) adopt mechanistic rational models in an effort to please and be accepted by those holding more "scientific" forms of knowledge.

I contend that we should radically change our way of looking at the "systems rationality." Actors do not always make "rational choices," nor do systems always "naturally"—rationally—evolve into more complex levels of integration. It has been noted that people may choose alternatives that do not always contribute to their welfare. In addition, it is clear that what is in the interest of one human being is not necessarily in the interest of another. Many studies of bureaucracies discuss precisely this point. Gouldner, for example, demonstrated that some rules could be rational for managers but not for workers (1954:16). In any given system, there is always a dialectic between these two "rationalities." However, this is far from being the complete picture of how a system works. We must also include in our analysis those features generally regarded as disruptive, irrational, and external. And we must look at them not as unintended and unexpected outcomes, but as constitutive elements. It is in this sense, for example, that we should incorporate the analysis of the political dimension.

Politics, for which the core actor used to be the nation-state, does not fair well in the neoliberal and globalized world of the 1990s, where efficiency is mainly linked with freeing markets and shrinking governments. The once-believed "rational" planning state structures are no longer favored because they are perceived as the sources of much corruption and political turmoil. It is in this context that we will see Yacyretá becoming a "monument of corruption." To rescue it from this fate and to make sure that it is finally placed in the right track, it is now proposed that it submit to the end of the century rationality, that is, pass to private hands and put its energy to the service of market forces, the needs of the MERCOSUR. This shift can only be understood by examining global transformations, and it can only be challenged by displacing the mobilization of collective actors into a transnational political field (Melucci 1996). This is what we will see happening with the grass-roots movements acting in response to the construction of the dam; they are now exerting pressures at national, binational, and transnational levels. Because most of the development policies and the popular action which makes sense and challenges these policies involve the manipulations of meanings in communication, we now turn to see how to analyze communicative practices in development.

STUDYING COMMUNICATION IN DEVELOPMENT

Earlier analyses of development impacts often concentrated on how a development project conceived exclusively as a technological innovation affected a population defined as a homogeneous and autonomous unit. Ensuing critiques turned to see the other side of the equation, the development agency, and showed that people were not solely affected by the introduction of an innovation but that the development apparatus with its specific discursive practices contributed to the production and transformation of "target" populations (Escobar 1995, Ferguson 1990). I contend that neither the population nor the agency can be analyzed in isolation. People are not only affected by the ongoing concrete, material planned process, they also suffer and respond to actions initiated by members of the development agency. Conversely, the project may be affected by the actions of the population. These two collective actors—the relocation agency and the population—are active components of the same process; they compose a distinctive communication system, a unit in which members have differential access to power, channels of communication, and decision-making. Rather than looking at the system as fixed, static, and bounded, as old system approaches did, I regard it as a dynamic unit in which both the limits and constitutive elements are in constant flow. I consider, for example, that at certain times, government agents or members of the civil society may become relevant elements of the systems, while they may not belong to it at other times. Consensus may never be the outcome; indeed, it is the evolving conflict that makes for the dynamism of the system. This system can not be understood unless we consider its intertwining with larger units as well as its linkage with spatio-temporal dimensions. Systems do not display a fixed and permanent form through time; they change continuously and simultaneously; they develop self-reproducing mechanisms.

This study is neither an exclusive analysis of agency—understood in a voluntaristic manner, for example, those individuals who rationally make options to achieve goals— nor of "structure"— the rational organization of means to ends which responds to its own laws irrespective of the will of individuals. On the contrary, I try to break with the dichotomic "either/or" alternative and attempt to bring to the fore the tensions between and within each of them. The examination of communication processes in a development project should reveal the permanent struggle of both forces at work. Neither communication nor participation can be regarded as neutral media. Both of them are inscribed in a context of asymmetrical power relations, and both quite often, if not always, serve to reproduce the existing relations of domination or to generate new ones.

Because these kind of projects are generally regarded as the expression of modern, purported, rational action, their study provides us with an invaluable vantage point from which to assess the notions of rationality brought into play, the functioning of institutional arrangements, and the actions and meanings of social actors. The processes I am describing in these pages are marked by ambiguity, contradiction, and heterogeneity; they simultaneously display patterns and common frameworks of reference and response. In writing, I try to re-create the systematic chaos of that which we call the real.

One of my aims in exploring Yacyretá's endless saga is to critically examine the role of social scientists in development planning. To paraphrase Bourdieu (1988), I attempt both to objectify the objectifying subject and to subjectify those who are generally objectified. In other words, I try to analyze the effects of social scientists' practice and how it contributes to the creation of a given reality through their participation, expressed in their interpretations, concept formations, and concrete actions. Conversely, I also look at the dynamic role played by actors who are traditionally regarded as mere passive recipients of messages. Both population and planners must be present for the other to exist. There can be no relocation agency without a population to relocate, nor can a population targeted for relocation exist without relocators.[7] Practices and meanings are both the products and the producers of a process of negotiation, signification, and resignification among the various participants. This constant interaction is responsible for the creation of multiple representations. The process is not unidirectional. There is no such thing as an active producer and a passive consumer of meanings.

To analyze the functioning of the communication system in a development project, we must consider the following: (1) The process unfolding in time and space, (2) the role played by the project-generated crisis, (3) the links between the process of positioning and communication practices, and (4) the communication practices, including those that facilitate accommodation and those that enable resistance. The chapter organization of the book reflects the following discussion.

THE UNFOLDING OF THE PROCESS IN TIME AND SPACE

While time was one of the organizing principles of modernity, space has become one of the major concerns of the postmodern reflexivity. Although development has always been time oriented (mainly through an evolutionary framework), and space has also informed some of the critical perspectives (mainly those which include concepts such as center-periphery, marginality, global-local), overall, time and space remained neglected dimensions in the design of social programs in development projects. Nevertheless, spatio-temporal dimensions cannot be ignored if our intention is to understand the structuration of social action (Giddens 1984).

Different categories of people within the relocation project relate differently to time. Participants situate themselves and others in time and manipulate it with various purposes. They make use of traditions to legitimize actions and to include and exclude others when they mobilize against dam construction. The uses of time are strategic power resources that contribute to self and collective identities and facilitate social control.

Akin to any other system, the communication system generated by the Yacyretá relocation process did not emerge in a vacuum; it was historically produced. The social arrangements we observe and the components we take as constitutive elements of a system carry the marks, the traces of past trajectories, when the components were not yet what they are and yet already existed as something. The communication system set in motion once it was realized that a population would be affected by the construction of a large-scale project was informed and conditioned both by the past experiences of social actors brought together by such an undertaking and by pre-existing knowledge, symbols, and meanings.

The exploration of past socio-historical conditions is not a mere pastime that provides colorful details to set a stage. It provides an understanding of how meanings and dispositions, in the Bourdieuian sense of habitus, were produced (Bourdieu 1988:22–27, 1977). This notion of habitus, comparable to Giddens's (1984:7) practical consciousness, refers to learned behavior and experientially acquired meanings that are applied in new situations without conscious reflection.

We can understand history in two senses: as a complex of "narratives," constructions about the past that have an effect in the present (as in Faye's [1972:18–19] *effet de récit*) and as concrete facts that occurred in time (cf. also Verón 1984:45). We should look at the interplay of both, at what happened, and at the different accounts of what happened. As analysts, we cannot directly deal with real past events but rather with various constructions of them. Despite these limitations, diverse accounts are important to disclose how people process and react to events: They help us reconstruct the conditions of production and consumption of discourses (Verón 1984:46).

Like history, the description of space allows one to contextualize social interaction (Giddens 1984:132). There are two senses of space that I will consider relevant to this study. One relates to the actual physical setting where people interact, be it a house, the relocation headquarters, or the office of a provincial administrator. The other refers to more broadly constructed spatial categories that are socially relevant, such as the neighborhood, the city, the region, the country. In examining space in the first sense, I will describe how it helps to shape the social encounters, how it can set constraints, and how it helps to enforce power relations.[8] Throughout this study I present the spaces favored by different participants and identify who operates in each locale. As we will see, the choice of particular spaces to call public attention to the struggles of the affected population expresses the prevailing power relations at different points in time.

The other sense of space reveals how spatial categories are used rhetorically in the confrontation between different groups. It also alludes to the way space (and place) is socially produced as the outcome of complex and often contradictory social processes (Gottdiener 1985; Gregory 1994; Harvey 1996). The use of spatial dichotomies in the Yacyretá case, such as the region versus the national center or the national space versus a foreign space as a means to legitimate the project, is expressive of particular configurations of power. The discussion of the spatio-temporal dimension is covered in various chapters, but mainly in Chapter Three and Chapter Four.

CRISIS AND THE SYSTEM

The older views of systems depicted them as relatively stable, maintained by homeostatic principles. These orientations asserted that disruptive forces, which originated in the external environment, could cause the destruction of a system. This was the dominant scheme among authors such as Wallace (1956) and Loomis (1960) who analyzed disasters[9]: Dam construction was sometimes considered a manmade disaster that created a crisis in existing systems comparable to those brought about by natural phenomena such as earthquakes and floods.

Similarly, analysts such as Bettelheim identified critical situations as dramatic disjunctures, characterized by unpredictability and insecurity which jeopardize learned daily routines (see Giddens 1984:61). Most authors also say that groups exposed to crisis move through several stages until finally they recover some sense of orientation and hence equilibrium. Others emphasize the differences between an initial and a resulting state. Turner, for example, speaks of liminality to refer to an interstructural or transitional situation linking two states (1967:93). Although these authors acknowledge changes, they tend to assume a continuity of structure.

The irruption of development projects in people's everyday lives indeed generates crises with long-lasting implications for all actors involved in the process. Nonetheless, such crises do not totally destroy existing social relations, nor are they an irreversible process: Certain relations may be temporarily suspended though not permanently interrupted; they might reappear in a modified form.

A process comparable to rites of passage—rites indexing critical situa-tions—takes place from the moment the future change (the relocation) is announced, until it comes into effect (see Turner 1967, Van Gennep 1960[1908], Bourdieu 1982). In this process, new identities and meanings are negotiated and specific rituals are performed, which also contribute to the construction of meanings. By virtue of the Yacyretá project, some men and women became "beneficiaries," while others were negatively constructed as intruders. The crisis is characterized by ambiguity and paradox (Turner 1967:97), by a recombination, reformulation, and transformation of old patterns. Because of the disorientation created by the crisis, mechanisms of condensation and displacement are very common (Laclau 1979:93; Turner 1967) as it is clearly exemplified by the way people attempt to make sense of the encounter with the powerful Yacyretá agency. The concept of condensation derives from psychoanalysis and refers to a fusion process of various components and conditions into a single representation. Laplanche and Pontalis (1976:117) speak of displacement when "the accent, the interest, the intensity of a representation is detached and passed unto others which are not originally as intense, and both representations are linked through an associative chain." Jakobson compared the concept of condensation with the rhetorical tropes of metaphors and that of displacement with metonymy (see Laplanche and Pontalis 1976; Lyotard 1974).

Participants in the resettlement process were hierarchically situated. Those with the resources and a reward to promise were in a more favorable position to impose rules governing the communicational exchanges; consequently, they metaphorically took the role of "authoritative elders." As in other rites of passage, this dominant position was ensured and reinforced by a continuous negation of the previous identities of those put in a subservient position. Whoever took the role of elder related to the others, the "initiated," as if they had no history; elders ignored the social persona; they devalued the culture (Bauman 1987; Lechner 1986a). These mechanisms of devaluation of selves and cultures, expressed in practices and meanings, engendered a kind of interaction where some participants were generally rendered passive and voiceless and others became active masters and teachers. Inability of the devalued to see alternatives and their increasing realization that existing social means of dealing with problems failed to respond adequately to the new situation contributed to create a feeling of *fait accompli*. Thus, the way the initial actions occurred and were interpreted, together with the resulting rules and resources, were both enabling and constraining (Giddens 1984).

The ordeals, disorientation, and lack of identity characteristic of crisis situations are not exclusively experienced by a population affected by a development project; other participants—such as different development experts—may also find themselves in a subservient position and experience uncertainty. This is likely because positions are not fixed but are conditioned by the working of the larger systems of social relations in which they are inscribed.

POSITIONING

People communicate through discourses which must be taken as social phenomena (Bakhtin 1986:259). Utterances (discourses) are constructed between socially organized persons who speak with a multiplicity of voices pertaining to (or stemming from) the various social positions each individual occupies (Voloshinov 1973; Bakhtin 1986; Young 1990; Moore 1994). Rather than looking at the formal elements of discourse, we should explore the social conditions that render communication possible or seriously hinder it.[10]

Positions—and identities—are defined, redefined, questioned, and confirmed in the process of interaction (Rossi Landi 1970:15; Giddens 1984; Smith 1988). But what is at stake in their negotiation cannot be totally grasped through an interactionist analysis which limits itself to the immediacy of a context devoid of time and of social structural differences.[11] As Bourdieu (1982) has noted, participants in communicational exchanges are carriers of a symbolic capital acquired through the process of socialization. That socialization guarantees the reproduction of social classes and other social categories. When interacting, participants do not produce discourses with the sole purpose of being understood. Utterances also contain signs denoting wealth to be valued and authority to be recognized and obeyed (Bourdieu 1982). There is a constant interplay between the formation of subjects in discourse and the production of discourses by subjects who are already holders of social identities (Berger and Luckmann 1966, Smith 1988, Althusser 1971).

The process of positioning is a complex one. It is based on a variety of markers present in social interaction: use of speech genres, forms of address, body gestures, and presentation of selves (Goffman 1959). It is of great importance to see how each participant positions the others because this reveals who is granted authority to speak. It also enables us to see whose discourse would be taken as legitimate, whose would be efficacious (Bourdieu 1982), whose would be "vraisemblable" (credible) (Greimas 1983:103), whose would be read "between the lines." By exploring the positioning mechanisms at work, we will discover how certain professional groups came to enjoy power within the relocation agency and subsequently lost it.

In communication processes, there is always a tension between the attempt to impose a unitary language and the reality of heteroglossia which acts as a reminder of social difference. Communication in development projects is no exception. There is an official language of planning and the languages corresponding to professional kinds of knowledge; there is a uniform, univocal national language and the language of class and geographical regions (Bourdieu 1982; Bakhtin 1986; Voloshinov 1973; Burton and Carlen 1979).

Acknowledgement of differences, however, must not obscure regularities in discursive practices and interpretations observable in specific social contexts, historically and spatially situated. The search for regularities should not lead to a dissolution of the human agents, as structuralists' studies do. The subject, as Verón (1984:50) puts it, is the one mediating conditions and processes of production. To recover the subject/subjects is a political act and an act of transgression. It raises questions of power precisely where this is not acknowledged; it challenges a representation of society as rationally and naturally organized. It unveils a conception of subjects as previously constituted uniform units liable to manipulation (Lechner 1986a:19, Bauman 1987:54–60).

I do not want to fall into a notion of a totally decentered subject incapable of reacting, a problem that has recently become central in feminism and among those concerned with various forms of emancipatory politics (see, for example, Spivak 1988; Harvey 1996; Moore 1994; Gregory 1994; Friedman 1996; Nash 1997). I propose to depart from the positions very dear to some poststructuralist thinkers, for in their emphasis on theories of language, subjectivity and difference, and relativization of all sources of knowledge, they have divorced themselves from the real.[12] We should recover the concrete agents behind discourses who are involved in political practices.

COMMUNICATIVE PRACTICES

In everyday interaction, people not only assign meanings to what is uttered but also to body signs and objects that may be neutral in other contexts. I will try to reconstruct how people elaborate and explicate what is said and also what actions and objects they take as meaningful. But this can only be done through establishing a dialogue with participants from previous dialogues who would provide me with an already interpreted text. As Bakhtin noted, researchers must work with texts already created; texts are our point of departure (1986:113). Thus, I will call *communicative practices* those processes by which people construct texts to confer meanings to actions, objects, and discourses. Communicative practices presuppose dialogical relations, that is to say, they involve an other, from whom the speaker expects a response, and they also imply preceding practices to which they are responding.

To describe these communicative practices we must identify what I will call *dialogical sets*, the particular communicative relations established with the advent of the project.[13] Each of these sets will have addressors and addressees, those who produce a text and those who consume it. The condition of addressor and addressee is not fixed; they are constantly shifting from one role to another. Some dialogical sets are relatively stable throughout the project implementation, such as the one composed by the staff and the population. Others may develop within specific conjunctures and later disappear. This is the case with groups or individuals who form temporary sets by being summoned or deliberately assuming the role of mediators. Not only individuals but also collectives, such as a family or a professional group, may become addressors and addressees. It may well happen that individuals reify institutions and perceive them as purposeful actors. Therefore, it is likely that we will find some dialogical sets in which one or both of the members are not concrete actors but organizations.

When looking at communicative practices, I am concerned with what is withheld and concealed. Secrecy, the withholding of information, and the absence of dialogue occur for a variety of reasons such as coping with uncertainty, asserting authority, or protecting oneself or another. For example, analysts have noted that secrecy is a common practice among bureaucratic officials interested in gaining power. Similarly, other authors have stressed the relationship between knowledge control and power. It is likely that some staff members of a relocation agency, seeking recognition or maintaining an already powerful position, may be reluctant to disclose information to others. We can also expect that the people to be relocated would lie or withhold some information they assume could be used against them. Contexts where mistrust, concealment and obfuscation prevail will favor the inversion of meanings and/or the creation or transformation of others.

PARTICULARITIES OF THE YACYRETA CASE STUDY

The case I will analyze displays some particularities which make it unique among resettlement projects designed to cope with the effects of construction of large hydroelectric dams:

- It affects dwellers of an urban environment and not indigenous or peasant families living in rural areas as it is the case with many hydroelectric projects.
- The team in charge of planning the relocation process included social scientists, both sociologists and anthropologists, who continued working through the implementation stage of the project. Although anthropologists had been involved in studying and criticizing resettlement projects, very few had been hired to take an active role in planning and implementing a relocation process.
- The project suffered numerous postponements which prolonged the period of uncertainty prior to relocation far beyond what is common in similar undertakings. Indeed, although uncertainty is often mentioned as a factor influencing the crisis and stress generated by population displacement, I know of no other experience in which uncertainty persisted as long as in the Yacyretá project.
- A great part of the prolonged relocation process occurred under a very repressive and authoritarian regime, a circumstance which impinged upon communication dynamics in a way which is probably unique among these resettlement projects.
- While the relocation process was underway, the economic situation of Argentina worsened and reached levels of hyperinflation and unemployment, which limited options and affected the type of strategies people would have employed under more stable conditions.

Undoubtedly, the exceptionality of some of these factors set constraints on the population's ability to make claims and on the freedom of members of EBY's staff to design social programs. These constraints are more severe than those one finds in other resettlement projects. Nevertheless, many of the responses and communication problems are not unique to the Yacyretá project, although access to power resources and negotiating opportunities would probably be greater in similar cases elsewhere.

NOTES

1. There are many studies on the impact of large dams on peasants and indigenous peoples. See, for example, Fahim (1981, 1983), Wali (1982, 1989), Colson (1971, 1976), Scudder and Colson (1987[1972], 1982), Salisbury (1986), Barabás and Bartolomé (1973, 1984), Gates (1988), and Fernea and Kennedy (1966).

2. In their 1988 book, Colson and Scudder said: "We think of societies as flexible organizations forming and reforming because they are composed of thinking men and women who are bound neither by primordial institutions nor by primordial identities. They can change and become something else. Rules and acquired wisdom, the stuff of culture, are guides to action but do not dictate action. Instead, people make opportunistic choices which they then try to justify. Sometimes this involves the revision of very basic assumptions, but

more commonly, people appeal to situational factors that particularize the choice to the here and now" (1988:2).

3. For an illuminating discussion that makes similar criticisms to populist models employed in agricultural extension, see Scoones and Thompson (1994).

4. For critical assessment of participatory perspectives see Rahnema (1992), Esteva (1985), van Ufford (1988), and Rosander (1992).

5. Marx (1987:352) said: "Technology discloses man's mode of dealing with nature, the process of production by which he sustains his life, and thereby also lays bare the mode of formation of his social relations, and of the mental conceptions that flow from them."

6. For discussions on these new trends in physics, see Prigogine (1980, 1984), and Prigogine and Stengers (1988). For an attempt to incorporate these orientations to the analysis of social processes, see Richard Adams (1988), *The Eighth Day.*

7. This is comparable to a sense of situatedness as "a dialectical power relation between the oppressor and the oppressed" (Harvey 1996:355).

8. Gottdiener speaks of the container function of a physical location—the site where events take place—and of the social order function—the social permission to engage in these events (1985:123).

9. Loomis says that disasters "occur when the social organization and units of considerable segments of society cease to function." Unlike Wallace, he recognizes that destructuration may also happen through the impact of internal forces (1960:130)

10. Foucault (1991) points that what he analyzes in discourse is not the system of its language nor the rules of construction. He seeks to unveil the "law of existence of statements, that which rendered them possible" (1991:59).

11. Bourdieu says: "We should depart from the 'interactionist' pespective which, caught into the direct, visible immediacy of actions and interactions, is unable to discover that the linguistic strategies of different agents depend upon their position in the structure of distribution of linguistic capital, where we know that, through the mediation of the structure of opportunities controlling the access to the educational system, they depend upon the structure of class relations" (1977:57).

12. In a recent article, Friedman (1992) warns against academic analysis which question the authenticity of traditions and collective identities by interpreting them as essentializations. This, he maintains might deny any form of agency to oppressed groups and delegitimize their political action. Similar concerns may be found in Smith (1988) and Lechner (1986).

13. The concept of the dialogical is comparable to the concept of intertextuality, although according to Todorov, the first bears a more restricted meaning: an exchange of responses by two speakers (see Todorov 1984).

CHAPTER 3

Regional Struggles for Hegemony

If development is an ensemble of discourses and practices organized around the goal of relocating peoples and cultures into a future full of promises, why should experts bother about examining the past when planning social change? This is undoubtedly the way most planners think about the relevance of history to development planning. Faithful children of the ideology of modernity, which relies heavily on the power of science and technology to promote progress, most experts used to blame history and culture for the backwardness and irrationality of "underdeveloped" societies. Consequently, if they ever hassled with these factors, it was with the sole purpose of recommending strategies to overcome these troublesome obstacles to innovation. Such views were partially replaced by one that stresses structural factors present at the moment an innovation is introduced. In this latter case, history was regarded as irrelevant, and planners did not include it as a variable to be reckoned with when designing a program of social change. Today, history remains largely ignored, even though some planners have become more sensitive to local cultures after critiques to the concept of development and various planning strategies of attaining it escalated. Even in those cases in which some authors express concern with tradition and the past, they generally do so in a romanticized manner and with an external analytical framework that projects into the actors goals and desires which are not necessarily theirs. They present the displaced as helpless and passive victims of a development which disrupts a presumably harmonious and unproblematic culture. But, as Birgitte Refslund Sorensen (1997) rightly argues, people are not simply victims of social change, they are social agents. When relocation occurs, "People live with and continue to reinterpret and elaborate their experiences, depending on context and purpose" (1997:144). Their narratives contribute to their sense of identity by placing themselves in "an event and a scene" and thus challenging some dominant perspectives of displacement that dehistoricize it.

The Yacyretá hydroelectric project is a good example of this lack of concern with notions of place and identity as reflections of historical developments. Preliminary feasibility studies analyzed neither the regional nor the affected population's history. Neither did they concern themselves with the local ways of constructing identities.

Nobody felt there was a need for dealing with such issues. Subsequent chapters will show that to ignore history is a mistake. Especially if our aim is to understand development practice, we have to acknowledge its temporality.[1] Communication and miscommunication among planners, government officials, landowners, and the displaced population can only be understood if we take into account their interaction prior to the announcement of dam construction and their use of narratives about the past to shape their daily encounters.

This chapter shows how the past and present of Misiones is depicted by diverse observers. Competing versions of the past and of the present are contradictory and ambiguous; they depend on the structural position of each narrator. I attempt to maintain the tension among narratives expressing conflicting projects for the nation and the region, to allow readers to perceive how participants construct and make use of their representations to justify and affect their own actions.

Accounts of past events provide us with clues for understanding legitimizing ideologies and behavioral patterns observed in the relocation project. They allow us to see how biases developed and persisted into the present. Discussions in this chapter let us see the marginal position of Misiones with regards to the national state. As a borderland, the Misiones space has always been regarded as a place where national identity is permanently threatened and contested. Because it constitutes a very particular national frontier, and also because the project is jointly owned by Paraguay, we need to see past and present regional interconnections: We cannot understand processes in Misiones unless we consider how they relate to developments occurring in Brazil and Paraguay and in the bordering Argentine province of Corrientes.

NATION AND REGION: MISIONES, THE REMOTE JUNGLE OF ARGENTINA

To the majority of Argentines, the province of Misiones is a wild and exotic place. They think of impenetrable jungle—hot, suffocatingly humid weather, the powerful Iguazú Falls, and the half-forgotten Jesuit missions. Argentines also think of this remote frontier as endangered. They worry that Misioneros are constantly exposed to foreign influences, namely Brazilian culture, and are unable to communicate in Spanish, the national language. In the 1980s, local government tourist promotions reinforced this image of wilderness and otherness: a smiling tucan invited everyone to "join the adventure" and visit Misiones.

This picture of Argentina's northeastern-most province is partly accurate and partly inaccurate. It is a picture that is largely a function of the economic, political, and cultural dominance of another region of the country—a region with a far different climate and ecology. Although dominant constructions of Argentine identity might acknowledge the tremendous differences between the various parts of their country, they tend to identify the whole country with the *región pampeana*. With one area within this region—the *pampa húmeda*—this identification is especially strong. In Argentina's *imaginary*, one region has become the nation. Argentines associate this grain-producing region, which includes Buenos Aires,

Santa Fe, Entre Ríos, and Córdoba provinces, with the golden years of the country when, they proudly say, Argentina became the bread basket of the world. Cattle production was well established long before the pampa's rich soil and the temperate weather were found ideal for the development of large-scale agriculture. Beef also contributed to the Argentines' identity; barbecued steak is regarded as the national dish.

That one region has assumed the symbolic construction of the nation is the result of fifty years of civil wars beginning shortly after the Río de la Plata provinces gained independence from Spain. Free navigation of rivers, collection of custom taxes, and provincial autonomy pitted the provinces against Buenos Aires, which often managed to control the wealth produced in the regions of the former Spanish viceroyalty. The port of Buenos Aires jealously patrolled river navigation and by limiting circulation contributed to the stagnation of many provincial economies. In *Las dos políticas*, attributed to Olegario Víctor Andrade, the author complains about Buenos Aires' monopoly of commerce and transportation and laments that "instead of Madrid, the capital [after independence] was called Buenos Aires. Instead of monarchical and foreign colonialism, we have had since 1810 domestic and republican colonialism" (as cited in Shumway 1991:218).

The battle of Pavón in 1861, which signals national unification, and the federalization of Buenos Aires in 1880 mark the achievement of political and military stability under the unquestionable hegemony of the port city over the provinces. It is the end, according to Romero (1979), of the *Argentina criolla*, and the beginning of a unified liberal republic. For nearly fifty years, an illustrated urban elite in alliance with powerful landowners directed the capitalist modernization process which pursued a deep transformation of the socio-economic structure of the country. The ruling classes strongly believed that the backwardness of Argentina would be overcome with the opening of the economy to the international market and by a deliberate "whitening" of the population through bringing in of massive numbers of Europeans. The newly organized state built telegraph lines, roads, and railroads to facilitate communication with the foreign markets and to maintain the recently subordinated provinces under its aegis. With the eruption of external conflicts—such as the War of the Triple Alliance (discussed later in this chapter—the imposition of internal pacification occurred, such as the Conquest of the Desert (the bloody extermination of the Indian population), and the end of provincial autonomy, national authorities devoted part of their energies to asserting territorial sovereignty through delineating international boundaries and surveying the largely unkown remote frontiers. One such frontier was the Misiones territory. Even though the settling of boundaries was wrought with conflicts, the subsequent construction of a collective imaginary of the national territory presented a picture of the state as having natural and static state boundaries, a key factor in the process of nation building (Escolar, Quintero Palacios, and Reboratti 1994).

By the turn of the nineteenth century and the beginning of the twentieth, a large number of European migrants settled in the *región pampeana* in response to a rather contradictory call from Argentina's ruling elites. The majority of them went to the major cities, accelerating the urbanization process. This was not what some members of the enlightened elites initially envisioned. Their intention was to encourage migration as a means to modernize the country through, among other things, the development of agriculture. However, they were not very ready to surrender their landed privileges to the newcomers. As a result, very few foreigners could remain in the countryside because there was no available land. Public lands had already been allotted to the existing elites.

Two versions of *argentinidad*, or Argentine identity, became dominant during the last decades of the nineteenth century. These two versions reflected the confrontations for hegemony among powerful elite sectors. Together with all their variants, these versions are still haunting Argentine society. They are related to the profound processes of transformation which were underway in the 1880s and both originated in the leading region, with Buenos Aires as its center.

One version is cosmopolitan and depicts nationals as European peoples committed to progress. It is generally anti-Spanish and secular and praises the power of reason and science. This representation has probably found its most vivid expression in Sarmiento's (1961[1845]) description of Argentina through his dichotomic model of *Civilización y Barbarie*, where the interior is seen as a backward area with cultural features which inhibit the development toward modernity. Although liberal in its economic principles, this version of *argentinidad* is exclusionary and aristocratic at a political level, denying effective citizenship to the majority of the population.

The other version identifies nationhood with *gaucho* culture. It often emphasizes the Spanish and Catholic heritage, and although it might praise the popular, it is often conservative and hierarchical. Around 1880, a faction of the elite began to romanticize the image of the *gauchos* (*mestizo* cowboys), who were previously pictured very negatively, as lazy vagabonds with no inclinations to form stable families. It was only after *estancieros* (landowners) ceased to procure their labor force through the invaluable help of judges and the police force, that transformation of gauchos into a positive symbol could occur.[2] Conservative landowners jealously guarded what they associated as the base of their wealth: cattle raising, which was facilitated by frontier expansion. Many developed antiforeign ideologies in the belief that the liberal project of agricultural production and the encouragement of foreign migration represented a threat to their old ways. But such fears were unfounded; the land tenure system did not change. On the contrary, with frontier expansion, the old elites stretched their control over land into the newly occupied borderlands.

Sábato (1988:24) maintains that Argentina's oligarchy has displayed a great adaptability to changes in production. This adaptability developed as a response to world market conditions, namely the expansion of industrial capitalism accompanied by an increased demand for food and raw materials from temperate regions. The dominant class, he argues, acquired its leading role not only by its ownership of land, but also through its ability to combine ownership with the control of commercial and financial activities. Throughout the nineteenth century, production in the *región pampeana*, switched from salted meats to wool, then to cereals, and finally to cattle in combination with grains. Although the liberal and conservative projects seem to contradict each other, in a short time both came to coexist quite comfortably: The cows ended up grazing next to the wheat and corn fields, and *gauchos* faces seemed to whiten, while the liberal-oriented school syllabus dictated the study of "national dances" encompassing the folklore *pampeano*, and hence, the *gaucho* culture. Although many nationalist authors tend to identify this latter version of *argentinidad* as the one that truly represents the invisible Argentina, the deep Motherland rooted in American soil, the defeated interior, and the popular classes, the truth is that by choosing the gaucho as its main icon, they help to erase from national memory the role played by other major actors, namely the Indians and the inhabitants of national regions other than the pampas.[3] Obviously, they also refuse to see the role played by migrants in the complex identity(ies) of Argentine peoples.

Misiones resembles the pampas neither in climate nor in soil. It is a hot, subtropical region with summer temperatures reaching 50 degrees Celsius. Rainfall averages more than 2,500 mm a year; it enables the growth of an exuberant vegetation cover, a *selva* (jungle) for many, even though this is generally associated with tropical regions. It is truly a forest, el *monte*, as many Misioneros call it with respect and admiration. Far from being flat as are the pampas, the province is rather hilly, and in some parts it reaches respectable altitudes (700 meters above sea level). Anybody coming from Buenos Aires province is taken aback by the contrasts; they are assailed by fragrances and bright and shiny shades of green over an astonishingly red soil. Undoubtedly, such a scene bears no resemblance to the dull, pale yellows and greens that spread endlessly to the horizon over a grayish carpet of earth which characterize the pampas. It is these distinctions that stirred the imagination of innumerable visitors to this remote and foreign region, when it was rediscovered at the turn of the century. Two hundred years earlier, Jesuits were also struck by the natural scenery and dedicated themselves to studying the great variety of fauna and flora. Observers either described the forest with admiration and enchantment or warned travelers about the dangerous poisonous spiders, snakes, insects, and different varieties of "ferocious wild cats," that could be encountered in an "untouched" natural environment.

Cavazutti (1923) rightly observed that many earlier authors stressed the beauty and economic potential of Misiones. Very few had a hidden agenda; their message was straightforward: They were interested in promoting the region to prospective settlers and investors. Imbued with the modernizing ideology of the late nineteenth century, they were eager to advertise its promise to stimulate European migrants to come and develop agriculture. Cavazutti quotes Guillermo Godio who in 1886 addressed a most distinguished audience of Buenos Aires at the famous opera theater *Colón*, a replica of the Parisian opera house. While there, he said:

The great secret of Misiones future, relies on agriculture. It is on behalf of agriculture that Misiones is destined to prove that the famous Eldorado which aroused the fantasy of the first conquerors, is not a chimera. . . . From now on even the deaf and the blind would know that Misiones is one of the most precious jewels in the diadema of the Republic. (1923:34)

Contemporary authors and common citizens sometimes describe Misiones as a wedge pushing its way between Brazil and Paraguay (see Map 3.1). This image may convey the idea of a will to expand into what it is now somebody else's territory, a likely representation of not very unconscious desires. Others would metaphorically regard Misiones as an arm, a part of the country's body which is dislocated. The examination of any map of Argentina reveals why it is described in such ways. It is indeed a salient part of the national territory, stretching to the northeast. Corrientes province, which constitutes its southwestern boundary, is the only connection to the republic. Beyond these limits, Misiones is surrounded by foreign lands—Brazil and Paraguay. The physical configuration of the area helps us to understand in part why isolation, distance, and foreignness are always major concerns for anybody dealing with problems of the area.

Map 3.1
Southern Cone Region. Yacyretá Dam

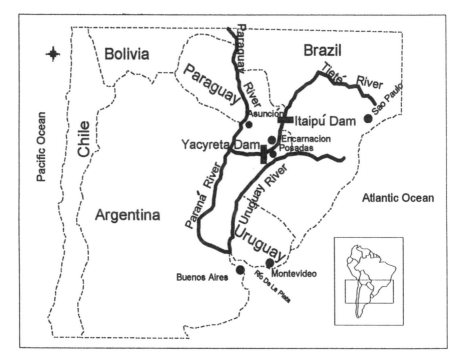

But what we now call Misiones was significantly different in the past. According to Argentine historians, Misiones was two-thirds larger throughout most of colonial times. To be able to interpret present events and to make sense of the tremendous transformations that affected the region in the past, we have to consider the role played both by Paraguay and Brazil. We will also have to take into account a larger region which goes beyond Argentina's frontiers. It is this greater spatial unit with undefined boundaries which represents the scene of struggles among the three countries.

MISIONES HISTORY

I have organized the discusion of historical processes studied from Argentina's vantage point in the following manner: (1) The colonial and Jesuit order, (2) the destruction of the Jesuit order and the return to barbarism, (3) the rediscovery of Misiones, "from wilderness to progress," (4) private projects of European settlement and the development of export agriculture, (5) provincialization and the introduction of new forms of production—namely, agribusiness and hydroelectric projects, and (6) the new regional integration: MERCOSUR.

The Colonial and Jesuit Order

The first Spanish settlement with an Atlantic orientation in southern South America was the city of Asunción founded by Domingo Irala in 1527. As early as the sixteenth century, chronicles addressed authorities, urging them to intervene among residents who "were men with neither law, nor King, nor God, nor morals." Authors like Lozano and Guevara compared them to pagans or berberiscos (Furlong 1978:30). Very few men formed families in accordance to principles prescribed by the Catholic Church, and many lived *amancebados* (in concubinage) with more than one woman. The concern with making the local population conform to metropolitan family patterns, as well as the ascription of such negative features as the lack of beliefs and morals and the failure to respect authority has been dominant throughout the region's history. These ideas either justified the replacement of the old inhabitants by European newcomers committed to the modernizing trends or the domestication of their labor. We will discuss this point further in coming sections and in Chapter Five.

By the turn of the sixteenth and the early seventeenth centuries, when Spain was under the rule of King Felipe III, the Jesuits were called into the territory in order to establish towns among the Guaraní Indians. Royal authorities also expected the fathers to convince their subjects to embrace Christianity. Thirteen towns were founded in the province of la Guayra on the left banks of the upper Paraná River. Shortly thereafter, the *bandeiras* of the *Mamelucos*[4] from Sao Paulo repeatedly invaded the area until it was destroyed in 1631. Both Indians and Spanish settlers were forced to take sanctuary west and south of the Guayra (Hernández 1973 [1887]:11). Such invasions reflected rivalries between Portugal and Spain over control of the New World's territories. Though legally settled by the Papal Bull of Alexander VI (1493) and the Treaty of Tordesillas (1494), these documents were differently interpreted by the contending parties (see, for example, Zeballos 1893, Zinny 1975). Ever since those times, the Portuguese and, later on, their American successors, the Brazilians, have been depicted as sanguinary, ambitious, wicked, and destructive peoples. Certainly some of the guiding myths of Brazilian nationalism provide a very different picture of the *bandeiras*. According to the

Brazilians, these were "mestizo" expeditions which opened the Brazilian interior, and marched to the west toward "independence and democracy while the lords of sugar plantations embraced European capitalism" (Ricardo 1956:248). The *malocas*, that is, the Mameluco invasions, penetrated the Missions territory with the purpose of enslaving Indians to be sold to Portuguese *fazendas* (large land estates). Authors estimate that as many as 30,000 Indians were captured during the seventeenth century. Although the Sao Paulo *bandeirantes* were defeated in the battle of Mbororé, they continued to be a threat to the Jesuit missions until their demise (Zeballos 1893:323, Furlong 1978:117).

Historians are divided when it comes to judging the role played by the Jesuits in this disputed region. While some maintain that they constituted a barrier that stopped Lusitans (Portuguese) from invading the national territory, others stress their isolationist policies and claim they formed an "Empire within the Empire" which had loose ties with the Spanish Crown (Bove 1923, Furlong 1978, Lugones 1981[1904]). Both detractors and admirers agree that the Jesuit enterprise was a completely new experience on American soil, worthy of careful research. This study does not attempt to address the many questions that remain unanswered about the role of this order in these subtropical lands. It simply highlights some historical events which enable us to understand how the past and present of Brazil, Paraguay, and Argentina became so intertwined.

The Jesuit fathers remained in the region for a century and a half. During their stay, they controlled the lives of more than 100,000 Indians. The missions became self-sustained units where both men and women dedicated their time to crafts, agriculture, and worship under the supervision of the religious order. The Jesuits undertook careful studies of the natural environment and experimented on the agricultural possibilities of the area. They were able to master the domestication of *yerba mate* (Ilex paraguayensis), a stimulant herb from which a highly popular drink is made. When the Spanish Crown expelled them from the area, they took with them the secret of the domestication of the plant. A hundred years later, the exploitation of the wild plants required the inhumane use of the labor force of the *mensúes,* descendants of the inhabitants of the missions. It was not until the twentieth century that new settlers were able to obtain new cultured plants, after years of experimentation and numerous failures.

During colonial times, both Asunción and Buenos Aires tried to gain control of the 30 *pueblos* of Misiones. By the eighteenth century, the area had become one of the wealthiest and most populated territories of the Spanish possessions in the Río de la Plata. Bishops from Paraguay and Buenos Aires, together with colonial authorities, started to accuse the Jesuits of conspiring to gain autonomous control and argued that the order was dominated by foreign priests and that the few Spanish within it were all in subordinate positions (Lista 1883:23). In 1726, royal letters ordered that the Reductions of the Company in the District of Paraguay be placed under the jurisdiction of the government of Buenos Aires. This move represented one of the last efforts to defend the Jesuits from their detractors. It did not last long. Roughly forty years later, in April 1767, Carlos III ordered the religious order to withdraw from the Spanish territories.

The Destruction of the Jesuit Order and the Return to Barbarism

We can hardly find historical accounts dealing with the 30 *pueblos* of Misiones during the hundred years that followed the Jesuit demise. Bucarelli, the governor of Buenos Aires sent Franciscans, Dominicans, and Mercedarians to replace the Jesuit fathers. It was the beginning of fragmentation and the economic decay of what once was a large and prosperous territory. Oral tradition, travelers' accounts, and local historians tell us that the majority of the Guaraní Indians were unable to administer their pueblos once the Jesuits left. They also say that they moved back to the jungle to live as "savages" again (Hernández 1973[1887]:19). Many use this argument to criticize the role of the missions. They maintain that the fathers were extremely paternalistic and that they failed to teach them how to live in a civilized and self-sufficient manner.

Another version, concerned with finding the identity of the Misioneros in opposition to the official national version centered in Buenos Aires, vindicates the heroic role of the Indians in the defence of the territory from Portuguese and Paraguayan attacks. The inhabitants of the pueblos are portrayed as people committed to the cause of independence. We are told that they sent envoys to join the new revolutionary governments and that a local hero, the Indian Andresito Guacurarí, a protegee of Artigas, the caudillo[5] from la Banda Oriental (Uruguay), fought fiercely against the Portuguese—fiercely but unsuccessfully. Those who resisted the Portuguese attempts to occupy their land were unable to stop them and witnessed the destruction of a great number of *pueblos*. Chagas, a Portuguese general, was held responsible for all kinds of atrocities. The Paraguayans, under the "obscure dictator Dr. Francia" are blamed for the destruction of the missions on the Paraná River (Lista 1883:25). While those favoring federalism and the autonomy of the provinces praise Andresito and Artigas for defending the pueblos, others who sympathize with Buenos Aires think that the pueblos were burnt and ransacked because of these contested heroes (Hernández 1973[1887]:18).

Misiones was generally denied the right to have an independent government. After the Jesuits were expelled, Asunción and Buenos Aires authorities continued trying to gain control over those lands. On the grounds that they lived in a strategic area which could easily be attacked by Brazil, nobody wanted to grant the Misioneros an autonomous government. Many believed that in order to protect the boundaries it was desirable to maintain the region under the control of a powerful central government and to appoint a military representative. Entre Ríos, Santa Fe, Corrientes, Buenos Aires, and Paraguay either controlled or tried to protect the Misiones region at different historical junctures. In 1814, Gervasio Posadas, supreme director of the Provinces of the Río de la Plata decided that Misiones and Corrientes should be one province. After this decision, the political control was in the hands of the Correntinos, and Misiones was scarcely inhabited. Authorities living in Corrientes failed to defend the *pueblos* of Misiones when they were attacked by Portuguese and Paraguayans. Some authors even contend that through secret agreements, Corrientes authorities allowed Paraguayans to occupy part of the Misiones territory during Rosas times (from the 1830s to the 1850s).[6]

Dictatorships and isolationism are features generally stressed when describing Paraguay. According to many nineteenth-century chronicles, foreigners and intellectuals were not welcome (Zinny 1975). Dictator Francia and some of his successors tried to keep national boundaries closed to external influences. The so-called *trincheras* (sometimes also called *tranqueras*) stand as a symbol of their closure. They were walls constructed to defend military encampments which spread along the right banks of the Paraná River. The trinchera de Loreto seems to be the first one of these walls. Part of what is nowadays Posadas, the capital city of Misiones, was once surrounded by these walls. As Rosas prohibited the navigation of the Paraná River, the Paraguayans had to change their commercial route. They started to send and receive goods through Brazilian ports and their caravans crossed what is now the province of Misiones, camping in front of Itapuá, Encarnación, which stood across the Paraná River. Troops also camped behind the tranqueras from 1849 to 1865. The area, delimited by the 2.50 meter high walls, was actually a fort known as Itapuá and Trinchera de los Paraguayos.

Paraguayans and Uruguayans alike believe that their country's history cannot be understood unless we consider it in its relationship to the two giants surrounding them. The Paraguayan war, often called the War of the Triple Alliance, is a good example of this.[7] Brazil and Argentina's support of an unpopular ruler in Uruguay triggered Paraguayan President Solano López's decision to declare war first on Brazil and then on Argentina and to invade their territories. It is argued that he did so because he saw the intervention in Uruguay as a threat to the existing balance of power in the Río de la Plata, which in his eyes, guaranteed his country's independence and territorial integrity.[8] The liberal elites from Brazil and Argentina—backed, some contend, by England—legitimated the war, which lasted from 1864 to 1870, in terms of a confrontation of civilization against barbarism; it was the war of those who favored "whitenization" and progress through migration against the autonomous and nomadic mestizo peoples (Bethell 1996, Pomer 1968, Hernández 1980[1870]). Near the end of the war, in a letter to Argentine President Mitre, Dr.Gómez, a fellow citizen, prophetically lamented that by "adulterating the struggle in Paraguay, we have transformed it into a war against a people rather than against a tyrant; we have given our enemy a noble banner for combat; we have engendered the spirit for a cause; we have created an eternal glory; which would raise against us and would wound us with the blades we have ploughed" (Gómez 1980[1869]). More than a hundred years later, his words ring true as the negotiations between Argentina and Paraguay regarding Yacyretá are still haunted by the scars of the war. The Paraguayans frame these negotiations as a revenge of this war. After its defeat, it found itself not only with fewer men but also with a smaller territory. Argentina, having regained part of the old Misiones, put it under the surveillance of Corrientes authorities.

On his return after triumphing over the Paraguayans, the victorious Brazilian general José Gómez Portinho, left battalion number 24 on a hilly site in what is now Posadas. It is said that the chaplain dedicated a mass to Saint Josep, and from then on the place was called Trincheras or Tranqueras de San José (Fernández Ramos 1931:215, Abínzano 1985:792, Manzi 1910:141, Bove 1923:36). Together with the troops came merchants and neighbors from the nearby villages of Santo Tomé, Aguapey, and San Borja. In a short time, they had built a row of *ranchos* (huts) which spread diagonally from the gate of the trinchera to the natural port on the Paraná River. The majority of the settlers were coming from the Banda Oriental. The rest were French, Italians, Spanish, and Brazilians. Argentines were a minority, only two, according to the records. From the very beginning, the village became involved in commercial activities. Its development is closely tied to the timber and *yerba mate* extractive fronts on the upper Paraná River. Cattle and mule raising became increasingly important in the south of Misiones.

Smuggling has always been a profitable source of income for the residents of the area. State representatives continuously denounced the practice of taking cows, timber, and other goods into Paraguay without official sanction. For many, it was one among other means of making a living. As such, very few regarded it as unlawful or worthy of negative moral judgments. But outsiders have always referred to it as one of the many issues deserving the intervention of the national state.

Records tell us very little about who inhabited Misiones and what they did for a living during the years of political turmoil in the provinces of the Río de la Plata. In 1813, Belgrano's forces were sent to protect Misiones from Paraguayan claims; 32,000 people lived in the region, representing as much as 7.2 percent of the total population of the country. Some decades later, immediately after the Argentine Confederation recovered control over the territory, authors comment that probably not more than 3,000 were struggling to survive either in the jungle or in poor huts built over the remains of the Jesuit ruins (Lista 1883:33,109; Hernández 1973 [1887]:46). We will never know the exact population figures. The 1864 census was not taken in the national territories on the grounds that the "population of these areas was not civilized" (Argentine Republic. Censo de Población de los Territorios Nacionales 1914: 12).

The Rediscovery of Misiones: From Wilderness to Progress

The Jesuit enterprise represents the first attempt "to tame the wilderness" in the remote northeastern part of Argentina. The second one, started by the end of last century, when explorers and surveyors sent by the national state reopened the area for "civilized" settlements:

Until quite recently, this marvelous land remained forgotten, but at the call of Motherland, that pronounced its name, we all remembered that Motherland is also there, with its green woods and rich soil, waiting for other men with other goals to reproduce the marvels made by the humble missionaries without any other help but their faith. (Lista 1883:4)

Agriculture was considered a critical necessity for a country "devoured by the desert so as to establish discipline and order among a nomadic population which corrupts and leads to barbarism the totality of society" (Mitre 1980 [1857]:321). Writers say that before the rediscovery of the area, the land was unknown, forgotten and left in the "hands of anthropophagus Indians, some of them even with tails" (Hernández

1973[1887]:98). The lake of Iberá in Corrientes, not too far from Posadas and the town of Ituzaingó, where the hydroelectric project is now under construction, was believed to be inhabited by semisavages and fantastic creatures (Lista 1883:5). The existence of the local population is acknowledged by very few of the late nineteenth-century historians and travelers: As a rule, they remain invisible (Hernández 1973[1887]. The space is presented as a desert to be settled and occupied. When those who hoped to convert Misiones into a prosperous and modern agricultural utopia acknowledged the existence of a population, they found it ill-suited for this transformation. The newcomers found the locals "semi-savage," nomadic, and ignorant of the symbols representing the nation: Such people deserved to be dominated and deprived of land. For Hernández, the native men were lazy, unwilling to work or till the soil (Hernández 1973[1887]:48). They were described as a "mixture of Indians, Paraguayans, Correntinos, and Brazilians" who vegetated in Posadas or wandered in the jungles of Misiones either hunting or fishing for survival or offering their labor to those newcomers to the region who started to pillage the natural *yerbales*[9] and woods. Brazilians, concerned as the Argentines were in asserting their identity and their national presence in the region, expressed similar concerns about the uprooted local population, most of whom spoke neither Spanish nor Portuguese. Nowadays, the lower classes of Misiones continue to be described in the same manner and arouse the same suspicions regarding their hybrid character (Gupta and Ferguson 1992, Bhabha 1994, Anzaldúa 1987, García Canclini 1990). Misioneros have been continuously regarded as peoples who are not fully Argentine:

National solidarity is totally fractured, it cannot be said that Northern Correntinos and Misioneros are truly Argentines in their feelings. Difference of language is a barrier more powerful than the Ocean. And because of this, it is easier for us to get along with Europeans than with this fraction of compatriots. We feel more as strangers here than an Englishman in Buenos Aires. (Hernández 1973[1887]:30)

By the turn of the century, many visitors to Misiones were praising the agricultural and industrial promise of the region. There were many barriers to the realization of this promise. Communications, the land tenure system, the existing economic activities, and inadequate human resources were seen by the advocates of the area as the major impediments to progress. As many of the enthusiasts of the region were Italians, it is not surprising that they suggested attracting migrants from their homeland to replace the locals (Bove 1923, Ambrosetti 1892, Cavazutti 1923).

All authors agreed that unless something was done to improve communications, the area would remain isolated and underdeveloped. Since colonial times, the Paraná River, and to a lesser degree the Uruguay River, have constituted the major routes connecting the Misiones region to the main cities of the Spanish Empire and to European ports. The rivers were the only realistic routes for Brazilian commodities; the Matto Grosso and the later-annexed Paraná regions had no land communication with major Brazilian cities until the 1940s. But river travel was not without its perils; shipwrecks could easily occur. Consequently, very few vessels would adventure beyond the Apipé rapids, three leagues north of Ituzaingó.

Navigation to the upper Paraná was only possible during the seasonal floods. Most of the steamships coming from Corrientes ended their journey in the small village of Ituzaingó. From there, travelers continued by land to Posadas. Another way of reaching Posadas was by ship along the Uruguay River up to Santo Tomé and then by wagons over muddy roads on an exhausting two- or three-day journey. It is not surprising then that one of the major preoccupations at the end of the century was the improvement of communications.

Shortly after Misiones was made into a national territory, communications improved significantly. Major steps to break the isolation were taken at this time, but others which were as necessary, such as road construction, were not considered for many decades. Commercial interests and the boom of yerba mate production encouraged the introduction of smaller vessels which could navigate the Paraná River beyond the Apipé rapids. The railroad, which cuts across the province connecting the two main rivers and remote cities of Buenos Aires and Asunción, was finished by 1912. The ferry boat trips from Posadas and Encarnación were inaugurated in 1913. Highway communication was a much later development, because it entailed building many bridges to cross the rivers and streams draining into the Paraná.

Once the Paraguayan war ended, Corrientes authorities sent surveyors to Trincheras de San José with the purpose of delimiting the area so that the town could be declared as the capital of Candelaria Department. By that time, it was already becoming a busy commercial center because of its favorable geographical position with regard to communication with the upper Paraná, the towns on the Uruguay River, and the Paraguayan village of Encarnación across the river. A decree from 1871 determined that the town should have a surface of 1,500 *varas*[10] divided into blocks of 100 varas each. It also determined that the *chacras*, 400 varas in size, should surround the central zone and be reserved for agriculture and animal husbandry.[11] Shortly afterwards, in 1872, municipal elections were held for the first time. The newly appointed authorities decided to grant plots to the first settlers of the town.

In 1881, Misiones became a national territory. The decision to put the region under the direct control of the central state coincided with the great political, economic, and socio-cultural changes in the Argentina of the 1880s. In order to achieve its modernizing goals, Argentina initiated the frontier expansion to open up territories to agriculture. The first appointed governor to the province was Rudecindo Roca, a colonel who fought against the Indians in the pampas (the other desert to be developed). Before Corrientes, in its "generosity," as chronicles of the time ironically said, decided to do away with the political control over this vast region, the majority of the land was allotted to a reduced number of families. Roca was one of the few favored ones.

In the beginning, Posadas remained a part of Corrientes province, but as a result of a claim raised by the new governor, the legislature decided to accede to the petition and the town became part of Misiones in 1882. Rivalries between the contemporary provinces are generally expressed with reference to the episodes of the late nineteenth century. Misioneros complain that Correntinos kept all the land to themselves, making it nearly impossible to start the colonizing process they had envisioned. Correntinos say Misioneros should be grateful as they managed to incorporate Posadas into their province.

By the turn of the century, visitors to Misiones repeatedly raged against the unproductive *latifundios (large estates)* in the hands of feudal lords. They blamed the ongoing situation on Corrientes authorities. Hernández complained that Governor Gallino sold the totality of the territory at a ridiculous price through granting certificates of public debt to members of the governing elite. Abínzano (1985) estimates that as much as 2,025,000 hectares were sold through these means. Fortunately, some of this land had to be returned to the state because the required surveys were not completed in due legal time. The lack of foresight on the part of the Correntinos who speculated with land created the availability for colonization. However, settlement of newcomers was only possible in the northern and central parts of the province where migrants became owners of family farms. The southern part remained in the hands of a few who owned large latifundios.

When Misiones was made into a national territory, its boundaries extended far beyond its actual legally defined limits. Brazil claimed a vast zone, which was once under Jesuit control. U.S. President Grover Cleveland was asked to intercede when the countries could not settle their disputes. Consequently, Misiones lost two-thirds of its land, and Brazil named one of its states Clevelandia in gratitude to the American president. Finally, in the early twentieth century, the extreme northeast of Argentina was ready for progress, although with a shrunken territory and very little land to offer to the prospective European *colonos* (settlers).

The First Years of Posadas. The level of activity in the new capital of Posadas surprised visitors. The region's boom paralleled that of the American West. Yerba mate extraction, the "Green Gold fever," and the exploitation of virgin woods accounted for its prosperity. Some of the first merchants, who came following the victorious troops, soon became the owners of steamship fleets, important wholesale houses, industries, and land. One of them, Domingo Barthe, owned as many as 25 ships and controlled some of the richest yerbales. In 1910, Manzi observed that the Posadas port was one of the most important of the republic, averaging the arrival and departure of seventy ships a month. As late as 1931, it occupied the fifth place in national customs revenues.

While fancy shops and "culture" flourished in a "cosmopolitan" Posadas, which suddenly rivaled in importance the older city of Corrientes, another hidden city life coexisted along the coast line of the Paraná River. Architecture reflects the denial of the elite responsibility for the existence of this other Posadas. The pretentious two-story houses of the prosperous families had no windows looking at the river; neither were they built in the waterway's proximity. It was as if they did not want to acknowledge that the source of their wealth was the river and the exploited men who lived nearby. The black legend of inhuman labor conditions and debt peonage started on the outskirts of Posadas port.

For Posadas to be seen as a modern and developed town, it had to be mirrored against others which were not. Observers have always praised the advancement of

Posadas by comparing it to the Paraguayan town of Encarnación and the village of Ituzaingó in Corrientes. In 1883, Hernández described Ituzaingó as a poor village of not more than 600 or 700 people, where it was nearly impossible to find the supplies and means of transportation that would enable him to continue his journey to Posadas. There were no brick houses; the majority of the homes were made of cane. Bove (1923) believed that this miserable settlement owed its existence to its location as the last port on the Paraná River before the barrier of the Apipé rapids; there was no other choice than to use it to deliver the merchandise to and from Misiones. After the War of the Triple Alliance, Encarnación was as poor as every other place in Paraguay. There were no adult men, only women and hungry children. Impressed by its poverty, Hernández remarked that because there was no lime and no concrete, houses could not be built. By 1910, unlike these two settlements, Posadas had, as described by Manzi, private schools, a school for teachers, a theater, social clubs, a Masonic temple, a market, a hospital, three newspapers (*El Oro de Misiones*, *El Pueblo*, and *El Noticiero*), and various magazines and periodicals (1910:144).[12] Bove (1923) says that with federalization, the city grew very rapidly, and the price of land inflated considerably, doubling in value in a few years. Although some early visitors speak about the agricultural production of Posadas farms, others insist that there was very little produced and that the government should encourage the settlement of farmers, "as the naturals are so lazy that they do not grow anything on the fertile soil where they live. They are surrounded by elements of progress, but they have no desire to improve their vegetative condition" (Hernández 1973[1887]:48).

The rural areas of Posadas included many of the contemporary working class and marginal neighborhoods, such as Villa Gutiérrez, Villa Mola, Villa Blosset, Hospital Regional (Fernández Ramos 1931:242). Many of them were named after the owners of the land and the big merchant houses. Some of these sites will disappear with the construction of Yacyretá.

Economy and Labor. Labor demand for agricultural and cattle ranching in the south and for some industries located in Posadas as early as 1875, such as the yerba mate processing plants, competed with the yerba mate and timber interests. Accounts of the abandonment of agriculture suggest that lumbering and yerba mate extraction succeeded in attracting the workers. Looking at historical records and descriptions of the area at different points in time, it seems that the local population was highly mobile and that it migrated very frequently to wherever there was labor demand. Such continues to be the case nowadays.

In an account written in 1916 in commemoration of the Centennial of Independence, the writer summarized the history of the educational system in Posadas. She wrote that close to the port, there was a school for children from poor families. She mentions another school to which the sons and daughters of *jornaleros* (day laborers) went. There was also a school of agriculture, around which the neighbors were said to be people "with little knowledge who had once worked in the yerbales, obrajes and fruit plantations" (cited in UNaM 1988). Some literature also suggests that when they left as peons, they did not totally abandon their peasant farming in the outskirts of Posadas. I believe that while men took on other work, subsistence production may well have remained in the hands of women.

The *mensúes* were the men working in the *yerba mate* plantations and sawmills in the wild subtropical forests of the upper Paraná River. On the Bajada Vieja, a street that went straight to the port of Posadas, *conchabadores* (contractors) hired their labor force and paid them in advance. In many cases, payments were not made in cash, but rather in merchandise, which the peons bought in Posadas stores controlled by the two or three owners of the companies. Before leaving, many were already indebted as they spent their cash in goods and in the brothels and bars that spread around the port. In 1912, inspector Ruiz Moreno observed that there existed 48 *boliches* (bars, groceries, and gambling places) and innumerable illegal prostitution houses (República Argentina:1914a).

From Posadas port, and sometimes from Encarnación as well, the ships headed to the Upper Paraná, where the mensúes were expected to harvest yerba mate leaves or to cut down the trees and send the logs downstream in *jangadas* (rafts). The workers could hardly meet the debts with their work, and very few were able to return when they wished. National and international papers denounced the situation. Anarchists, socialists, and other concerned citizens visited the *obrajes*[13] and *yerbatales*[14] to assess the labor conditions.

Some people imagine the mensúes as solitary fellows with no families. The reality was somewhat different; many of them traveled with their women, who shared their labor and hardships. Cavazutti, quoting Bouvier, tells us that women were sold to cover the debts left by their runaway companions (1923:153).

Nearly every foreigner coming to Posadas and Encarnación for the first time was amazed at the sight of busy women involved in petty trade and contraband across the river. They were called either *paseras*, because they "pass" goods or *villenas* because they came from Villa Encarnación. Besides bringing fruit and vegetables to the market, but some were also said to be involved in the trade of large quantities of yerba mate, which they sold to the cities of Paraná, Corrientes, Santa Fe, and Rosario. A hundred years later, paseras continue to come to the local market of Posadas and to private homes, offering their merchandise with the familiar ¿*Qué le vendemos patroncita*? ("What shall we sell you my little patron?") Many of the displaced on both margins of the Paraná River are still involved in this trade.

Despite rhetoric on the contrary, the presence of the nation-state was very limited and, at that, mainly in the areas where the big companies reigned. Wherever and whenever it was possible, the government intervened more actively. In the southern part of Misiones, it initiated the first colonization experiences and, in addition, tried to give deeds to the existing population. The refusal to become proprietors through paying a small sum for the registration of the deed was interpreted by Spegazzini (1914:33) as a proof of "little attachment to land" on the part of the local population (cf. also Hernández 1973[1887]). When the government announced it was going to found the colonies of Santa Ana and Candelaria and that it planned to grant land to the residents, rumors suggested that the authority wanted to enslave them and many were ready to migrate. This example also illustrates one of the first attempts (1887) of the central authorities to "domesticate" the regional population. They promised to give the land to those who would meet the following conditions: (1) to cultivate crops, (2) to keep their animals from destroying fields of others, (3) to send their children to the town school, and (4) to marry. As was the case with the Jesuits about two hundred years before and with projects such as Yacyretá a hundred years later, the federal state was determined to "civilize" the Misiones population through labor, education, and marriage.

As late as 1930, the state still did not know the location and the extension of many of its public lands. However, it had already allotted part of them to families newly arrived from Russia, Austria, Germany, the Ukraine, Sweden, Galitzia, Switzerland, France, and Italy. One group of migrants was not interested in agriculture but rather, in commerce. They were the "turks," the generic name given to Syrians, Lebanese, and people coming from Arab countries, who rapidly gained control of the majority of the bars and stores on the Bajada Vieja.

Private Projects of European Settlement and the Development of Export Agriculture

Beginning in the 1920s, the majority of migrants were recruited by private colonization companies. Unlike those preceding them, many of the new settlers had come with more money to invest and thus had access to larger and more productive lands. Most of these were of German origin. The colonizing companies acquired land in the Upper Paraná and new towns developed with a predominantly European population. Until the construction of Highway 12 linked Posadas with the Upper Paraná region roughly thirty years ago, the northern part of the territory remained isolated from the capital of the province and from Argentina as a whole.

In the north of the province, there existed for some decades a stratified society which was ethnically differentiated; the rich, the landowners, tended to be white and fair haired, and the wage laborers tended to be dark *criollos*.[15] Although many descendants of the European migrants now live in Posadas, their "culture" has not yet been recognized as an integral part of the *cultura Misionera* by the self-appointed guardians of local "tradition." Those who claim the right to define what is truly *misionero* are the Posadas residents, generally those related to the first "families," originally coming from Corrientes, Uruguay, France, Italy, and Spain, and from other parts of Argentina. Among them, there are still many that believe they have the mission to "argentinize" the foreigners and to "misionerize" Argentines from other regions (see Ferradás, González, Urquiza, and Sintes 1988).

Many of the European pioneers grew yerba mate on their family farms and made a profit for some years. Successive crises created by a fall in demand combined with overproduction later compelled them to diversify production. Thus, through the years, they incorporated other cash products into their production schemes, such as tung (aleurite), tea, tobacco, and citrus fruits (for a detailed discussion on these processes and their effects, see Bartolomé 1975, Baranger 1978, Boleda 1983, Palomares 1975). All of these crops are subject to cyclical booms and busts, determined by world market conditions. To avoid the intensification of the yerba mate crisis, the government subsidized producers from 1953 to 1962. At different conjunctures, it did the same with other export crops.

There are very few records from this interwar period, as opposed to the previous one, where innumerable written documents registered the potential of the region and described the scenery. Gone were the days that depicted Misiones (and for that matter, Argentina) as the promised land. Misiones was finally settled, but many in the region found that survival was a daily struggle. The depression years (1930s) slowed down the growth of the capital city and its hinterland. Very few public works were initiated or planned, and private investment also diminished. Nevertheless, important things were accomplished during these years: The streets in the central part of the city and the avenues surrounding them were paved; two municipal markets were inaugurated; new schools were built; and the urban bus service started. In the neighborhood known as *El Chaquito*, Mr. Heller opened a factory which became so important that the railroad made a special extension to connect with it. A meat processing plant and a lumber mill were also built in the area. All these activities attracted workers from Posadas, from Paraguay, and from other parts of Misiones who settled in the outskirts in areas which will be flooded with the Yacyretá hydroelectric dam (see UNaM 1988). During the 1930s, many *chacras* were subdivided and sold, giving birth to new working class and lower middle class neighborhoods. Other lots were sold in the 1950s, after Misiones became a province of the national state.

Provincialization and the Introduction of New Forms of Production: Agribusiness and Hydroelectric Projects

In December 1953, Misiones was made into an autonomous province under Federal Law 14294. By that time, most of the public lands had already been allotted and the colonizing process had ceased. Instead of receiving migration flows, the province gradually became a source of labor to industrial centers. This loss of population was related to an agrarian crisis which deteriorated in the 1960s, simultaneously affecting the major crops of the province.

While the prices of industrial crops were falling, timber production started to develop. Stimulated by government policies, middle-class sectors, such as professionals and merchants, together with representatives of strong capitalist sectors invested in the northern part of the province. Timber production is now under the control of what De Janvry (1981:111) categorizes as "capitalist estates and commercial family farms."

Large agribusiness began to dominate the Misiones scene in the 1960s. Its interests were opposed to those of small producers and family farmers who joined the MAM (Agrarian Movement of Misiones) to fight for price adjustments and other claims, such as availability of credit, regularization of the land tenure system, and a social welfare system.[16] These protests, which included mass demonstrations and the closing of highways, ended abruptly with the military coup of 1976. Some leaders were sent to jail, while others "disappeared." Repression was felt both in the countryside and in the urban-based organizations—such as neighborhood commissions, unions, and university groups—that supported the movement.

During these last decades, many small producers unable to maintain their "subfamily farms," have been forced to leave. Some, have gone to Posadas and built their homes in the lowlands of the city, but the majority have left for places as far away as Córdoba or Buenos Aires. During the 1960s, the population of Posadas averaged an annual increase of 30.5 per thousand; this was the lowest growth rate recorded. In the 1970s it began to grow more rapidly. The population of Posadas was 95,864 in 1970 and 143,889 in 1980. More significant to the population growth were the Universidad Nacional de Misiones, created in the 1970s, and the announcement of the construction of the Yacyretá hydroelectric plant. Workers, technicians, professionals, and investors settled in Posadas, hoping to make a profit with such dam-related activities as construction, real estate, and tourism. As years passed and very little happened, many left the province again.

For the older Posadeños, the 1960s and 1970s represent a period where the configuration of the city totally changed. It ceased to be a place where they knew everybody. They suddenly found themselves surrounded by outsiders. The locals do not like newcomers and generally call them *parachutists*. They complain that they take the best jobs from them; they occupy many decision-making positions without having any familiarity with and commitment to the province; in general, they are only interested in making money and leaving.

Today Posadas faces major problems resulting from the failure of public works to follow the population growth. A great part of the city lacks running water, there is no gas supply, very limited areas are connected to a sewage system (10 percent), and energy costs are the highest in the country. (Part of the electricity is bought in Paraguay at prices adjusted in foreign currency.) Many of these problems are expected to worsen with dam construction because the city has not built many of the engineering works necessary to meet new demands. Water supply is insufficient, and many of the new housing compounds (both the ones built by Yacyretá and others built by the provincial state) lack water because new plants and pipes are not large enough.

As early as the 1950s, national authorities began to discuss the potentialities of rivers of the Río de la Plata Basin for hydroelectric projects. But it was not until the beginning of the last decade that national authorities and regional residents became truly concerned with the construction of dams. National and regional goals were not necessarily the same. The national government was trying to find a cheaper means of providing the industrialized center with energy and to respond to the "aggressive expansionism of Brazil." The Misioneros wanted to have energy sources cheaper than the existing ones in order to attract investments and to develop industrial poles that would provide more jobs for its surplus population.

Many hydroelectric projects have been proposed. Some are under study, others—such as Uruguaí —were constructed by Misiones at social and conomic costs the province could not afford. Among them all, the Binational Yacyretá hydroelectric project is still the most ambitious and one of the most controversial.

The New Regional Integration: MERCOSUR

The fact that geopolitics has gone out of fashion in the majority of the Western countries is generally attributed to the appeal the subject enjoyed in Nazi Germany.[17] Probably because the nationalist right of the Southern Cone countries was sympathetic to developments in Italy and Germany, geopolitics had a different fate in this part of the world, mainly among members of the armed forces (Dijkink 1996). In Argentina, the neighboring countries, especially Brazil and Chile, had been deemed as a threat to national sovereignity, and even common citizens ignorant of the ideological roots of geopolitical debates largely suscribed to this discourse. Most of the frontier policies had been designed under conflict hypothesis.[18] Misiones, for example, was divided in frontier areas and zones which indicated different degrees of risk to the disintegrating cultural influences of the dreaded neighbor Brazil. These spatial units were constructed as barriers blocking the penetration of everything foreign: people, commodities, language, and media messages. During the rule of authoritarian regimes in Argentina, Brazil, and Paraguay, doctrines of security marked the daily rythms of the frontiers.

With the advent of democratic regimes in all the Southern Cone countries, border anxiety and concerns with sovereignty have largely been abandoned. With the new economic order of the 1990s and the rhetoric of globalization, carefully guarded borders are seen as an anachronism (with the obvious exception of the armed forces, which are not very convinced about abandoning their *raison d'être*). A new rhetoric of integration has replaced the *cultura de la des-integración,* culture of disintegration (Abínzano 1993), promoted mainly by the former military dictatorships. In 1985, presidents Alfonsín of Argentina and Sarney of Brazil started negotiations for binational economic integration. These negotiations led to the creation of the MERCOSUR through the Treaty of Asunción in 1990. Initially signed by Brazil, Argentina, Uruguay, and Paraguay, it has recently incorporated Chile. The treaty explicitly states that it was created in response to international events, "especially the consolidation of large economic blocs." The interpretation of the scope and goals of the treaty is not monolithic. Some argue that its creation is tied to Bush's *Enterprise for the Americas Initiative* and therefore it would put the Southern Cone countries even more under the caprices of transnational capital and the hegemony of the United States. Others claim that it could represent a way to achieve regional autonomy because it has been concocted as a mechanism of weakened nations to negotiate in more favorable conditions with the global powers (Abínzano 1993, Giarraca and Teubal 1995, Yamamoto 1996, Bekerman 1995).

Many authors wonder how a country like Brazil got involved in MERCOSUR. What are the advantages for a country whose internal market is probably larger than the sum of the other three associates? Bekerman (1995) suggests that access to energy resources (crucial for the support of its industrial growth) and accesibility of cheaper foodstuffs from temperate ecological environments might explain Brazil's drive to integration with its neighbors. Developments in recent years seem to confirm her assumptions: It is now proposed that the energy produced by Yacyretá and by Corpus—if it is ever built—would be consumed by Brazil. On occasion of the inauguration of the Yacyretá dam in September 1994, the Brazilian president sent a letter to Argentine president Carlos Menem which intriguingly read, "I wish to highlight the meaning of the Paraguayan-Argentine *understanding* (sic), not only for the two countries, but also for the increase of energy generation in the region" (*Clarín,* September 4, 1994). I wonder who can be held responsible (the newspaper, an unknown translator, or the Brazilian president?) for the *lapsus linguae,* mistaking *entendimiento* ("understanding") for *emprendimiento* ("undertaking"), the implications, however, are manifold and quite suggestive of the regional dynamics. Moreover, talks about the interconnection of the electrical system are presented as an ideal way to guarantee a steady source of energy under unfavorable climatic conditions (e.g., droughts that lower reservoir levels). Natural gas from northwest Argentina will now be piped to Brazil. It is not yet clear if Misionero homes could connect to these gas lines.

Experts on regional economies are warning about the devastating effects of these agreements on small producers in peripheral areas traditionally dependent on state protective measures. As in Mexico's experience with NAFTA, the trade agreements will deepen regional inequalities (Marqués and Rofman 1995, Gledhill 1995). Without the regulating role of the state, which used to come to the rescue, and having a subtropical production which cannot compete favorably with that of Paraguay and Brazil (for example, tea, yerba mate, tung, paper pulp) Misiones is now submerged in one of the most acute crisis in its entire history. Furthermore, differences in the national taxation systems create staggering asymmetries with devastating effects for the provincial commercial activities. In the last chapters we will return to these issues and discuss how they affect the strategies of various local actors.

NOTES

1. Pickering, who is concerned with scientific practice "as the work of cultural extension and transformation in time," suggests that as "historians our business might be to explore open-ended transformations of science and society in terms of the temporally emergent making and breaking of cultural alignments and associations with the worlds of production and consumption, transformation understood as having no determinate destination in advance of practice"(1996: 232). He distinguishes his work from others involved in science-studies, such as Latour and Woolgar's (1986) "laboratory life," which are more concerned with spatial and geographical metaphors than with time.

2. Puiggrós (1969: 200) comments that the *gaucho* was prior to the *estanciero* (big landowner) but that the "*estanciero* killed him, buried him, and (afterwards) built him a monument."

3. I cannot elaborate in detail an analysis of the various versions of liberalism and the regionalist and populist forms that challenged it. Because of space constraints, my presentation is rather schematic, and it sacrifices some of the nuances of the various movements. I am emphasizing some of the most extreme positions on both sides and highlighting some of the arguments that have proved to be very resilient in each discourse. For more thorough studies on these debates, see, for example, Romero (1986), Shumway (1991), Cohen Imach (1994), and Halperín Donghi (1980). To see the contribution to the discourse of the Argentine right by nativists and traditionalists see Rock (1993).

4. The Mamelucos were the offspring of Whites and Indians. They joined the bandeiras, which were expeditions into the interior organized under local auspices for offensive warfare, mostly for the capture of Indians (Morse 1965).

5. Caudillos were charismatic political leaders in post-independence Latin America.

6. Juan Manuel de Rosas was a caudillo and rich landowner from Buenos Aires. He became governor of Buenos Aires in 1829, and in 1835, he was granted absolute power. He confronted the provinces of the littoral because he did not want to allow the free navigation of rivers or the opening of customs in cities other than Buenos Aires.

7. This war was the blodiest and longest interstate war in the history of Latin America (Bethell 1996).

8. The role played by England is this war is very controversial. Nationalist and anti-imperialist versions of the war generally empasize the role played by the British Crown, which they argue was interested in breaking the isolationism of Paraguay to be able to introduce their industrialized goods and freely use the rivers for their free trade with the Río de la Plata region. Undoubtedly, the crown supported the war efforts by granting loans. Recent studies, however, suggest that England did not really benefit from the war and that trade with Paraguay did not increase significantly after its defeat (Abente 1987, Bethell 1996).

9. Until the twentieth century,when colonizers found a way to domesticate the *yerba mate* plant, the only way to obtain the precious leaves was through exploiting the wild plants. The upper Paraná River had the largest of these wild yerbales. Sometimes, the location of the plants was kept a secret, as legend says was the case with the Tacurú Pucú (giant ant hill), one of the sites more widely mentioned.

10. Old Spanish linear measure (.84 meters).

11. The word *chacra* initially referred to municipal divisions reserved for rural activities. Through the years, many of these sectors became urbanized but kept the name of *chacras* to remind us of their rural origin. *Chacra* is now used as the equivalent of neighborhood or quarter. In subsequent chapters, it will be used as the equivalent of neighborhood.

12. Even as early as 1892, it was significantly important compared to the other two. At that time, Ambrosetti (1892:117) said that it had two hotels, saddleries, blacksmiths, carpentries, leather shops, photography stores, postal and telegraph office, a municipality, customs, prefecture and an agency of the national bank.

13. The *obrajes* were places where timber was extracted and later sent down the Paraná River to the city of Posadas and other towns nearby.

14. *Yerbatales* (also *yerbales*) were the places where yerba mate leaves were harvested from wild plants.

15. The connotation of *criollo* in Argentina is quite different from the meaning of the term in other parts of Latin America. Although originally it meant the American-born children of Peninsular parents, as years passed, it acquired a new racial referent—mestizo peoples—and, depending on the user, a rather derogatory connotation by stressing the "popular" elements in their cultural repertoire.

16. Bartolomé (1982) considers the MAM as a movement comparable to the agrarian populism of the American farmers. Elsewhere (Ferradás 1986), I have argued that these movements bear many resemblances with other Latin American peasant movements. They developed in the 1960s under the influence of Catholic groups which encouraged participatory actions to counterbalance the predicaments of the left after the Cuban revolution. They generally developed in backward regions which were suffering the effects of the world and national markets. There was an internal differentiation within these movements. Each group represented was interested in making different claims but they

stayed together as long as there was a particular conjuncture which affected all of them in a similar manner.

17. Peter Taylor (1989:49–50) sustains that the role played by geopolitics in Germany, centered in the work of Haushofer, has been exaggerated.

18. Brazil showed similar concerns regarding Argentina. For a discusion of Brazilian geopolitics see Schilling (1978).

CHAPTER 4

Damming the Region, Empowering the Nation: The Yacyretá Hydroelectric Project

As we have already seen, the Paraná River has always been at the heart of disputes among the countries of the Río de la Plata region. Those who could control it possessed an invaluable resource (the regional economies depended upon riverine transportation for the commercialization of their production) and a strategic means of controlling the whereabouts of everybody in the region. With the construction of highways and the development of agribusiness, the river was half-forgotten. Nevertheless, in the 1970s, against the background of the oil crisis shocking the world economies and the failure of attempting other means of activating the region's economy, both the Argentine national state and local authorities of Misiones have once again reconsidered the river potential for development and concluded that construction of hydroelectric dams would be the best solution to achieve their goals.

This chapter summarizes how the Yacyretá project was conceived and negotiated. In examining the history of the project, I show the effect of political and economic processes (local, national, and global) on decisions related to the hydroelectric dam. In the previous chapter, I analyzed the emergence of rivalries among the Argentine province of Misiones and the neighboring countries Brazil and Paraguay. In this chapter, I will show how these rivalries have been played out to justify the project and also to jeopardize it.

Throughout the history of the project, various interest groups became involved in the negotiation, financing, and decision-making processes related to the engineering works and population resettlement. Not all of them played the same role in trying to legitimate the hydroelectric project to the general public. While initially some of the ideological constructions were quite successful in gaining popular support, as years passed it became practically impossible to find anybody sympathetic to the project, especially in the areas where the impact is experienced more intensely. Here, I reconstruct some of the events surrounding this project that engendered generalized feelings of distrust, resentment, and skepticism. I show

how the power dynamics of the project has changed as a result of democratization processes in the Southern Cone region and the encroachment by multinational lending banks on debt-ridden nation-states' ability to make major decisions. Has the bargaining power of municipal and provincial governments improved with the return to democracy and the somewhat fashionable rhetoric of localism and regionalism? How weak have national governments become under the pressures of global promoters of structural adjustment and trade liberalization? How have these global changes affected the project's outcomes? The last sections will explore some of these issues and will show that the confrontations are never fully solved; there is a permanent struggle in which participants often have quite contradictory agendas (even though some of the contenders seem to always enjoy comparative advantages). To get a better understanding of what is triggering most of the disagreements, I include a brief characterization of the hydroelectric project and a description of the relocation agency. To get some sense of the areas suffering a prolonged and uncertain relocation process, I briefly describe the sites selected for the study.

THE YACYRETA HYDROELECTRIC DAM IN THE ARGENTINE AND PARAGUAYAN BORDERLANDS

One hundred years ago, the barrier of the Apipé rapids accounted for the interdependencies among Trincheras de San José (now Posadas), Encarnación, and Ituzaingó. The first two depended on the port of the latter to deliver all the timber and yerba mate from the upper Paraná River and to receive the basic staples. If the rapids had not been there, the Paraguayans and the Misioneros could have easily sustained themselves without Ituzaingó. However, the rapids were all too real and constituted a major concern for anyone willing to develop the region. Not everyone wished them away; some believed that the rapids might be used to their advantage. In the late nineteenth century, a Basque, don Francisco de Basaldúa, "who toured the Iberá and the Upper Paraná, considered it feasible to construct a hydroelectric plant, making use of the Apipé and Carayá rapids (see *El Territorio. Suplemento*. July 1983:2).

Today, the three cities are again tied together in connection with the rapids and the islands of Yacyretá, Apipé Grande, and Talavera. This time, the construction of a huge hydroelectric plant is creating new bonds and affecting each area in various ways. Ayolas, a Paraguayan town, has become the fourth member of this new interdependency (see Map 4.1). During the peak years of construction of civil works, thousands of workers, technicians, and professionals moved to the encampments in Ituzaingó and Ayolas, the cities next to the working site. Both Posadas and Encarnación will be suffering the major impact of this huge project. Once the gigantic reservoir is filled, about 81,500 hectares in Paraguay and 25,000 in Argentina will be covered by water. Important areas of the urban infrastructure and highly populated neighborhoods will disappear with the flooding. Studies from the late 1970s estimated the relocation of approximately 40,000 people, and the two countries were expected to build homes for resettlement (about 2,000 houses in Encarnación and 4,500 in Argentina). Burdened with financial problems, the governments put the relocation program on hold on various occasions. After numerous delays, the initial assessments are no longer valid—household composition has changed dramatically and new families have moved into some of the areas, despite warnings that they would not be granted resettlement rights. Although new studies tried to obtain more reliable information on the current needs, it is still quite uncertain what the real situation is. Most of the information from these studies is in Paraguay, which out of the old-fashioned nation-state competitiveness, has concealed it from its Argentine counterparts. The Environmental and Resettlement Program of 1993 spoke of the construction of 10,142 housing units, assuming the relocation of more than 50,000. Early studies from the late 1970s and early 1980s minimized the significance of some traditional economic activities such as brickmaking and did not recommend specific policies to relocate the producers and their families. As years passed, this proved to be a serious oversight. An intense challenge to the relocation agency came from the brickmakers in the two countries (see Chapter Nine).

Map 4.1
Yacyretá Dam

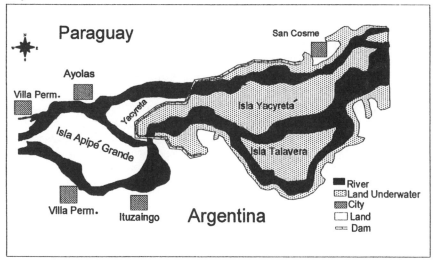

Relocation does not only include large sectors of the population, it also includes a significant part of the urban infrastructure on both banks of the river: train stations and railways, ports, sections of highways, public and commercial buildings. In addition, new constructions and improvements were also originally planned: sewage system, water supply, telephone networks. After more than fifteen years since the major civil works were started, it is still quite uncertain whether many of these works will ever be completed, despite recurring promises to the contrary made by the Argentine government.

The major works include the main dam and a control dam. The main reservoir was formed after building a dam across the navigable channel of the Paraná River, immediately downstream from the Apipé rapids. It was predicted that the lake would cover 1,600 square kilometers "13 times the surface area of Asunción and 8 times that of Buenos Aires" and that the gigantic reservoir would extend 200 kilometers with a maximum width of 21 kilometers and a depth of 35 meters. So far, these levels have not been reached because it was decided not to work at full capacity until the EBY finds a way to cover the costs of relocation and environmental requirements. The works include a navigation lock in Rincón Santa María. The project also has two spillways and two irrigation gates to stimulate agricultural development on both banks of the river. The hydroelectric plant was built on the island of Yacyretá. Years behind original schedule, the first Kaplan turbines started to operate in September 1994. The total planned 20 Kaplan turbines might be in operation in 1998 if EBY succeeds in obtaining loans.[1]

HISTORY OF THE PROJECT

There is no general agreement as to when discussions of the Paraná's potential had begun. Yacyretá's public relations leaflets and the articles in *El Territorio*, the local paper, trace the origins to as early as 1905, when technicians "appointed by the General Office of Navigation and Ports from the Ministry of Public Works made hydrometric observations and systematic appraisals of the river and the rapids." Some years later, the Argentine national government asked two engineers to determine the feasibility of hydroelectric development using the various rivers of the region. Their studies included recommendations on two historic concerns in regard to the Apipé rapids and the nearby islands: the construction of a dam and the facilitation of navigation. In 1926, the Argentine and Paraguayan ambassadors to Washington signed an agreement contemplating the possibility of initiating this construction. As time passed, enthusiasm for the hydroelectric possibilities of the Paraná faded.

The project, which was originally called Yacyretá-Apipé, has been haunted by countless delays ever since its inception. Contributing factors to the postponements include financing problems; the unstable political situation of Argentina; the clash of interests of the two participating countries, common in bilateral projects; and pressures exerted by powerful economic groups. The combination of all these circumstances has impinged upon the total cost of the project and the completion date, making both vary greatly through time as is shown on Table 4.1. Uncertainty and lack of credibility have been a byproduct of these constant changes.

Throughout the thirty years of Yacyretá's history, Argentina alternated between democratic governments and military regimes with diverse ideological and economic orientations, while Paraguay was ruled, for the most part, by only one man, General Alfredo Stroessner.[2] Although today the two countries have govern-

Table 4.1
Anticipated Date of Completion, Estimated Dam Cost, Type of Political System and Causes of Delay

Year	Due Date	Cost ◊	Political System Argentina	Paraguay	Causes of Delays
1974	1981* 1984	1.35	Democratic Frejuli J. D. Perón	Authoritarian Gen. A. Stroessner	Binational disagreements. Technical Problems. EBY's internal regulations. Project design.
1977	1985	7.19	Authoritarian Gen. Videla	Authoritarian Gen. A. Stroessner	Project design. Compensation to Paraguay for the loss of land.
1980	1986		Authoritarian Gen. Videla	Authoritarian Gen. A. Stroessner	Bidding process. Action of regional, national, and inter-national power groups.
1983	1990*	4.29	Authoritarian Gen. Bigno-ne	Authoritarian Gen. A. Stroessner	Labor strikes. Budget problems.
1985 1988	1992	6.00	Democratic U.C.R. R. Alfonsín	Authoritarian Gen.. A. Stroessner	Budget cuts. Labor strikes.
1989 1992	1993* 1996*		Democratic C.S. Menem	Authoritarian Gen. A. Rodríguez	Argentina's economic crisis.
1993 1997	1993* 199?**	10.00	Democratic C.S. Menem	Democratic J.C.Wasmosy	Argentina's economic crisis. Disagreements with privatization. Lack of relocation homes.

* First turbines   ◊ In billions of U.S. dollars.
** All the turbines

ments chosen through free democratic elections, authoritarianism is still ingrained in the power structure. In Argentina, for example, the executive branch tends to interfere in the functioning of the legislative and judicial branches, which, by constitution, are autonomous. When the 1958 agreement was signed, General

Aramburu was the de facto president of Argentina. He came into power shortly after President General Juan Domingo Perón was overthrown. The vice-president was Isaac Rojas, an ultra-nationalist rear admiral who had always been concerned about the geopolitics of the river basin and continuously warned of Brazilian expansionism.

Successive democratic and military regimes did not take any action with the project. In 1973, democracy was given another chance and Peronism won elections under a different name: FREJULI (Liberation Justice Front), with the support of both right and left wing factions within the party and in alliance with various parties of the most diverse ideology. As Perón could not seek the presidency, Héctor Cámpora was made the candidate of the front. It was the first time in ten years that Argentines chose their president. Votes favored Cámpora, and he became president of the country. After governing for two months, he resigned along with the more radical members of his cabinet. He argued that the population should have the right to choose its beloved leader. In October 1973, General Perón became president for the third and last time. By the time he took office, right wing members were gaining control of the state apparatus. After his death, when his widow, María Estela Martínez de Perón, Isabelita, became the first female president in Argentine history, the ultra-nationalist groups already controlled the majority of the key posts.

The military led another coup in 1976. They imprisoned Isabelita and thus prevented her from completing her presidential term. The Process of National Reorganization or the Proceso, as people called it, began with this coup. The military took over with the excuse of putting the "house in order," one of the obsessions of the Argentine right (Rock 1993). This meant state control of every citizen and the physical annihilation of anyone under suspicion. Under this extremely repressive regime there was very little room for protest or resistance. The armed forces had no intention of letting civilians govern the country again. They would have probably remained in power for many more years had they not been defeated in the Malvinas War of 1982. The disastrous failure in that war opened the eyes of common citizens, allowing them to realize the horrors the country had passed through during the previous years. Unable to make any legitimate claims to stay in power, the military retreated once again and called for democratic elections in 1983.

With great expectations, Argentines voted the Unión Cívica Radical (UCR) candidate, Raúl Alfonsín to the executive office. He took over a devastated country: a gigantic foreign debt, a shrinking industrial sector, thousands of "disappeared" citizens, unemployment, illiteracy, and hunger. Many would have liked to believe that with the advent of democracy, conditions could magically improve. But Alfonsín faced the opposition of such powerful groups as the Church; various economic sectors, including the financial and landed elites and the so-called "industrial captains"; the labor unions; and the armed forces. A crisis of hyperinflation brought social unrest culminating in riots. Early elections were called. Argentines voted Carlos Menem, the candidate of the Justicialista party (a formerly Peronist organization) with the hope that he would bring back social and economic well-being. To the surprise of many old Peronists, and to the resigned attitude of the majority of Argentines who believed that there was no other solution to avoid economic instability, the leader of a traditionally anti-imperialist party embraced neoliberalism and became one of the most ardent defenders of privatization and free trade.

Four major events in the history of the Yacyretá project occurred while Argentina was facing very different political and economic circumstances. The Yacyretá Treaty was signed during Perón's presidency; bidding processes for project design and major contracts took place during the military government; civil works were started under democratic rule, during Alfonsín's presidency; and the partial filling of the reservoir and the initiation of energy production occurred during President Menem's administration.

The Notas Reversales of 1970 exchanged between Argentina and Paraguay determined that a consulting firm should be chosen through international bidding. The *Consortium Harza y Asociados* was selected to undertake the economic, financial, and technical assessment of the project. This assessment was to be used as a basis for the Binational Treaty.[3] On December 3, 1973, Vice-president Isabel Martínez de Perón went to Asunción to meet President Stroessner with the purpose of signing the Tratado de Yacyretá (Treaty of Yacyretá). During the visit, the two ministers of foreign relations stressed brotherhood and friendship between the two countries. The treaty, it was said, was a major step toward Latin American integration, a fashionable theme in the Argentina of those days: "Argentina is determined to give what it ought to in the understanding that all the countries in the continent would also contribute, as we believe that Latin American integration and unity are unavoidable if we are willing to accept history's challenge" (*La Opinión*, September 7, 1974).

Peronists believed that their President, a Third World leader, should follow San Martín's path, by playing an influential role in the unification of the Spanish-speaking countries. This dream of *La Patria Grande* envisioned by Perón's followers could not be accomplished because the old general died shortly after he became president of the republic for the third time. When Isabelita took office, Argentina was in political turmoil. Fights among competing factions within the Peronist party continued and were becoming increasingly violent. López Rega, the minister of social welfare, popularly known as *El Brujo* ("the sorcerer") because of his dedication to the "occult sciences," was very influential in Perón's government. To get rid of political opponents, he created a paramilitary group, known as the Triple A (The Argentine Anti-Communist Alliance) that threatened, kidnapped, and killed hundreds of people. Meanwhile, guerrilla groups attacked military barracks and led different actions in cities and in the countryside. Because of this situation, the government declared a state of siege, which remained in force throughout the military regime that seized power in 1976.

With the excuse of the threat of leftist assaults, all citizens were put under surveillance. Guards asked visitors to leave identification documents and registered their names and persons they would see before allowing admittance into public buildings. These controls also occurred at Yacyretá's headquarters. The EBY had its own special services which scrutinized visitors and investigated employees before and after being hired. During the military years, they also controlled and limited access to the neighborhoods that would be flooded with the dam. Even university teachers and students doing research at the request of the EBY needed a special permit to enter the area. Permission was only granted after carefully studying the personal records of each participant.

In Ituzaingó, the local population was not allowed in the neighborhoods built for the EBY staff and for the contractor's employees. Fences separated the original town from the new buildings. These fences no longer exist but Yacyretá still maintains many of its restrictions.

Control in public buildings was loosened with the advent of a democratic government in 1983 by removing the guards from the entrance. For quite a few years Yacyretá was one of the few exceptions to this. Admission to EBY's premises was still limited: people had to identify themselves and give reasons for their visit. Security personnel continued to behave as if nothing had changed in the Argentina of the 1980s. This situation changed only recently, when the Posadas headquarters of Yacyretá was reopened in 1993 after a year of interruption of relocation activities.

The political struggles of Isabel's years help us understand how some policing features of Yacyretá emerged. However, they do not explain why they had become an integral part of the institution. Similarly, the political situation of those years was a contributing factor to the weak response of the local population, but it cannot be taken as the sole cause for the lack of involvement.

On December 3, 1973, the day the Yacyretá Treaty was signed in Asunción, Misioneros were attending the funeral of their governor and vice-governor who died in a plane crash two days before. Many suspected that their death had not occurred by accident. Whatever the causes were, the tragic end of the province's authorities opened a period of heated disputes for succession. Misiones became an arena where the ongoing ideological struggles would be tested through the election of the new authorities. Every party had invested large sums and sent cadres to campaign in Misiones. The sinister minister of social welfare had made use of the entire state apparatus to win the favor of the voters and defeat opponents. The right-wing sectors of the Peronists were particularly interested in defeating a radical faction, which separated and formed a new party, the Partido Auténtico. This party had a following among members of the MAM, a fairly active rural movement which the central government was eager to weaken. All means were considered valid for the destruction of the left: threats, physical annihilation, and political defeat through elections. Given these circumstances, it is understandable that Misioneros did not show much concern when the treaty was signed and the EBY was created—they had more immediate worries.

CONSTRUCTING YACYRETA: MONUMENT TO CORRUPTION OR DEVELOPMENT?

The construction of huge dams such as Yacyretá involves a particular kind of development project. The literature includes hydroelectric projects in the category of "large works," "large projects" (Rofman, Brunstein, Laurelli, and Vidal 1987), "large scale projects" (Ribeiro 1985), and macroprojects (Murphy 1983). All these concepts emphasize grand dimensions, a characteristic shared by such projects and easily observed in the engineering works, the machinery employed, the earth movements, the lakes that are created. Capital investment is also large and so is the demand and movement of labor—features that made Ribeiro emphasize the gigantism of these projects.

The rhetoric promoting these projects also stresses the enormous size of everything connected with them. Leaflets and press releases convey this idea of grandiosity through pictures and comparisons such as: "The power plant is 70.4 m high; the Obelisk in the city of Buenos Aires is 67 m and the Pantheon of Heroes in the city of Asunción is 37 m." "3,800,000 cubic meters of concrete will be poured. An equivalent volume is necessary to build a highway connecting Asunción and Buenos Aires (1,400km)."

Features distinguishing this undertaking from others help to depict Yacyretá as exceptional, unique: "Together with Itaipú it is the biggest Latin American public work"; "It is the Work of the Century." Through emphasizing the exceptionality of certain outcomes of these projects, negative effects such as population displacement and the flooding of land are presented as positive to the general audience:

YACYRETA IS NEWS IN POSADAS. . . . Because the transformation of Posadas will include the largest relocation of population of its kind in the world. (EBY, Bulletin 1, July 1980)

According to World Bank experts who evaluated this case based upon studies made by local professionals of the EBY Social Area; what is going to happen here has no worldwide precedents with regards to the number of people and the surface of urban nuclei—Posadas and Encarnación together—receiving the impact of the dam. With the exception of the Aswan dam in Egypt, which required the relocation of 100,000 people—but from the rural sector, there has never existed the need of moving 40,000 urban dwellers because of the construction of a hydroelectric dam. Because of this, as analysts will say, Yacyretá is unique in its type. (Esto es Yacyretá. Suplemento *El Territorio*. July 1983)

In 1958, a group of UN experts defined the integrated development of watersheds as "the orderly management of hydraulic resources of basins, in its utilization for multiple purposes to promote human welfare"(Viladrich 1972:12). Yacyretá is advertised as a multipurpose project. Its benefits, EBY maintains, "go beyond the use of electrical power: it will facilitate navigation, tourism and irrigation." It promises that "the settlement of new populations and industries will invigorate a largely forgotten zone of the Río de la Plata Basin. Most of these goals are expressed in the majority of large-scale projects, but only on exceptional occasions are they achieved successfully. It has long been noted that investments on these projects are made with only one purpose in mind: energy production. The rest of the objectives are for public consumption; they aim at legitimizing dam construction through portraying it as something that contributes to the common good.

Although various benefits are advocated, project design rarely includes any indication as to how these benefits might be achieved. Efficacy in obtaining citizen's consent largely depends on the type of objectives emphasized in the projects. Those projects addressing shared concerns are more likely to succeed in winning public support. Undoubtedly, no population is homogenous and interests do change through time. However, some ever-present symbols and themes exist which do have a wide appeal.

As discussed in the previous chapter, navigation, tourism, and irrigation were already a major concern when travelers, government envoys, and private prospectors were assessing the development possibilities of Misiones more than a hundred years ago. Some visitors observed that the lack of good water supplies could be one of the factors inhibiting the development of agriculture in the Posadas surroundings. Every traveler complained about the hardships and dangers encountered when trying to navigate upstream beyond the Apipé rapids. And many also insisted that the natural marvels of Misiones would attract tourists. Today, many Misioneros believe that tourism, "the industry without chimneys," should be one of the main areas of development.

Very few areas of Posadas have running water. The closest ground water is below thick layers of basalt reachable only through the use of dynamite, a very expensive process requiring very specialized labor. Agricultural activities rely heavily on generally abundant rainfall. However, occasional droughts do occur and crops fail. The Municipality of Posadas cannot cover the demand for water when it is scarce, and the majority of the population lack the economic resources to buy it from private providers. Because of this situation, promises of more water are always welcome. As far as water is concerned, feasibility studies and the Yacyretá project design only refer to irrigation in a very vague way. It is not clear whether specific plans exist on how to distribute irrigation water; neither is it known if complementary works such as channels or small reservoirs would be built with the purpose of improving agriculture.

Trains, trucks, and planes have long replaced the steamships on the Paraná River; but the taming of the Apipé rapids still stands as a symbol of what must be done to connect Posadas to the country and to the world. Some social sectors seem to assign more importance to navigation than others. An editorial in *El Territorio* (March 29, 1988), entitled "The Paraná, river of life," compared this river to the Nile and said that both of them have "nurtured the seeds of civilization and progress." Regretting the gradual abandonment of water transportation, it summarized various hypothesis:

The Argentine flag has nearly disappeared from the River Plate Basin, but we will not attempt to formulate a hypothesis about the origins of these complex phenomena. We will only mention that some attribute it to the lack of freight; others to bureaucratic impediments, and to obsolete elements; others to a supposedly disproportionate weight of maritime union claims; others to the convenience and speed of surface transportation; and even some others, to the existence of powerful extranational interests, related to the industrialization and commercialization of trucks.

The newspaper article continued by saying that it was quite surprising that we neglected navigation when the so-called developed nations were increasingly valuing these means of transportation, even though they have the best roads and cars. It concluded by wondering if Misiones could afford the luxury of wasting "this liquid road, 4,700 kilometers long." It is not surprising that an ex-Navy official, the ultra-nationalist and anti-Peronist Rear Admiral Rojas (1979) insisted on the use of rivers. According to him, Peronists were responsible for the substitution of ships for other means of transportation.

Kaul Grünwald (1982), an author with a similar geopolitical obsession, was concerned that Itaipú might alter the river water level and thus impede navigation. He advocated the construction of Corpus, another hydroelectric project on the Paraná. He was convinced that this was unavoidable if Argentina wished to maintain the desired volume of the river. He also favored the construction of Yacyretá on the same grounds. These works will also help, he asserted, to break with Bolivia's and Paraguay's mediterraneity. From Argentina's geopolitical point of view, the support of Paraguay, Bolivia, and Uruguay was decisive to maintain the balance of power in the Southern Cone. Interestingly, some of Grunwald's concerns were not unfounded: When Brazil constructed Itaipú, it did not include navigation locks to prevent possible attacks from Argentina. Ironically, now that Brazil has changed its vision and its geopolitical think tank, the Escola de Guerra, suggesting regional integration and the development of hydroways connecting the rivers of MERCOSUR, Itaipú stands as one of the major obstacles.

The renovated interest on the construction of a dam developed in relationship to the oil crisis. The same day the newspapers announced the signature of the treaty and the creation of the EBY, a pathetic photograph published in La Nación showed the barren streets of Rome under the prohibition of the circulation of private cars during weekends with the purpose of saving gas. Oil prices also had a devastating effect on the Brazilian economy as its industrialization process was highly dependent on fuel imports. This situation encouraged Brazil to find a way to supplement oil with other energy sources. The decision to build hydroelectric dams on a great number of their rivers is a response to that problem. Itaipú, a large dam built jointly with Paraguay on the upper Paraná, was the most ambitious project. Negotiations between Brazil and Paraguay stirred the nationalism of many Argentines who pressed the government to improve diplomatic relations with Stroessner's regime. Yacyretá and Corpus were seen as national responses to counterbalance the possible effects of Itaipú, a project that was decided unilaterally by Brazil without consulting the governments sharing the river downstream. Because of this issue, Argentina proposed to the United Nations that countries desiring to use a common river should consult all affected parties before making a decision (*Clarín*, December 17, 1974).

Newspapers said that Peronists blamed the previous military governments for the impairment of relationships with Paraguay. According to the press, it was thanks to Perón that Argentina reached an agreement with Paraguay, overcoming the "Paraguayans reluctance inspired by the hidden hands of Itamaraty" (Brazilian diplomacy).[4] It was also because of his "personal intervention" that the national congress finally ratified the 1973 treaty, despite some doubts raised by political opponents who wondered whether Argentina had been excessively generous with Paraguay by conceding a credit of 50,000,000 dollars, promising the construction of a bridge connecting Encarnación and Posadas; and conferring too many compensations. Opposition parties also showed concern with the first article of the treaty because it said that the dam could "eventually minimize" the effects of floods, but no serious provisions were taken to study a way of controlling them *(La Nación*, February 2, 1974).

In 1974, Paraguay enjoyed a very favorable position. It was as if it could finally take its revenge, a century after its defeat in the War of the Triple Alliance. Ironically, the two countries that stopped it from becoming an industrialized nation were now offering it the energy to run the factories it did not have. Argentina made various offers to win Paraguay's favor: Experts visited Asunción to study the possibility of establishing aluminum and cellulose factories; government envoys proposed to open lines of credit to develop agriculture and other productive activities (*Mayoría*, April 13, 1974). As Paraguay needed very little electricity, it could set the conditions to give permission and to participate in the construction of the dams. The Argentine press, expressing the concerns of many citizens, frequently complained about the neighbor's requirements which caused innumerable delays and raised the costs: Once, they wanted the project design to be modified because they understood that too much of their territory would be flooded; another time, they argued over exchange rates. Conversely, Paraguayans blamed Argentines for the delays. They still do. They argue that the mismanagement of EBY can only be blamed on Argentina, the country which always appointed the executive director, even though the treaty established that the two country members would alternate in project control. They also attribute most of the delays to Argentina's economic crisis because Argentina is solely responsible for project financing. The Paraguayan press sees any Argentine move as an attack on Paraguayan sovereignty and rights. Commenting on Yacyretá and the recent MERCOSUR agreements, a journalist doubted that anything good would result from an alliance with the Argentine "brothers" and added that there is a popular saying: "There are two kinds of Argentines, the ones who screwed you up and the ones who would do it soon" (*El Diario*, October 6, 1992).

Indeed, Paraguayans continue to suspect Argentina's intentions. In 1989, shortly after President Menem took office, he declared that Yacyretá was a "Monument to Corruption" and unilaterally decided to stop works without consulting its partner. This pronoucement has to be understood in the context of the global economy of the 1990s. Burdened with the service payments of one of the largest Latin American foreign debts, and pressed by the multinational demands to straighten up the financial situation, Argentina embraced neoliberalism and started to advocate privatization as the solution to the country's ills. The sale of the nation's assets, including Yacyretá, was justified by a discourse that described the state as corrupt and inefficient. Regarding Yacyretá, Menen claimed for example, that the dam project that initially had an estimated cost of 1.5 billion dollars had already spent 3 billion dollars to complete only half of the major works in 1990. Also, anticipating a decision which would be announced some time later, the Argentine president complained that in Argentina, EBY had a seven-story building with nearly 3,000 bureaucratic employees "who have nothing to do" (*El Diario*, April 4, 1990). These comments coincide with contradictory and alarming warnings repeated consistently—but officially denied—between 1990 and 1993, which suggested that the government would only continue with the "major works." Relocation and environmental programs seemed to be threatened. Therefore, employees in charge of these matters became useless. In 1990 and 1991, EBY established a system of voluntary retirement. EBY's functionaries were reduced to 450 in Paraguay and 500 in Argentina responding to a requirement from *El Banco* (World Bank). A little after that, EBY closed down in Posadas and Encarnación. In recent years, Argentina made most decisions (at the suggestion of the World Bank and Inter-American Development Bank, IDB) regarding rationalizing personnel, privatizing, hiring of consulting firms, retaining part of the profits to pay debts to contractors, and modifying or suspending relocation programs without considering Paraguay's views on these issues. Paraguay responded with accusations of Mitrismo (Mitre was Argentina's president during the War of the Triple Alliance) and viceregal arrogance (in reference to the attitudes of Buenos Aires authorities regarding Paraguay province during the years of the Virreinato del Río de la Plata) *(La Nación*, August 19 and 20, 1995).

Ultima Hora, a Paraguayan paper, commented that corruption was real and blamed earlier rulers of the two countries who "lacked any morals in the management of the common good" (*Ultima Hora*, April 4 and April 14, 1990). Suspicions of mismanagement included the bidding processes, insurance, and compensation payments.[5] In reference to Menem's remarks, common citizens and journalists noted in amusement that it was indeed a director appointed by Menem's administration, a former Posadas mayor and candidate for governor, who squandered more resources. He bought new buildings, spent large sums in refurbishing the headquarters, and he enjoyed riding cars equipped with sirens, which had to be adapted to meet his needs (*ABC Color*, April 5, 1990). It is also suggested that he employed EBY's economic and human resources for his political campaign.

Today, Argentina is desperately trying to sell Yacyretá, one of the last "Grandma's jewels" (as the Argentine press ridicules the state's privatization frenzy). In 1995, neither Paraguayan nor Argentine citizens accepted the proposed terms of the concession of the sale of energy for 30 years. Congress in the two countries has voted against various proposals for privatization.[6] The Argentine government asserts that it will take responsibility for a debt of roughly 5 billion dollars. They are offering Yacyretá for 1.8 billion dollars. It is estimated that the dam will produce a profit of 600 million dollars yearly. In 30 years, it is argued, those who get the dam will have a profit of nearly 18 billions, ten times their original investment. Menem's administration is determined to privatize Yacyretá, regardless of what the National Congress and Paraguay think. In recent months it was studying the possibility of making the decision through a presidential decree, a common practice of a nation-state which still has to learn some lessons about democracy. One of Menem's ministers, who used to be an advisor of the contractor, is now suggesting that the operation of Yacyretá should be given to his former employers, who are also demanding the payment of a debt of 800 millions dollars. Has the era of corruption in Yacyretá ended?

What role did the World Bank and the IDB play in this story? They suggested lines of action that favored contracting out, mainly consulting firms and NGOs, a practice characteristic of the times of postfordism and flexibilization of the labor market. They pushed for privatization because they no longer believe that nation-states are the appropriate vehicles for efficient management and the promotion of development. They became aware that history matters in the binational relations of the two countries and arbitrated in many of the disputes. They strongly recommended that the consulting firms should be from countries other than the co-owners of the dam. When the relocation and environmental programs were reinstated in 1993 following the banks directives, the two countries agreed to appoint a "neutral" Colombian national to coordinate the activities on both sides of the Paraná River. It would be too simplistic, however, to think that the two banks had the last word. On many ocassions, EBY authorities and the central governments from the two countries defied their creditors' advice and managed to impose their will in certain matters. Other actors generally had less luck in negotiating their interests. That is the case of regional authorities and the local population.

REGIONAL PARTICIPATION

When treaty negotiations were under way, local governments had practically no participation on the decisions connected with the dam. They were neither consulted when feasibility studies were made nor told to what extent their territories would be affected. Nevertheless, the Paraguayan-Argentine Committee claimed that it was the first time that a project of that kind let local governments participate by "providing ideas and bringing up their concerns." Although the press reported that provincial authorities expressed similar opinions, their request to have a group of technicians explain the characteristics of the project in the understanding that it might affect a considerable number of local families indicated they felt insufficiently informed and dissatisfied (*La Nación*, November 18 and 27, 1974; *El Ande*, November 27, 1974).

According to *El Litoral*, a Correntino paper, in the opinion of some distinguished residents, Yacyretá was a challenge "plenty of best wishes." When referring to the dam, the local press made use of the same rhetoric as the one employed by the country's leading papers, foreseeing a future of progress, industrialization of backward areas, and regional development. Unlike these major papers, provincial journalists echoed the ever-present local concerns: competition between Misiones and Corrientes, and fear that the "center," Buenos Aires, would make a profit out of their sacrifice. To achieve the promised goals of the project and avoid the risks of being cheated once again, Correntinos were told they should have "to defend the natural rights of the province" (*El Litoral*, January 1, 1974).

With the return to democracy in Argentina in 1983, the provincial governments started to make more demands regarding the project, and political parties played a more visible role in the negotiations. However, it was not until the electoral victory of the Justicialista party in national elections that some of the provincial demands were met. President Menem appointed a local politician as executive director of EBY. For years, Misioneros and Correntinos had resented the decision to establish the main office in Buenos Aires; they regarded this as an expression of the national state centralism. The main headquarters was moved to Posadas, and a short-lived experiment in local power was put in motion. Contrary to widespread expectations, the move did not improve interaction with the displaced population. On the contrary, procedures became more bureaucratic, and visitors to EBY had to talk to numerous staff members before they could reach the employee they attempted to see. Because the new head of EBY was using his appointment for his own political agenda, he created new positions for his supporters. He thus developed a complex bureaucracy in which few employees had the adequate skills to perform the activities for which they were hired. He lasted at EBY less than a year and never became a governor.

ENVIRONMENTAL AND SOCIAL IMPACT

Neither the studies made by Harza and Associates nor the treaty itself paid special attention to the environmental and social impact of the dam. Newspapers from the early 1970s were very vague when referring to these issues, and none of them really asserted that vast sectors of the cities of Posadas and Encarnación would be flooded, let alone that a great number of residents should be relocated. When relocation was mentioned, articles began by saying "it is believed" or "everything leads to the prediction that the waters will flood. . . ." Remembering that the first studies were made 50 years before and that negotiations were very often interrupted, some journalists doubted that the project would ever be finished *(La Nación*, August 26, 1974). On page 16 of a press release, experts from the Comisión Mixta Técnica briefly commented that effects of the project on urban centers would be felt in Posadas and Encarnación. They estimated that about 10 percent of the population of each city would be relocated. They added that, by and large, the cities would benefit from the relocation. It is worth quoting the reasons why they believed so: "Those zones, lacking sanitary installations and which are now subject to recurrent floods, will be replaced by modern units provided with these services. During the floods, the inhabited areas facilitate the propagation of contagious diseases, constituting a threat to public health and therefore they should be eliminated."[7]

In August 1974, the *Coordinadora de Barrios de Posadas* (Posadas Neighborhood Coordinating Committee) representing 52 *Comisiones Vecinales* (Neighborhood Commissions) expressed concern about the future of the population of Posadas as feasibility studies estimated that 2,800 square kilometers of the city would be flooded. They also worried about the possibility of a rise in the price of land and that this would particularly impinge upon the poorer residents of the city. The law of *no innovar* (status quo law) passed by the provincial legislature aimed at preventing real estate speculation.[8] It did not allow the sale or improvement on property that was supposedly affected by the dam. It was meant to avoid massive eviction of illegal occupants or tenants from private land that until then had been of very little value. The regulation originally created to protect the deprived social sectors resulted in a negative effect on their lives in the long run as discussed later in this book.

In 1993, environmental issues were taken more seriously. In combination with experts from the World Bank local groups concerned with the environmental costs of these projects pressed for the search for concerted solutions. This led to the hiring of experts to advise on an environmental and relocation program which was presented to government experts, university researchers, NGOs, representatives from the populations, and politicians. This event marks a shift in the development strategies of the banks. Responding to new trends in development planning, they advocated participatory approaches and the inclusion of NGOs. Local authorities also expressed the desirability of these orientations. Unfortunately, very little changed despite this new rhetoric. As we will see in the last chapters, clientelistic relations still play an important role. Also, despite the promising start in 1993, most of the environmental recommendations have not been implemented and nobody knows for certain whether they will ever be.

THE YACYRETA RELOCATION AGENCY

After the Yacyretá Treaty was signed, the EBY was formally created. The joint agreement determined that the "Entity" (as many people call it) would have headquarters both in Buenos Aires and Asunción, the capital cities of Argentina and Paraguay. A board of directors composed of representatives from the two countries would meet periodically to make decisions related to the project. Throughout most of the project, the headquarters remained in Buenos Aires and decisions were made from the capital city without even visiting the relocation sites. In Posadas, various professionals struggled to influence decision-makers living in the remote center of the country. The Posadas office had a sector in charge of legal aspects of relocation, a technical sector in charge of inspecting construction works in the city and of surveying the relocation zone, and a social sector in charge of the relocation program. The organization of each sector changed as years passed. Nowadays, the majority of the professionals working in the relocation program are hired on short-term contracts.

DAMNED PLACES AND PLACES OF HOPE

The area to be flooded was first determined in 1974. Many years later, Decree 1585 established that all areas below elevation 84 would be affected, including those spaces that should be cleared because of the construction of complementary works, such as the bridge connecting Posadas and Encarnación, the water pumping station, the port, highways accesses, railroads, and customs. The area included the chacras that spread along the river banks of Posadas and the areas encompassing nearby streams that flow into the Paraná River (see Map 4.2). All these lands are very low and, therefore, they are exposed to periodical floods. Because of their vulnerability, most of these lands have always had very little real estate value.

Map 4.2
Encarnación, Paraguay and Posadas, Argentina

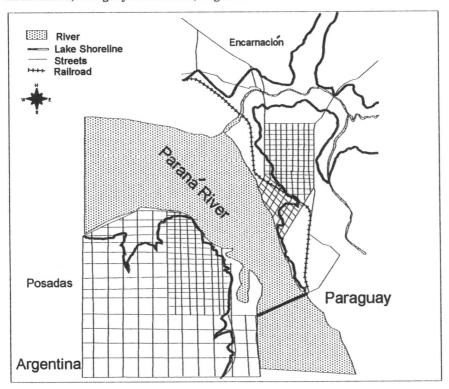

With the exception of a few residential houses built on the outskirts of the pretentious Aguacates neighborhood, the majority of the homes are very precarious. A great number of these humble dwellings are built on public or private lands (69 percent).[9] The 1979 census estimated that 31 percent of the household heads to be relocated owned the plots where they lived. While some settlements are at a walking distance from the city's center (a square delimited by four main avenues enclosing 256 blocks), others are quite far away from it. Those living in some of the densely populated sectors depend on either permanent or transitory occupational opportunities offered in the (nearby) downtown Posadas.

The further we go from the city center, the more scattered the houses are. As there is more available land, people raise more farm animals and grow more vegetables. Here and there, we find olerías—small brick factories run by local craftsmen who take advantage of the soil's qualities and proximity to the water sources. All along the coast, we can see small boats fishing for some dorados, pacúes, and surubíes—much appreciated local fish, which will be sold in the streets or consumed in the fishermen's homes. Some of these same boats can be seen late at night wandering quietly on the Paraná's waters. Small candle lights draw fantastic shadows over the river. These fishermen say they are catching fish— many Posadeños whisper that they are smuggling merchandise from Paraguay: bringing electronics, cigarettes, whiskey, or drugs.

Each sector has a different history of space occupation. A few are as old as the capital city itself; some emerged during the first decades of the century when river-related economic activities flourished. Houses are also grouped on both sides of the railroad all the way down to the ferry boat connecting Posadas and Encarnación. When the river and the railroad stopped functioning as the main communication links, some areas lost their dynamism but did not disappear. Many of the residents stayed, waiting for better days while working in activities in the informal sector of the economy. The opening of new highways connecting Posadas to its hinterland and to the rest of the country attracted squatters who settled in the surroundings and formed new neighborhoods, some of which became densely populated.

There are neighborhoods where residents recognize fairly well-defined boundaries which do not necessarily coincide with the limits of the chacras. Other quarters only exist as such in the municipality records and have no reality to their inhabitants. The existence of any kind of local identity and community bonds, however, was not the concern of those defining the relocation stages and the districts to be included in each of them. Like other projects of this kind, space and time are controlled by engineering needs. Thus, space is artificially divided in accordance to the order set for the major and complementary works.

The EBY divided the areas to be relocated into three stages. There was a fixed time assigned for each stage as well as a "target," a desired outcome: to relocate a certain number of people. As Robertson noted, development planning is characterized by an orderly progression from one balanced state to another, where the neat, mathematically defined units of time refer to cycles of project management rather than to fragments of "real" historical time (1984:113).

To the social scientists working on EBY's relocation program, the stages were a given, and it was unthinkable to question the rationale involved in determining them. It was something imposed from above, designed by unknown actors, in an imprecise time prior to the hiring of the social professionals. The relocation planning had to conform to technical considerations and priorities, which conditioned spatial demarcations and the intensity and frequency of encounters between residents and Yacyretá's agents. Lines drawn following the engineering and economic priorities cut across significant social units. Through artificially dividing the neighborhoods, they might separate an old grandmother from her relatives living next door, or a compadre or comadre from the other member of the diad who may reside one or two houses away. They also disorganized community life where it had existed.

Certain types of encounters, such as those generated by the 1979 census and the Swap Operation, which will be discussed in the next chapter, occurred between every household and Yacyretá's employees; other encounters were limited to those included in the first stage. Not every household pertaining to stage one maintained the same kind of contacts with the EBY; various factors contributed to differences in communicational exchanges. The effects of the 1983 floods, legal problems with the deeds, and changing priorities in engineering needs produced a very curious pattern of relocation where whole blocks were moved except for one or two houses left in isolation, surrounded by barren spaces, gigantic dynamite holes, and contaminated puddles.

Given the impossibility of interviewing all the household heads from every affected area, I decided to choose chacras representing different experiences with the EBY according to their position in the sequence of relocation. I will now summarize some characteristics of the selected chacras; they will be more fully described later in the next chapter.

El Chaquito and San Cayetano (known as chacras 206 and 209) were part of stage one. In 1988, they had been partially relocated. They were periodically visited by a social worker and occasionally EBY would summon household heads to its Posadas offices to discuss issues connected with their legal problems.

The Heller neighborhood (chacra 207) was also part of stage one. Some of the original residents left when they got compensation money or were relocated early. The houses were built through a housing project and were comparatively better than those prevailing in the relocation areas; most of them were made out of bricks as opposed to tin or wood, the dominant materials in the zone. The uniqueness of this sector was its employment as a transitory residence in special cases: It provided shelter to some families affected by floods and to others that had to leave their houses for engineering needs before their new homes in the relocation sites were finished. Without being planned, it came to be some sort of an experimental site where relocation techniques were put into practice. As was the case with the other neighborhoods of stage one, social workers visited the households periodically.

The neighborhood of Bajada Vieja and the area below Posadas amphitheater was included in stage two. Like those in stage three, they had been visited by Yacyreta's employees only during the initial years of the relocation program (1979–1980). After that, they had sporadic contacts with the EBY when it promoted technical and literacy courses. A few households were also visited in 1985 to verify data from the 1979 census, to see if there had been changes and to estimate the number of new occupants without relocation rights. EBY's social workers did not visit the area regularly.

Finally, chacra 93 represents the last phase of the relocation process. It is one of the resettlement sites hosting the displaced population. As a new settlement, with families coming from different areas, it has no common tradition and no name. Undoubtedly, those living here had maintained the most frequent contacts with Yacyretá's staff.

From each of these places, I selected a sample of households heads to interview. I wanted to have both the EBY's categories of proprietors and nonproprietors represented in my sample, as well as female- and male-headed households. My assistants and I consulted the social workers' records of each household from all these chacras in order to obtain a sample to be interviewed in depth. This time consuming selection process could have been avoided; a lot of the records did not coincide with what we later found in the field. In the next chapters, I will explore some of the reasons why EBY's data differed from ours. Our work with the records, however, was not a waste of time. On the contrary, it allowed us to do participant observation in Yacyretá's offices quite unobtrusively: We could see the consultations between people and social workers, the interaction of professionals, technicians, and employees, and the organization of regular daily work.

NOTES

1. The original construction design provides for the addition of 20 more turbines in future stages of the project. Given the current circumstances of Yacyretá, I doubt very much that anybody is dreaming of installing them. For additional information on engineering specifications, see *La Ingeniería*, # 367, Centro Argentino de Ingenieros, July 1986; Esto es Yacyretá. Suplemento de *El Territorio*, July 1983; EBY 1979, 1980, 1987).

2. General Stroessner remained in power until February 1988 when General Andrés Rodríguez seized power, putting the longest dictatorship in Latin America to an end.

3. For a detailed analysis of the bidding process see Ribeiro (1994).

4. There are numerous articles commenting on the role played by Brazilian diplomacy (Itamaraty, the Ministry of Foreign Relations). See, for example, *Revista Cambio*, December 1974; *El Cronista Comercial*, January 9, 1974; *El Litoral*, December 30, 1974. Brazil has been Paraguay's major commercial partner (major creditor and major investor) for the Last 15 years (Franco 1988).

5. The Paraguayan press reports that people who received millions of dollars in compensation between 1976 and 1989 were front men of important members of Stroessner's entourage (for names and amounts paid in compensation, see *El Diario*, May 10, 1990).

6. In April 1997, the agreement to privatize signed by presidents Menem of Argentina and Wasmosy of Paraguay was canceled because the Argentine and Paraguayan congresses did not endorse it.

7. These comments, which clearly show the biases of the authors, who equated poverty to disease, were curiously included on a section called "Benefits of the project Yacyretá-Apipé with regard to the future control of the floods."

8. On the regulation of the law, see *El Territorio,* November 11, 1974. On its contents and purposes, consult *La Nación,* November 18 and November 26, 1974.

9. When the 1979 census was taken, 31 percent of the households heads declared to be owners of the plots where they lived, 21 percent were either tenants or occupants of the plots under the permission of the owners, and 44 percent were intruders on public or private land.

CHAPTER 5

The Encounter of the Relocated Population and the Relocation Agency

The decision to build Yacyretá and the need to move population out of areas that would be affected either by the dam or by complementary works such as bridges, highways, and water works have brought together people who would never have met otherwise and others who were previously involved in various asymmetrical relations such as patron-client and capitalist-laborer. In this chapter, I will discuss the encounter between the population to be resettled and the various agents who communicated that dam construction would affect their lives. To understand such an encounter, I will first describe where the various actors came from and how they lived before relocation-related actions transformed their daily lives. The description of their past has primarily been constructed on the basis of the accounts of the population that has already experienced the effects of Yacyretá's policies. Consequently, what is stressed in the narratives of the early years in the neighborhood stems from their evaluation of the present situation.

The encounter was not a gratifying one. On the contrary, it marked the beginning of a very critical period in the lives of both the EBY's staff and the people to be relocated, characterized by anxiety, uncertainty, and a rather resigned anticipation. All these are symptoms of Scudder and Colson's "multidimensional stress," the particular state created by compulsory relocation, a notion that has also been used by Yacyretá's social planners. Nobody, however, had seen that the crisis is suffered both by planners and the affected population.

When a crisis situation erupts in everyday life routines, social actors recognize breaking points, time-space boundaries separating a "before" and "after," usually having symbolic or physical markers (Giddens 1984:282). To those affected by Yacyretá's relocation policies, the "census" and the "granting of the blue folder" constitute such dividing devices: They mark the transformation and/or the creation of settings of interaction, social relations, symbols, and meanings, as well as the acquisition of new identities, such as becoming "beneficiaries," the "licenciada/o," or "Mr. or Mrs. Yacyretá."

However, people did not regard Yacyretá's announcements as the sole event that dramatically changed their lives. The tragic floods of 1983 were vividly recalled and blamed for their sufferings as much as and, in many cases even more than Yacyretá was. Yacyretá's works and the floods of 1983 account for most of the spatial transformation of Posadas. Throughout the 1980s, parts of old neighborhoods disappeared, other spaces were used for transitory relocation, and rows of bright new tile-roofed houses emerged in previously quiet semi-rural environments.

Before seeing how the population interpreted their first encounter and how they elaborated what was told to them, in other words, how they consumed messages and actions, I will describe some aspects of everyday life in the neighborhoods which may provide clues for understanding the population's reactions.

LIFE IN THE NEIGHBORHOODS BEFORE THE CENSUS

The name Bajada Vieja refers both to the first street opened to communicate with the port and to a district. There now exists a distinction between the street and the well-defined surrounding blocks, and the area spreading down the cliff from the port to the Posadas amphitheater. Above the cliff, houses are made of bricks and a few are still made out of wood, but they all have running water and electricity. Down the cliff, people get water from a public tap. Houses are made of cardboard and tin; very few shacks are connected to electrical sources. The dwellings are hidden inside a heavy forest: some cannot be seen from above. There are no streets running down to the river coast or parallel to it; only a few steps here and there which start on the sides of sightseeing balconies marking the end of the planned paved streets. The contrast is great: People come to these balconies to see the view of Encarnación and the Paraná River. On both sides of the balconies, there are elegant homes with beautiful cultivated gardens; down at the bottom there are poor shanty homes enclosed by thick subtropical vegetation.

As there are no streets and very few paths, people from the low areas must go through their neighbors' homes to reach their own place. To get to other parts, it is even more difficult, since some sectors are separated by streams, and there are only very unstable little bridges connecting them. Walking along the river banks to get to some of the houses is only possible when the water level is low enough.

In the past, most of the area belonged to the brothers Tabia. Their firm owned the shipyards in that zone. Don Hilario Gómez, a grocer who used to work for the company as *mita-í* (foreman), commented that "half of Posadas used to belong to them; they helped to create the city. . . . They employed as many as fifty people."

Don Peralta, a worker in the firm, helped some men get permission to build their homes inside the property, and he also joined men and women when they cleared the field and built their *ranchos*. That was about thirty years ago. At that time, old residents recalled, "It was a thick jungle and an *estero* (swamp), full of snakes, it was so muddy, that it felt like soap."

In general, the population distinguished between private and public land. They preferred to build their homes on public land because they thought it is unlikely they would be evicted. Thus, many informants expressed their desire to build their houses in plots reserved for future streets rather than in privately owned sectors.

How Ubaldo Delgado decided where to build his house illustrates their strategies:

Ubaldo: In order to enter here, I went to [the] Prefecture, to the police station. And they told me, that [the] Prefecture had nothing to do. [They said] That this is a property, it is a property [private property] and they tell me [that] I am inside, I am an intruder. If I am outside, it belongs to the Prefecture, then I was outside the thing. But for more security, I went to know these people of Tabia, and I asked them and we found the map, it is a triangle. We used to be there, in the coast, now we are in the center of the triangle.

Carmen: What did Tabia tell you at that time?

Ubaldo: Tabia told me, "go and make it, after all, I know you are going to look after it (the plot). What I would not like is if you were an intruder."

Old Posadeños speak in very derogatory terms about the coastal people, who used to work as *changarines* (porters) in the port. The poorest from la Bajada Vieja and other coastline areas used small carts to carry the merchandise. Mola, the same person who owned land and business in Posadas and after whom one of the riverine quarters was named, had a company that was in charge of carrying the merchandise from the ships to the coast when there was no port. They used a big carriage with twelve horses.

Subsistence of the population was, and in many cases still is, largely based on the river. In the old days, many men worked as stevedores, loading the freight. When the activities of the port decreased, some retired and others left or turned to the informal sector of the economy. Some still do some odd jobs in the port. Fishing is another source of income and a means of getting free food for the household. Women use the river to wash clothes both for their families and for others who pay them per load. Smuggling is another important activity, which remains unrecorded in all surveys.

Julio Fuentes's account illustrates the life history of many neighbors:

Carmen: What did you tell me you worked as?

Julio: Maritime worker, navigator, I am retired. I retired 18 years ago. I retired in 1967, there was not anything else to do. The highway started to come. Everybody, those who deliver the merchandise by surface, it is more convenient for them. With only two people, it is enough from here to Buenos Aires, in a day and a half, they are right at your door, therefore, it is more convenient. That killed navigation. There are a lot of maritime workers who could not retire; all of them left to Buenos Aires. Because over there, there were still boats, here, there is nothing left. A few stayed, and work for the sand ships, with the hope they will be able to retire.

Carmen: Are you from Posadas?

Julio: Yes, I was born in San Ignacio, but I was raised here, Posadeño, and very soon I started to navigate, it was in 1935. . . . Thirty-seven years and eight months was my calculation of the years of work before I retired, it was time to do so. Navigation is unrewarding, because the sailor loses all the affection, even of his lover, because you are never at home. . . . You have no entertainment, nothing. When you arrive in port, they put you "everything red."[1] People want to have fun, and all your money goes. When you realize, you have nothing left in your pocket. It is their fault, they shouldn't bet money. He, who likes to have fun is not careful. Very few are careful.

Although the Bajada Vieja street is increasingly becoming a tourist attraction and a fashionable place to live, some old city residents still think of it as an undesirable area. While the upper part is slowly losing its bad reputation, the low part is still regarded as

truly a *favela* (Brazilian shanty town), where there exists a sector of the population with a strange social organization. They all have their lights, their dancing saloons, many work in the service sector, but a considerable number traditionally work in smuggling, trafficking, they are dangerously tied to smuggling, a lot of marijuana comes through that part. (A middle-class Posadeño.)

Old men from other quarters affected by the floods still remember when Bajada Vieja was full of *piringundines* (brothels), bars, and dancing places where men could pick women up: "One would go to the *bailantas* and nobody would say anything because it was National Territory. It was dangerous, if you didn't know the way you couldn't get where you were going, the lights went out at 12 p.m."

Neither the people living in El Chaquito, nor most of the Posadeños knew where the quarter got the name from. Some suggested it was because the majority of the first residents were Paraguayans and a large number of them were veterans from the Chaco-Paraguayan war. When the war was over, extremely poor Paraguayans migrated en masse to Argentina looking for better living conditions or escaping from political persecution, which became very severe after General Stroessner seized power.

I interviewed people who claimed to have lived in the surroundings since they were born and whose parents were the first settlers of the area. Doña Damasia came from Paraguay in 1936. She and her family first settled on the coast, the favored area for occupation during those early years. Its convenience was based on two factors. First, it was next to the river, a major means of subsistence; second it had no owner because it was a very floodable sector. When they subdivided large extensions of land to sell them in installments, her family bought some plots and moved a little inland and higher to El Chaquito, where she maintained her peasant way of life. She woke up at five in the morning to cultivate her vegetables, to milk her cows, make cheese for her household and for sale in the city market. While she was busy with her small farm chores and five children, her husband worked as a sailor on ships making the journey to the upper Paraná River. Born in Paraguay at the turn of the century, Don Cortés came to Argentina as a child and later became an Argentine citizen. He had always worked in activities related to the port.

Every account of the early days of any quarter started in the same way. In the beginning, it was impenetrable jungle. Residents told me that before the Heller factory was built in the 1940s, it was all "swamps, weeds, and guava trees." Barthe, one of the first merchants to arrive at the old Trincheras de San José and who made his fortune through the control of various firms related to the river economy, used to have ship repair shops in the zone later owned by Heller. Although most of the accounts refer to a wild swamp before the factory was inaugurated, and some even mention the existence of lots of *yacarés* (a kind of alligator) which they used to hunt, there were some activities along the coast that were well established long before the 1940s. These included the ferryboat and some sawmills.

Villa Coz was next to El Chaquito. The name was formed with the initials of the original owner, Don Carlos Ovidio Zayas (C.O.Z.). He also owned part of what later became San Cayetano, one of the latest settlements in this sector of Posadas. El Chaquito and San Cayetano were separated by Avenue Quiroga. There seemed to be no clear-cut distinction between Villa Coz and San Cayetano. Many thought both chacras 208 and 209 were called Villa Coz before the San Cayetano church was built and that soon after that everybody started to refer to the area with the Church's name. Next to the Heller factory, there used to be rows of houses constructed, according to some versions, by the National Mortgage Bank. Some EBY staff members do not believe the bank built those houses, arguing that a national institution could have never financed a housing project in a floodable area. These opposed views do have policy implications. They can influence decisions made with regard to compensation values.

Monetary considerations apart, the Heller housing project seems to have been originally allotted to the political clients of the Peronist party. Those who lived there from the very beginning comment that they were "lucky they got the houses a little before Perón's fall." They stressed that many important authorities from Buenos Aires had come to the inauguration of the neighborhood. A Peronist woman, who remarked that they obtained the houses during the Peronist government, "which gave so many possibilities to the *middle* class," kept the foundation stone in her backyard. The fate of this stone was also the preoccupation of an old neighbor who is now living in chacra 93; he wondered where the stone was while telling me that the Heller neighborhood was first called "Eva Perón" but was immediately changed after the Revolution of 1955. This was not the only transformation they witnessed during those days. Trucks loaded with armed men would come, harass them, and threaten to burn the homes; moreover, sympathizers of the victorious group razed every symbol of the previous regime. They were not totally successful, however. Peronists hid as many things as they could at great personal risk— the case of the stone was one example among many.

The Heller factory, built in the 1940s, had its own port. There was a railway siding made specially to connect the coastal installations with the railway. At its peak, it employed as many as 400 people. The main factory made plywood, and there was also a sawmill which used the discarded wood.

Don Farías, an old *correligionario* (member of the Radical party), who claimed to be a former owner of some land in El Chaquito, as well as an administrator at Heller for two years, described the beginnings of unionization in a manner that illustrated anti-Peronist biases. He commented that when the Law of Professional Associations was passed in the late 1940s, workers joined the newly formed union; they were "very active and insolent;" they "would do all kinds of things." He continued saying that Peronism "complicated people's life, they became arrogant, nobody respected or complied with anything." And finally, he complained that "they wanted all rights and no obligations." He remembered a very long strike before 1950 in which workers opposed the firing of undocumented Paraguayans and demanded they be hired again. He spoke very derogatorily of Paraguayans, who, according to his view, made up the majority of the riverside people and thought they should not be given a home because once "they had it they would bring all the family."

Animosity against Paraguayans was not uncommon in the neighborhoods, although many "Argentine" residents could have easily been born in Paraguay. Indeed, in most cases it was totally fortuitous where one was born relative to national boundaries. Great numbers of the inhabitants of the region move constantly from one country to the other in response to changing political and economic conditions. Among those born in Paraguay, some expressed their preference for the Argentine nationality and asserted they felt more Argentine than many who were born there.

In all neighborhoods, conflicts might arise with regards to national identity, rivalries among political factions, and soccer. Soccer games were an arena where neighborhood rivalries were played out. El Chaquito and San Cayetano confronted each other in the field, and invariably, most of the games ended in fights: "Before it was tough, because I could not go to Quiroga Avenue. When there was a championship, there were big fights and I could not go across the street." Every neighborhood competed with every other, and very often, the police had to send men to put an end to the disputes: "There were some tough people too. Don't think that they were all beautiful people, no Chaquito was at one time respected."

Soccer teams were sponsored by the owners of groceries which had adjoining bars. The grocers played an important role in community life. Residents could get goods from the store on credit. Each sale was registered on little booklets and people could pay for their debts monthly or whenever they obtained enough money. Some of the groceries had a dance floor which on weekends got crowded with all kinds of people. Men belonging to the grocery *barra* (clique) met women who worked as domestic servants during the week. Drafted men from the various armed forces would also come, and it was customary that many of the dances ended in brawls.

The grocer generally acted as a broker with the larger society. He could be a labor contractor, recruiting his soccer players and other clients for various odd jobs. In addition, he assured a political clientele to the faction he belonged to. These stores were places from which great social control could be exerted. Men would spend most of their time drinking, playing cards, boccie, billiards, knucklebones, and gambling. Most of the movement and gossiping of the neighborhood was controlled from these places.

A man who used to own one of these stores told me that he used to be the president of a soccer club which had six teams. He proudly said that on one occasion, he ordered all the team shirts from Paraguay: "They looked exactly like those of the national team and customs let me pass them." One day, he commented to me that he knew everybody in the neighborhood and their whereabouts; "nobody can fool me," he added.

The grocer was also somebody the client could rely on in difficult times. The first important strike after the Revolution of 1955 was one led by railroad workers. One of my informants had to hide for days because the police searched his home daily. The governor tried to cut supplies from the strikers but the grocer from whom he always brought the staples told him and his friends they could take all they needed, including money; "It is something," he said, "we always have to be thankful for."

The Church rivaled with the grocers for the control of a large client population. It also organized soccer games both for adults and children, held dances, and sponsored various social activities on occasion of religious festivities. The most important was the procession on August 7, in honor of San Cayetano, the patron of workers. The importance of this festivity was reinforced by the presence of a lot of outsiders, especially those from the "center."

When the "missionary fathers" first came to the area, there was no church and they used to hold mass in a tent. Shortly afterwards, they moved to a wooden chapel. Father Segismundo, later chaplain of the army, was very active in organizing the community to build a new church. They collected money through organizing various activities such as raffles, charity fairs, and dances. Everybody was very proud of their accomplishment and insistently remarked that the church was erected with all their effort, with "the sweat of workers." Another neighbor pointed out that it was only neighbors that did it; there was "no municipality, no government, nothing."

The Church, people from San Cayetano believe, helped them understand each other and was "fundamental to our being more united." The following summarizes what the Church meant to most neighbors:

For us, the Church was everything, we were all for the Church, the whole neighborhood. Because there, all the neighborhood used to gather, in the church. There, they organized charity fairs, there was a soccer field, the kids had fun there. Then, of course, on Sundays, the masses, there it was based, around the Church, the whole neighborhood was based.

The Church assumed a role of moral guidance. It set the standards of what families should be like. An old woman pointed out that the fathers "did a lot because they married all the couples, nearly all the couples in the neighborhood." The priest had a paternalistic relationship with his parishioners: "He was very good because he took care of all the people and helped them a lot."

ENCOUNTERING EBY

The first encounter between the population to be relocated and EBY was through the EBY census; my first interaction with the displaced ten years later dealt with their accounts on that turning point of their lives. On our first visit to the chacras, we told household heads and/or other family members that we were interested in writing a history of the neighborhoods—of what they were like in the past and how they changed after the decision to build Yacyretá was made. Different questions were addressed to us to check where we came from and what our purpose was. In one house, after explaining our purpose for the second time, a woman expressed her approval and her daughter yelled jokingly from the kitchen: "You are going to be in the history books like San Martín."As a rule, people were willing to talk about these topics and would speak about them with ease. Many, however, did not want us to tape their accounts, and we did not insist on this. Although field work was done under a democratic government, the initial contact between the people to be resettled and Yacyretá occurred under a very repressive military regime, and the population in general—and not solely the people to be relocated—were still very afraid of having their opinions recorded in a manner where they could be easily identified. In addition, there were a few informants who believed that the EBY punishes those critical of its proceedings, either by postponing their resettlement or by giving them smaller homes. This group did not want us to work with a tape recorder because they feared their statements would reach Yacyretá. Not everybody was so much concerned with anonymity, many insisted that their names be mentioned when I wrote about those issues; they wanted everybody to know what had happened to them and what they thought about it. Don Ramírez asked if what he was saying would be told to the general public because he believed it was important that people know what had happened with Yacyretá, and how they treated the people: "What I tell you anybody can tell. I do no lie. Neither do I exaggerate. Things are like they are, and it is good they be known."

In the following sections, I reproduce parts of the dialogues between the population, my assistants, and myself.

Pedro was in his late sixties, he retired as a navigator because of an accident which left him crippled. He felt very lonely because all his children had left home and his wife died. He had not been visited very often by EBY's staff and his understanding about the relocation process was very vague.

Nancy: When was the first time that you were in contact with people from Yacyretá?

Pedro: It's been . . . many years ago of that. I could not say it exactly but it was probably in 1977 I can't remember it so. . . . It's been a long time ago.

Nancy: What did they tell you?

Pedro: That it was not allowed to *innovar*[2] (make changes). In other words, that houses could not be built, and the one who left could not return. It was because of the dam that was to emerge (salir). And then, they came, and in another opportunity they returned. . . . They did census. That was in 79, 80 (1979, 1980). They always came to see, to see how the floors[3] were, because there were always floods, but it was not big, no. They (the floods) always *bothered* the people, and the people had to *bother* the authority, where he is, if not. . . . It is communicated. But I never *bothered* them, we always went up the cliff. I would erect a little place (where we stayed) until the water lowered. But many could not do so because they did not have the means to do so. Civil Defense (employees) came to see the situation. They had to *bother*. The trucks from the municipality would come to take them. And after it was over, they would come to check if the place was in good condition to bring him back here. But that flood of 82 (1982) . . . there it was lost. But they left, but many lost.

Nancy: And how did you feel about the idea of leaving the neighborhood where you have lived for so long?

Pedro: And as . . . that came, that idea came because of the dam because afterwards it is going to sweep over everything, this is going to remain under water. The mirror of Ituzaingó,[4] the dam . . . but this . . . is going to inundate that where they are going to erect the dam here. Here in Encarnación[5] our low zone is going to be under water and this is a great mirror of water that is going to make . . . the coastal area is going to be under water: Prefecture; a little more up there, the port. And so, these things, everything is going to be under water.

Juana, another neighbor, said that some years before, "those from Yacyretá came, a girl and two guys. They measured the home. They asked how many were in the family" and then they gave them a folder that she still keeps. She added that they told her that "water would catch her." Like Juana, Vicente also remembered that they asked him how much money they made and how many there were in his family. Like his neighbors, he said he knew about Yacyretá through the census, "seven or eight years before." Nobody was very sure about the year. Brígido said he could not remember well, but that it was during the military government in 1977 or 1978. Ramón placed that initial encounter in 1974 or 1975. The two, as the majority of the neighbors, immediately added after mentioning the census, either that "they were then given the folder" or "that they had one." Indalecio complained: "A long time ago they promised us they would give us a house and nothing happened, we were *censused* about four times."

Ramón, Juana, Julio, Brígido refer to various visits. They also remember what Yacyretá offered to them:

Juana: The guys that come to take notes do not know anything and they tell (you) that this will take long and who knows when they will be given. The only thing they do is to write down how many members there are in the family, how many children, the money we have, the meters of the lot (plot) to see the size of the house.

Brígido: These people returned twice. . . . They offered us different places to go to live, like the area of the Regiment and *Coca-Cola*, but I preferred the zone of Itaembé.[6] They came afterwards to see if I still wanted to go there and I said yes.

Julio: Here, we had visits from them many times. There was a time, nearly a month, two months, three or four would come. I had a little grocery store . . . and they would drink a beer, a soft drink, and begin to talk. I started to ask, as I am curious, what is this business about?

Carmen: What did they tell you?

Julio: They said that this was fast (that the dam would be done in a short time). He (an EBY employee) says, "this is going to happen!" And I say "What is going to happen to us." And they assured that they were going to give a place to whoever wants one and those who don't want one will get compensation. The plot will be assessed, the property will be assessed, and you will be paid. And I say, "but with (the amount of) money that you are going to give me, I cannot do anything."

Like the neighbors at Bajada Vieja, there were a lot of neighbors at El Chaquito and San Cayetano who were uncertain on the year they first heard from Yacyretá. Braulio, the son of a 66-year-old-widow registered as the household head, gave us his view on when and how they got the news. Unlike those living in Bajada Vieja, residents in these neighborhoods understood that there had been more than one census.

Braulio: Yes, that was when . . . that, I do not remember well, in . . . , but it seems to me that it was in 1980, when they made the 1980 census. It seems to me that it was then that they gave the news that we had to go from here. And people do not give much importance to it. You see, because I do not know. You know how they are . . . politics. They know that everything is politics. And then, it started to mobilize here, around the business of the bridge. I remember that it was in 1980, in the census, and there, it was started, the talk about Yacyretá. Because in 1978, I remember, when the World Cup came, I was near 2 de Mayo, around that zone and nothing had happened yet. It was after I came here . . . and with the business of the census, that they left those little labels at each house, you see, "censused" and what do I know? People did not give a damn.

Felisa was a fifty-year-old woman who lived in San Cayetano with her companion, their son, daughter-in-law, and grandchild. She was not legally married and the property was under her name. She commented that she had never heard of Yacyretá until they had taken the 1979 censuses and then added that she still did not know "what is that business about a dam." As most of the people interviewed, she remembered they took a picture of the house; that they then asked how many there were, whether the house belonged to them or not, and if they had a sales contract.

Casimiro of El Chaquito, father of ten children and grandfather of three, was in his fifties and occasionally worked recruiting labor for the railroad or for other transitory chores. He recalled that "First, a census came . . . we were given the folder. And they told us from Yacyretá that we were within the status quo law. . . . At the beginning, we didn't believe, but when the second census came, then, we did."

Julio González was the household head, but I interviewed his wife because he worked all day and it was very hard to find him at home. Dora was in charge of doing all the errands. They had five children, and although in their early forties, they already had two grandchildren. Before telling me any other thing about the first time she met the Yacyretá people, she called them *sinvergüenzas* (shameless ones):

Dora: In 1979, it was the first census . . . and they said that they were going to take us out. They told this to everybody and said that it was "direct swap." . . . That nobody was going to lose anything, they took the picture of the house, and they gave us the folder with the picture of the front.

Carmen: Who did that?

Dora: Well, employers, those who took the pictures would come, they didn't have an important position, . . . they were sent by the others. They looked at the roof, the walls, the trees. They said they would pay for everything. . . .When they took the Census, they said that we went (into) direct swap . . . that whoever had a plot, there was no problem, that they changed it for another house, that they changed right.[7]

Adolfo, a forty-nine year-old man who made bread and pastries for a living made some remarks that the others did not. According to him, in 1968 or 1970, there was already some news about the plans of constructing a dam. During those days, approximately nineteen years before, he commented, it was said that there would be no more fuel in forty years. He was better informed than others, and it was obvious that he read the papers discussing the project.

Evaristo, a retired seventy-year-old man who had fathered 11 children, did not mention the census, but rather, a measurement taken in 1977. An active member of the Comisión Vecinal of El Chaquito, Domingo talked extensively about the community's problems. Most of what he told me, he also reported to the press, the local authorities, political parties, and to the EBY. It was not surprising that he was one of the few persons that referred to past events related to Yacyretá's history other than the census:

Domingo: The works, we knew they would be made during the Peronist government of 1973. It reached an agreement with the Paraguayan government to construct this dam. . . . If we have deeds it goes for a direct swap, if we do not present the deed in time and form, we will have to pay all of it. And there are neighbors that have been paying taxes for nearly thirty years, who are paying taxes, thirty years.

The first time I visited José Ríos at El Chaquito, it was a hot Sunday afternoon. He was sitting outside his house drinking *mate* with his daughters, sons, in-laws, and grandchildren. Except from one house next door all other surrounding houses had already been demolished. From his house, I could see earth mounds, ditches, the ramps they had already erected for the highway leading to customs, and the international bridge. Because it looked as if they were having a family reunion, I limited myself to telling them the purpose of my visit and asking Don José when I could come back. He said that he would love my coming back because he liked visits and enjoyed talking.

On my second visit, a married daughter, who lived in Barrio Iprodha,[8] told me that her father would be coming soon, he was fetching some water from the public tap. Don Ríos was old and a widower; the only company he had was, according to his daughter, a grandson whom he adopted from one of his daughters. He came soon afterwards, carrying two heavy buckets of water. When I asked when he first knew about Yacyretá, he said it was with the census and went inside the house to bring the blue folder. He checked the date and then asked me to have a look at it. He was registered as an owner. Then, he remembered:"There had been a blank census, they would give you a little paper. Later, they came and gave us the folder."

Nobody in Bajada Vieja and Anfiteatro had identified the profession and/or names of the Yacyretá people; but both in El Chaquito and San Cayetano, all informants mentioned the *licenciada* ("titled ones"), the word by which they address the social workers.[9]

One of us asked an informant: "Who came from Yacyretá? Do you know any of them? Have you gone there to talk?" The informant, a football player and a province employee answered: "No, the licenciada, she came and said, "Look, a census is being taken: afterwards the bridge is going to be open, here, in Posadas-Encarnación."

Florencio is a middle-aged mechanic who followed the same trajectory of many men in his age group. Born in a Misiones rural area, he went to Buenos Aires to try his luck. He wanted to study how to repair cars and he did so for a while. In 1978, he came back. In 1979 he married and settled in San Cayetano.

Florencio: Here, in this place . . . we came two years ago. Because the flood chased us, in 1983, the flood chased us.

Carmen: How did you know about the Yacyretá construction?

Florencio: And I knew about it after I got married. I got to know because in 1980, you see, there was a census, they took a picture of the houses . . . previous to that they gave us a croquis similar to this one, just simply a little paper like this one. They took the picture (he shows it) . . . and this is from the time I got married. It was then that they brought a leaflet that said "B_1," "B_2," "B_3."[10] That group 1, something like that, the first group had to leave. It was all those people, over what was going to be this, the ramps; then, there were people who had deeds and were owners, proprietors of the plot. And the third group, which corresponded to me, it was people who were on public land, in municipal land, public, the B_3. And they took a lot of people. What was delayed a little was the first group.

The categories he used did not correspond to any of EBY's official stages. He thought the order of relocation was established according to categories such as owners and intruders.

Doña Teresa lived with two unmarried children, two married ones, their consorts, and two grandchildren. She owned a badly kept brick house which she complained had been ruined with the 1983 floods and could not be fixed because of the law of *status quo*. She considered herself part of an impoverished middle class. Her late husband used to work for the Argentine Railroad Company and in 1973 became an elected representative of the Peronist party. She said that the idea to construct the dam had been in "the mind of many men for fifty years, but only recently, they started to build it."

Most of the informants constantly repeated that they "were waiting" when asked about Yacyretá. This was the case of Rubén, a father of five children, who worked at the muncipality in the morning and fished the rest of the day to make ends meet. He said that they had nothing to do "other than waiting." He first heard "comments" (gossip) in his neighborhood, but in a very "superficial manner"; he acquired a "greater knowledge when those from Yacyretá took a census in 1979." He then said again that he knew about the dam through comments, but that he still did not know what a dam was.

On another visit, Florencio said that they had twice come to his house but they did not find him because he was in Buenos Aires. He then added that he was lucky they had found him the third time because "those 'social visitors' went three times to each house and if you were not there, there was not anything you could do." He then asked his wife to bring a supporting document saying that on May 26, 1979, they had taken the census at his house.

Dominga was waiting for her husband to come for lunch in a short while so she could not be extensively interviewed on this visit. However, we sat in the patio and chatted for a while: "You see, 'she said' they would give me another house, so I knew they wouldn't leave me on my own."

Susana used to rent the house where she lived before moving to Barrio Heller. When they came to take the census, she identified herself as the household head. At that time she was living with Gerónimo, ten years younger than her, and with three children, each of them with a different last name. The youngest was the son of her present partner. She admitted to have been rather concerned when she first heard the news and that they would ask the EBY's people what they were going to do with them. They later felt relieved when they were "given the folder" and were told that "nobody would be left in the street."

María del Carmen, Don Ramírez' companion, was watching a soap opera when one of my assistants arrived. She invited her inside the house and told her they used to live in another neighborhood but she temporarily moved when they lost their house with the 1983 flood. She complained that the situation was now very different from the beginning because they initially said they would have a house which could be paid in "affordable installments." She repeated these last words several times. She then explained that in the beginning there were two options: money or a house in exchange for the one they had. As her house was lost with the floods, she bitterly complained, she now would have to pay for the new one.

At Barrio Heller, they remember one of the social workers by name; one of the neighbors stressed that "she had even come to our house a few times." They also mentioned a lawyer, but not by name; the engineer Pérez, "the boss"; and a male social worker, García.

THE FIRST RESETTLED HOUSEHOLDS

Doña Soledad and her husband came from Paraguay in the 1940s. At that time, they had a little son and they had to work hard to become owners of the house. She worked as a washerwoman and also grew a lot of vegetables and raised some chickens in the backyard. One of my assistants, Susana, asked her if she could remember when they first heard about Yacyretá. She started by saying that she could not remember and then added:

Susana: Did people from Yacyretá come?

Soledad: Yes.

Susana: Do you remember who came?

Soledad: No, I don't remember. They said that we must go and we say it is impossible, how are we going to go? That we are inside our *ranchito* (little hut) that we got[11] with a lot of work. We kept building it little by little. . . . Then they came and began to say that we must go because we will be under water. Under force we have to go and well, my late husband accepted it.

Susana: And what did people say in the neighborhood?

Soledad: Nothing, because we are going to tell you, frankly, they are all ignorant, there is nobody who is going to say that we cannot go. And that is how things are, and then we accepted. All of us accepted. And those who own the house, they would have direct swap.

In general, residents of chacra 93 recalled the first news about Yacyretá as a positive event. They took Ramona by surprise; being born and raised in the neighborhood, she received the announcement with happiness because they told them "it would be a total change in their life, the house, everything." According to her, it was a happy thing, as she had always had a very "precarious little wooden house."

The reconstruction of their (the residents of chacra 93) past history with Yacyretá seemed to include more censuses and more visits. They described the "counting procedures" in more detail. They seemed to be more aware of what data the EBY wanted and what it was for.

FIRST ENCOUNTERS AS SEEN BY YACYRETA STAFF MEMBERS

Anybody listening to Yacyretá's staff accounts of the first encounter with the population would have some difficulties discerning the various actions they refer to. I interviewed present and former members from the various sectors to see what they recalled.

With the exception of some of the lawyers, who, as I shall discuss in Chapter Seven, were famous for being inaccessible, the rest of the EBY's staff had been friendly and open to my queries. The following comments are an example of what they reported to me about their initial participation:

Juan: Finally, the EBY attempts a timid rapprochement with the social scientists from the University. It consisted in asking us to do a study. It was clear that the census from 1975, even though it had a lot of tables and many volumes, it lacked a humanistic, historical, anthropological dimension showing how people really lived. It was very hard to imagine and generate a relocation project based on the existing data; it was basically data of a sociodemographic kind. What then happened is that they asked us to do a study, given the fact the initial housing plan was considered inadequate; this problem probably being attributed to the use of inappropriate census data gathering techniques. This study was some sort of a letter of introduction, its purpose was basically the description of ways of life, quality of life. . . . It had a lot of photographs. It was called "Housing and labor in the areas affected by Yacyretá." It included a lot of things: temporary labor, the study of porters, labor demand. . . . It aimed at looking for how to compensate for the impact of relocation on their sources of labor. Our study was phenomenal. We had to do it in two weeks, with four or five teams working simultaneously. A lot of students participated because we were very few teachers. They took a photography class to get those pictures. And then, people from Misiones appeared producing something impressive. People affected by the project appeared, those who up until then had only been comments, statistics. Suddenly, the pictures appear, the house plans . . . like something tangible, absolutely *carne y hueso* (flesh and bones, very real), in comparison to the previous study. . . . In Yacyretá, I started with a rather complex operation, in its logistics, its organization. It consisted in changing the supporting document given in the 1975 census, for a luxurious plastic folder with some sort of a location certificate, with a water mark . . . like bonds, with a polaroid picture of the house. Then, each of the three, four thousand households beneath the security level were given one of those folders. This lasted for months. This was my initial task, we had to plan a massive entrance to the field, with a fairly large group of people. We went with pick-ups provided with loudspeakers. Field workers called people by their names and they would come and receive the blue folders.

There was no general agreement whether there had been one or two censuses before the 1979 EBY. Neither did EBY's staff members know for sure what institution was in charge of them. What everybody agreed on was that they were inappropriate instruments to develop resettlement policies. One of the major problems with the 1977 census was that, because it was taken before establishing the definitive level, it included a greater area than the one effectively affected. Somebody from Yacyretá told me that even if they had wanted to use some of the data it would have been impossible to do so because rats had a feast with the protocols. The Argentine navy, which was said to be in charge of data processing, kept them in its deposits in Buenos Aires docks, universally known for its overpopulation of rodents.

Although they acknowledged many problems with the 1977 census, the EBY employed the same cartography for the 1979 census. It also incorporated into the resettlement files the data they could recover from the Buenos Aires port.

Members of the social team remembered that the 1979 census and the Swap Operation were done simultaneously. Some of them referred to both by using the word census. A sociologist was in charge of the census and an anthropologist coordinated the Swap Operation. The majority of the field assistants doing the census were students in social anthropology, social work, and social science research. By and large, the Swap Operation was in charge of social workers. All of them did their work on short-term contracts with the consultant firm. Everybody remembered that at one point there were more than eighty people working in their sector. In Posadas, both actions were coordinated by an anthropologist who was responsible for the PRAS (Relocation Program and Social Action).

A social worker who participated in every stage of the project recalled that they started the Swap Operation by leaving pamphlets in the whole area. That was done only once because so many of the people for whom the pamphlet had been written could not read. Subsequently, they used loudspeakers. Liliana, one of the social workers, told me that, while she was in the field registering data, neighbors would approach her to ask when this would happen. The professionals had taken courses to participate in the operation. In those courses, they discussed what to tell the population.

Many at Yacyretá believe that the idea of giving the blue folder was a mistake:

It was the idea of De los Ríos, the director of the legal area, He had seen this in Spain. But you can do this when the beneficiary is defined. Here, the problem is that there are a lot of people with a folder who are not beneficiaries. Even though it says in small letters that it does not grant the condition of beneficiary, people understand that it does. In other words, initially, the supporting document from 1977 was changed for a folder. Then, it was enlarged when it was realized that reality had little to do with the 1977 census. It was a useless operation.

After finishing these operations, which lasted for many months, social workers started working house by house in the neighborhoods corresponding to stage one. Each social worker had a zone. Their supervisor did the zoning. At that time, as the registers elaborated on the basis of the 1979 census were not finished, the social workers did not know how many people there were in each area and had to check this in the field. Dora remembers:

We visited the houses periodically. At that time we were a lot. We visited each family every fortnight. Besides getting information, we gave them advice on what they needed. For example, documents, we would tell them what they had to get. We got preferential appointments. There were a lot of people without documents . . . it was a significant number. . . . There were a lot of six-year-old kids that had been born . . . and the mother was with the "pink paper."[12] We arranged contacts with the register office [registro civil], with Migrations. In general, they considered us. . . . At the time of the *milicos* [slang for military men] everybody are soldiers . . . now, [regretfully] they were all captains. Even the minor office clerk behind the counter.

MY RECONSTRUCTION OF THE FIRST ENCOUNTER

So far, we have heard the accounts of the first encounters as told by Yacyretá's staff and by people in the neighborhoods. Both reconstructions of these past events were mediated by my selection, organization, and ordering of voices; brief descriptions of characters, comments, and interpretations to facilitate the understanding of the plurality of voices. I will now reconstruct events through the use of written records such as newspapers articles, reports, memoranda, and various studies.

What follows is a summary of the major actions of the early years of the Yacyretá project. It includes purpose, participants, geographical areas, and socioeconomic categories surveyed.

Study of a Sample: August 1975. The sample included 1,068 people, 914 of whom resided in Posadas. It registered demographic information, including the analysis of time of residence in the area, labor and income, and family size data. In addition, researchers analyzed the affected population's opinions and attitudes toward the project. It was done by a consultant firm. It included the analysis of some affected areas in Corrientes. There is no information on who did the fieldwork.[13]

Register of Population and Housing: March 1977. It surveyed the characteristics of the houses and household members in the affected areas. This study registered 4,572 houses, inhabited by a total of 18,440 people.[14]

Census of Population, Housing, and Economic Activities: April to September 1979. The EBY-Posadas was responsible for designing and taking the 1979 census. A section of the PRAS conducted this action. The goal of the census was to "identify both spatially and socially all families and people living in the area below the future lake level in the urban sector of Posadas." It registered both proprietors and nonproprietors. It aimed at getting as much information as possible to orient policy making. University students were hired to do the fieldwork. In the introduction of the published results, the director of the program said:

From the analysis executed on this report, emerges a socioeconomic profile, characterized by a young population component with a high potential for growth. This sector is inserted in a way that although it seems to be marginal, it is highly functional to the fragile labor market of a city lacking important industrial activities. The low average income, occupational instability and a depressed *standard of life* in comparison to the local media, do not authorize, to qualify the majority of the population as "marginal." Thus, a more careful analysis allows to detect a potential of economic growth and social improvement, on which the Relocation Program of the Entity is based. (EBY 1981b:ii)

Swap Operation: 1979–1983. Initially, it consisted of giving a folder containing data on the beneficiary's household in exchange of the supporting document granted to each household head interviewed with the 1977 census. This folder was blue in Argentina and red in Paraguay. Red is the color of Stroessner's party, the *Colorado*, while blue is identified with the opposition. When it was decided to establish 1979 as the final date to grant the condition of "beneficiary," people who had not been registered in the 1977 census also received a folder (EBY 1987:25). Social Workers were in charge of the operation and it was supervised by an anthropologist. It lasted until 1983.

Social Worker's Visits: From 1980 to the present. Social workers periodically visited households included in stage one. They were in charge of various social plans: regularization of documents, granting of permanent residency to foreigners (*radicación*), vaccination, literacy programs, and labor training.

Surveyors Visits: From 1980 to the present. Surveyors were in charge of measuring, registering, and mapping the plots, buildings, fences, and any other thing attached to the soil. They estimated the cost of the property. Appraisers coming from Buenos Aires set the final value. They did technical work and kept all information in individual folders in the EBY.

Visits of Field Assistants of the SIDP (Section in charge of Research and Project Development): Those in charge of analyzing and keeping the records of the 1979 census went to the households to confirm and update information.

Study on Means of Subsistence and Household Ability to Pay (MESUBS): 1981–1982. Three researchers from the UNaM, a sociologist, an anthropologist, and a social worker, conducted a study at the request of the EBY. The population studied was a sample of squatters to be relocated by Yacyretá in stage one. I was the anthropologist of that team. We supervised the work of 20 field assistants who did in-depth interviews for eight months. The assistants were university students.

Urban Settlement Verification: 1985. This study was coordinated by the SIDP and was done together with the UNaM. Students in social sciences participated as field assistants. It aimed at verifying changes in the settlement patterns in the affected areas. It checked both households that were no longer in the area and new ones that settled after 1979. Two present major problems of the relocation project were assessed in this study: the existence of 1,190 homes of "intruders," and of 416 "derived households" (the married offspring of original households). Both situations were not anticipated and search for solutions originated disputes among decision-makers of the two nation-states, the affected provinces, and the two cities on the Paraná River.

All actions just described brought together various people who had related to each other in accordance to social positions they had before these initial encounters. We will now examine the past experiences of these people to see how the existing social arrangements might have impinged upon the new ones created because of the dam construction.

In the previous sections, I reconstructed the dramatic encounter as it was recalled by the different actors involved. I reported this critical moment by letting participants speak so as to convey how each of them experienced this unexpected change in their everyday lives. Authors such as Bauman (1987) have stressed the peculiarities of modern social planning and its effect on the lives of common people. He metaphorically speaks of "gardened" cultures to refer to social policies that attempt to educate and manipulate subordinate groups whose culture is devalued or ignored. Others have noted that this is one of the effects of the development apparatus that puts populations under the aegis of the state (Ferguson 1990).

In planning the relocation process, Yacyretá's staff did not acknowledge many cultural particularities of the poor of Posadas. When they took the census, they did not include any questions to determine the language spoken at home nor did they check variations in speech genres. Many of the displaced either speak Guaraní at home or employ a form of Spanish in which many meanings differ from the official national language. All pamphlets and radio announcements were made following the style of speaking used by dominant groups. Consequently, many messages were not consumed in the intended way.

Social policies also negated existing forms of social organization. When designing their programs of social action, social workers did not consider the role played by local leadership such as churchmen, grocers, and political brokers nor did they look at the importance of community spaces such as soccer fields and dancing places. The destruction of many social bonds and familiar settings of interaction affected people's identities and self-esteem. The devastating effect of these policies was expressed in the narratives recalling their past in the neighborhoods, which was seen as a time marked by solidarity and friendship.

Informants expressed how they felt deprived of their previous identities, insistently recalling some of EBY's actions. Nearly all men and women we interviewed remembered how they were counted and how their houses were measured. The manipulation of identities was also expressed in the requirements for identification documents and—in the case of Paraguayan-born neighbors—in establishment of legal residency. The transition from being a resident of a quarter to becoming an individual with relocation rights was expressed symbolically in the possession of the blue folder granted by Yacyretá. As one surveyor once told me, it was as if people thought they were getting a diploma. This indeed was the way they understood the meaning of the folder. The majority of residents thought that those who possessed one were entitled to a new house without having to pay for it. There were numerous cases in which people sold the folder as if it were a deed. One of my informants even told me that the folder came with a key with which they could open the door of their new house. When looking at leaflets given to the people at the beginning of the relocation process, I discovered how they came to misunderstand what the folder stood for. The leaflet had a picture of the blue folder and a hand with a key, a map including the relocation sites, and the various possible designs of houses. It said:

Who is the beneficiary? If you live in a house in the areas affected by the Yacyretá project; if the census was taken at your home; if you have proof of your house location or "blue folder," and if you are registered in EBY, you are a beneficiary of the Relocation Program and you have the opportunity of owning a home.

On my subsequent visits to the area, I found that the population of both Posadas and Encarnación still felt that the posession of the folder granted them relocation rights. Residents were not alone in misinterpreting what the folder stood for. Some social workers, who were in close contact with the affected population also misinterpreted the power of the folder. This created serious problems at the time relocation negotiation started because it was only then that people found out that not everybody with a folder could get a new house.

The crisis generated by the relocation process was expressed both in the narratives describing a harmonious past and in the narratives depicting an obscure and dreadful present. To the majority of my informants, Yacyretá turned their neighborhoods into inhospitable and lonely places. After EBY was announced and some engineering works started, neighbors said that their area was made into a swamp, full of snakes, poisonous insects, and dangerous animals. This happened because of a combination of factors such as the devastating flood of 1983 and construction works underway. The municipal government stopped providing garbage collection, and the electrical and water companies stopped supplying their services to the few sectors which had enjoyed them. Although EBY cannot be held responsible for some of these inconveniences, people blame all their present problems on the agency. In the following chapter, I will be examining some of these constructions in greater detail.

NOTES

1. He refers here to red lights and signs indicating the presence of prostitution houses.

2. The man is speaking about the law of status quo passed in 1974.

3. The informant is referring to municipal and other government officials who visit the household when floods occur and check if the floors of the houses had been damaged. Most houses only have earth floors which become very muddy as soon as the areas are inundated. If the homes are seriously damaged, household members are temporarily taken to special shelters.

4. Many newspaper articles and leaflets promoting Yacyretá spoke of the dam as a "mirror of water." Ituzaingó is the Argentine town close to the site where the engineering works are done. It is also the location where workers, technicians, and professionals live. The informant fused both meanings into a single one.

5. Pedro speaks of Encarnación, the Paraguayan city which will also be flooded, as if it were the same thing as Posadas.

6. The areas Brígido mentions are sectors of the city where the municipal authorities temporarily resettled the families who lost their homes in the floods of 1983.

7. Informants used "cambio directo" and "cambio derecho" interchangeably. It will appear as direct swap.

8. A dormitory public housing project, 6 kilometers away from downtown Posadas. It was built during the same years Yacyretá was building the relocation homes.

9. In Argentina, university students obtain a Licenciate degree after five or six years of study. It is a professional diploma which enables graduates to either teach, do research, or work at public or private institutions. In the past, social work schools did not offer a five-year program of studies; they granted diplomas of asistentes sociales (social assistants) after two or three years of study.

10. He referred to a leaflet describing the stages of relocation E1, E2, E3, which were shown in a map. It also provided examples of the types of houses that were assigned according to family size. House design changed according to the relocation sites A1, A3.2, A3.3, A3.1, A4.

11. In Spanish, Soledad said *procuramos* (procured), implying a great effort to accomplish the goal of having a house, which may include from borrowing money to obtaining discarded materials from different patrons to make improvements. It implies that they had to mobilize their social networks and develop special strategies.

12. When a baby is born, the hospital registers the basic data about the birth on a form which is then taken to the registration office.

13. Some results were published from the following reports: *Comisión Mixta Técnica Paraguayo Argentina de Yacyretá-Apipé*, 1977; EBY, 1975.

14. For details on this study consult EBY (1978).

CHAPTER 6

Constructing the Power
of a Dam

While the previous chapter was concerned with the first encounter between the population and the relocation agency, this chapter analyzes the basic dialogical set created with such critical encounter. Through grasping the way participants positioned each other during the relocation process, we may comprehend the conditions under which communication processes occurred. People's response to resettlement policies cannot be fully understood unless we examine their representations of the agency. Conversely, we can only make sense of social policies if we know how EBY's agents think about the poor of Posadas. The process I will examine is a complex one. Positioning does not entirely determine communication, and communication by itself is not entirely responsible for the various positions and identities here examined. There is a dialectical relationship between the two. Moreover, interaction is shaped not only by a local system of social relationships, but also by much broader systems in which the Posadeños (and Encarnacenos) are inserted. I here investigate the knowledge produced by the participants in the project. As Smith (1990) suggests, it can be explored "as the ongoing coordinated practices of actual people." This, she says, means considering ideas, beliefs, and concepts as expressions of social practices inscribed in specific local historical contexts (Smith 1990:63). I will show how everyday practices are transformed "into the abstracted generalizing language of bureaucratic and professional organization" in which individual and diverse experiences are generally lost (Smith 1990:156). I cannot escape, however, from inserting my own professional (and therefore, ideological, according to Smith) interpretation in the construction of this text. In the first part of the chapter, I analyze how Yacyretá became constructed as an omnipotent actor, and I show how this had an effect in the structuring of collective and individual action. The last part of this chapter scrutinizes the multifarious respresentations of the poor of Posadas and their effects on processes of identity formation.

YACYRETA REIFIED

EBY is an institution, and as such, it can neither speak nor do things to people. Although this is obvious to the reader, it needs to be stressed because participants in the relocation process feel otherwise. Indeed, people to be resettled, the EBY's staff members, and politicians alike reify the agency and refer to it as if it were a very powerful actor. I will first examine how Yacyretá is depicted among the affected population.

In the last chapter, I showed how the advent of Yacyretá and the floods of 1983 were generally combined in the narratives and how the ordeals neighbors went through were blamed on both events. I will now examine the associative chains of elements within which the term "Yacyretá" is situated. As already discussed in the introduction, in crisis situations a process of condensation occurs: "All component elements and conditions fuse, as a whole, into a ruptural unity" (Althusser, quoted in Laclau 1979). I will thus identify the combined elements and how they were associated.

FLOODS FROM NATURE AND FLOODS FROM DAMS

Past floods, the affected population said, were natural. Many people remarked that floods "visited" regularly, every five years, and stated that they had never been as big as the one in 1983. If the water ever reached their house, they asserted, it would not stay long; to prevent damage, it would be enough to raise the house from the ground through a procedure they called *sobrado*, which consisted in putting pieces of wood under the tin and/or cardboard walls to lift them. To people in the lowland areas of Posadas, water and floods were things endowed with a will: They came, they chased and grabbed the defenseless victims, and they left.

Felisa once complained: "The river intimidates us, because every so often it visits, and when it comes, it takes away from us everything we have . . . and we leave our house and we suffer."

A great number of informants blamed the devastating floods of 1983 both on Brazil and on the huge hydroelectric dam of Itaipú:

Dominga: The river only brought sacrifice, sorrow, and loss. This flood was different from the previous ones, because it came suddenly. This was because Itaipú controls all this region from there. It is the biggest dam in the world.

Casimiro: With the flood of 1981, everything was ruined in 24 hours. It was the most impressive flood we have ever had. There had been hundreds of them. But before, we would be back in one or two weeks. Here, we lost everything. Until now, we are convinced that it was Itaipú that opened the gate. The water came in a few hours. . . . The papers said it was a lie, that it was a normal flood.

Rubén: And that flood is not natural, because I believe, they had opened a gate. It was as if they had thrown a large bucket of water. It came, and then left. And again, three days later. I woke up and the water was half a block away and it was quiet and I did not think anything bad could happen (he was here referring to a more recent flood in 1987).

José Ríos: Yacyretá started to come to our house. They would say that we had to leave the place because of the water, they say that they are going to throw the water from Brazil. I don't know, they lie so much.

Itaipú, the large Paraguayan and Brazilian dam, was under construction on the upper Paraná River during 1983. When the floods occurred, the lake was not yet formed. What did happen that year was that the Itaipú engineering works permitted the lowering of the river level when the gates were closed to fill the reservoir. This was done shortly after the end of the dramatic floods. No informant mentioned this event. Facts were inverted in the collective memory of the population.

I have already described how, historically, Argentina, Brazil, and Paraguay struggled to gain control over the Paraná River region. In our summary of the negotiations leading up to the construction of Yacyretá, we also saw that Argentine authorities felt urged to start the works because of the geopolitical rivalry with Brazil and the fear that Brazil would become more influential through building the Itaipú dam jointly with Paraguay. The press echoed these depictions of the Brazilians as ambitious and wicked, always trying to corrode the national identity. It was during those years under a military regime that Gendarmería, a special corps of armed men in charge of guarding national frontiers, initiated a campaign to assert Argentina's sovereignty in the country's borderlands.

In El Chaquito, Heller, Villa Coz, and San Cayetano, the majority of the residents were convinced that the ramp built for the Posadas-Encarnación bridge was making things much worse. It caused what they call la *enchorrada*, a sudden burst of water that covered everything with the stinking refuse from the city:

Silvia: It rained. And the *enchorrada*, because of that little stream, would flood everything. All the dirt from the city. All the dirt from the Vicario stream would come and deposit right there, where we were. The ramp was already high, and the dirt would trickle and would stay, forming a dike, because of the ramp. It had never been like that before. The water would run when we had floods. . . . In 1982, we had to leave. Because everything came with that ramp. It started to exert pressures on us. They did, they filled everything. And when we could no longer bear it, because we were uncomfortable, then, they said: "Well, you want the houses. All right." It was a kind of pressure, you know. We had to accept anything.

Alicia: Then came that rain. All the houses started to get covered by water. There, the problem started, with that street. Because we had never had problems with the floods. As my mother-in-law said: we were like those toads, we would float as soon as there was some thunder.

Marta: The first big, big flood which caught us was in 1965. It started because of the bridge.
Carmen: Did they start the bridge in that year?
Marta: Yes, of course. Because they built that ramp and that attracted a lot of water. The water spread over a greater area. Then, that big one caught us. Each time it was even worse.

Most of the informants spoke of the ramp under construction and of the bridge as if the two were the Yacyretá dam itself. When Argentine authorities were trying to convince the Paraguayans to accept the joint venture of Yacyretá, they offered to build the bridge to make the deal more attractive. Everybody links the two projects, although ever since the initial negotiations, the Argentine government and the EBY had been striving to make the public believe that each of those undertakings was independent of the other. In Argentina, the bridge is mentioned as one of the many "hidden costs" of the project. Paraguayans argue that the cost of this gift has been included in the overall debt of Yacyretá.

The majority of the residents said that they were not quite sure what a dam was. They reported that on the first encounter with the EBY employees, they were told that water would get them or that "everything would be flooded." In describing what was communicated to them, they employed the same words they used when referring to the actions of a "natural" flood. Unfortunately, there was no way we can recover the original dialogues between Yacyreta's staff and the so-called beneficiaries. What we do have at our disposal are the information leaflets distributed in the affected areas. One said as follows:

"Yacyretá is news"
Transformation of Posadas in the 1980s. In less than ten years, Yacyretá will mean to this capital:
An international bridge; a new port and its infrastructure; *defensas costeras*–streambank erosion control; a new bus terminal; a new freight terminal; 30 km of new railroads; new highways, including bridges; a water pumping station; a power station; a sewage treatment facility; and new housing complex for the families occupying houses that will be affected by the Yacyretá works.

The written material mentioned neither water nor flooding: The closest it got to those concepts was through reference to a lake that would be located in front of Posadas. The way the information was spelled out, at least in its written version, contributed to the merging of meanings. For years, there was no way people could see the engineering works of the dam itself. First, they were not started until 1984. Second, the dam site was miles away from their houses. The first years after the 1979 census, men and women in the affected areas were very skeptical about any news regarding the future relocation. The majority of those interviewed affirmed they had not believed anything. This was mainly because they could not see any physical changes around them. Gradually they began to take the ramp, the bridge, and the floods as proofs of Yacyretá's existence. It was not until until these tangible signs that earlier accounts acquired verisimilitude.

To some, the floods were intentionally caused either by Brazil or by the EBY. The aim, many believed, was to make them go or submit to the authority of Yacyretá. One informant, who was already living in the newly constructed houses, commented that Brazil was creating the situation, but that they had stopped doing that once neighbors left the area. He complained they had not been warned "that the big flood was coming" when the EBY informed that in the future everything would be filled with water.

THE END OF FLOODS

When recalling what they first heard about Yacyretá, a few of those interviewed said that they would not be relocated because of the dam but because of the *Costanera*—a promenade generally built next to a river or a lake. Some others asserted that Yacyretá is a costanera which will prevent floods once it is finished. When preliminary studies on the hydroelectric project started, EBY's leaflets, press releases, and newspapers articles included the control of floods among the most important benefits of dam construction. This might have been associated with the coast defense mentioned in the leaflets. Only in the 1990s did Yacyretá officials admit that the dam would not control major floods.

In El Chaquito, Heller, San Cayetano, and Villa Coz, the most common associations we registered were those fusing the concepts of the ramp or the bridge, the floods, the natural, the exceptional, and Yacyretá. This did not occur in Bajada Vieja, a neighborhood where none of the complementary engineering works were under construction. This sector of Posadas only changed dramatically with the 1983 floods. Furthermore, contacts with the EBY staff were very limited; therefore, there were very few opportunities for residents to obtain information of any kind. It was not surprising then, that Yacyretá was most commonly associated with the floods. There were no references to the bridge, the ramp, or the streams, but there appeared other elements with which the project was associated. One was the costanera; another was other public housing projects which the province was building with national funds. Nearly everybody related Yacyretá with the floods. Within this associative chain, a frequent condensation was the one that fused the transitory relocation sites assigned by the province to shelter the victims of the 1983 floods with the Yacyretá resettlement areas.

Yacyretá, together with other works to which it was associated, such as Itaipú, the ramp, and the like, served to explain things in retrospect. For example, the works were posited as the cause of earlier events, such as the big floods of the 1960s. Other people, although not overtly attributing the disasters to Yacyretá, made some connections between the two: They asserted, for example, that the disastrous flood was in 1979 instead of 1983. (As discussed in the previous chapter, 1979 was the year EBY took a census of the affected population and also the year when they started the Swap Operation.)

In sum, there were numerous ways various elements became associated with Yacyretá. Quite often, the resulting combinations was contradictory and ambiguous, a characteristic feature of the condensation process. As noted before, condensation is likely to occur in critical situations; because it develops in such circumstances, it may carry fatalist overtones. A quite common remark was that the neighborhoods—and the country—were cursed. Javier, from San Cayetano, thought: "They have kicked the liver of Argentina and if we add the floods, . . . everything is in such a bad shape." Dominga, expressed the same thought more tragically and more religiously: "I have suffered enough. Tomorrow . . . only God. Because I have suffered five things and of those things I can no longer suffer. . . . I can only wait for death."

When the informants commented that what had happened since Yacyretá's announcements was not "natural," they did not necessarily imply that they were facing a manmade disaster. On the contrary, to many "not natural" was something out of the ordinary; as one had put it, it was a "phenomenon" and hence, mysterious, powerful, and frightening. It was something with such a strength that it can "lift whole houses and carry them in one piece," so fearsome that even among those who had already moved, there were still some who said they woke up at hearing the first drop of rain and started packing and moving the furniture automatically.

THE POWER OF A DAM

When speaking about ideological constructions, authors point to a recurrent feature: Symbols and meanings working to the benefit of specific dominant groups are presented in such a way that they seem to be part of the natural, objective world, endowed with a logic of their own. Yet, an analysis of how ideology works can be oversimplified when, for example, it is thought that meanings are intentionally produced with the purpose of controlling and reproducing a system of social relations. Many ideas which are taken for reality are not deliberately and consciously fabricated, although they do help power groups and contribute to sustaining relations of domination.

Because the common man/woman regarded these constructions as independent of the will of human beings, he/she thought there was very little left for him/her to do. He/she was likely to experience the same helplessness when he/she confronted things presented as natural and found himself/herself in situations perceived as unnatural and exceptional as those represented by Yacyretá. For years, in the areas affected by the hydroelectric dam, everybody thought there was nothing they could do in response to the project. When my assistants and I asked people to be resettled whether they had done or said anything with regards to relocation, we always received in reply an answer that was really a question: "And what could we have done?" Insofar as the dam became naturalized—even to the point of being considered supernatural, an exceptional "natural event"—residents from the affected neighborhoods felt there was no alternative. Nobody could oppose a great powerful structure such as Yacyretá; one could only submit to it. In return, those who submitted had expected to be taken care of and protected. As seen above, most people believed that there was a relationship between Yacyretá and the floods. They thus thought that they were entitled to demand help when water damaged their houses. If authorities from Yacyretá informed them the Relocation Agency had no responsibility in the matter, they felt deceived and betrayed. Informants grumbled that nobody from the EBY gave them a hand in the disatrous floods of 1983. "The least Yacyretá could have done was to furnish a truck to carry our belongings." "The neighborhood was expecting another thing from them," a woman told me.

YACYRETA IS MORE POWERFUL THAN THE POPE AND ANYBODY ELSE

The church of San Cayetano played an important role in the lives of those living in the surroundings. As I have already pointed out, it competed with the grocers in organizing soccer teams and with the neighborhood commissions in sponsoring social events such as the celebration of Mother's Day or Children's Day. I have also noted that through their actions, these institutions both reproduced and contributed to create the social and economic relations of the neighborhoods. Yet control of moral and spiritual issues was virtually the exclusive concern of the Church. Very few would dare to dispute its power to deal with such matters. Thus, the Church would set moral standards by striving to convince neighbors to get married and by guiding them in the education of their children.

Yacyretá did sweep away these previous social arrangements and in doing so proved its power over them. The church of San Cayetano served as focus of the few opposition movements to the relocation project, and failed. The priest, now an army chaplain, called for meetings to design strategies to resist resettlement. Actions against Yacyretá included masses, demonstrations, and petitions presented to the local authorities and to the press. The bishop of Posadas took issue with the demands and made claims with regards to the church building, which was the pride of the neighbors.

Don José Ríos had worked for the priest for six years and said he was paid weekly but that he asked not to be paid on Saturdays because he "felt sorry to take money from the chapel." He did not mention any actions in which residents took part. According to him, it was only church representatives who pleaded: "It was left in the hands of the bishop, he was the one who 'administered' more. He succeeded in getting what he had to, we do not know how much it was paid in *dollars*." By saying that compensation was paid in dollars, he implied that a very large sum was paid. Although he imagined that the church was able to make a good deal, he felt that relocation could not be resisted, not even by the church: "I gave importance to Yacyretá because I knew it would happen. There were many who did not want (to be relocated). But there was no (possible) resistance against force." A very active *puntero de barrio*—a grass-root political organizer—said that at first he would not believe that Yacyretá would become a reality, because of "the force the church has." As many others, he realized that it was a "serious issue" and that the dam would be built "when they knocked the chapel down." A resident of San Cayetano who belonged to the congregation of the "Apostolate of the Prayer of the Sacred Heart of Jesus," one among the five in the quarter, remembered the church as an institution in permanent growth. He said that it created the situation of "understanding each other more, of uniting, working, and living more . . . then, Yacyretá came, it destroyed it, and everybody dispersed." Immediately after remembering this, he complained: "They did not communicate this plan to the people. That is part of the pride and arrogance of Yacyretá. The church belongs to everybody."

I asked Doña Felisa from El Chaquito whether they had done anything when they knew they would demolish the church, and she answered:

Who would say anything, if it is not us who rule . . . the bishop, yes. . . . They promised
they would make one in the Barrio Yacyretá. But the church was done with the sweat
of all the workers, all the neighbors. We could not do anything because they had to take
it out, it bothered. What can you do, even if people protest, they will not be able to do
anything. [asked about how long it took to take everything from the church] I do not
know when the deadline was, but in the end, they did not take everything . . . maybe it
had not really bothered them yet. The only thing is that it was going to be left alone.
Everybody went, everybody was crying. There was no party, nobody wanted to know
anything more about it. We only had a farewell mass.

Nearly everybody commented how miserable they felt when the church was
destroyed, and many said they resented this loss more than that of their own home.
Many parishoners recalled that, when the day was due, they all cried in despair and
that some of the workmen hired to demolish the chapel did not have the courage to
do so. Rubén thinks that after the big flood had "disintegrated"[1] the people and had
convinced them to go, "they" gave the *coup de grace* by knocking down the church.
"They needed the Pope's permission, I don't know, from Italy, to demolish the
church. You cannot simply demolish it." He then repeated that everything "rotted"
when they destroyed the building. When asked who was responsible, he replied:
"Well, Yacyretá. I believe they were the ones who had built another one. Because
there was no other company. Yacyretá *ordena* everything (meaning both it arranges
and orders). It was then that they disintegrated everything." Rubén continued,
detailing the great power the Church enjoyed: neither the bishop nor the radical
representatives could do much against it; it controlled everything, even the
neighborhood commission; it had the *manija*—the handle, a slang expression
meaning great power.

The accounts were eloquent enough: In the eyes of the people forced to relocate,
Yacyretá proved to have greater powers than even the Pope. If such a grandiose
religious authority was unable to prevent the EBY from demolishing the chapel,
what was left to them? In acknowledging the EBY's superiority, people also
expected it would replace the church in many of its functions. Some of these roles
were indeed performed by the EBY's staff. In the long run, these same actions
reinforced the representation of Yacyretá as a church-like institution. Such proved
to be the case with the programs initiated by the social workers to provide people
with documentation, including proof of marriage and birth registration. Likewise,
the EBY attempted to set moral standards by establishing the criteria of promiscuity
and by planning to "educate" the affected populations. Education was understood
in various senses, which are covered by different social policies to be discussed
later. What needs to be stressed here is that through its actions Yacyretá came to
occupy a position previously reserved to the Church. This entailed particular
privileges and obligations.

YACYRETA KILLS

But Yacyretá had not only shown that it could impose its will on the Church. In the view of lowland dwellers, it manifested its supremacy through other means. It demonstrated, for example, that it could play a role in such mysterious matters as life and death. While interviewing a woman who was one of the first to be resettled, her husband insisted that she tell that her grandmother died of sorrow. In 1982, when it was necessary to clear an area for the bridge works, they told her grandmother she should leave. They offered her either compensation or transitory relocation until the new houses were finished. Her grandmother asked for the money because at that time the majority felt it was quite unlikely the houses would ever be built. So, she had to move away from her daughter and son and their children who lived next door but were not yet affected. They explained to me that she could not bear this separation from her relatives and the familiar surroundings and felt so unhappy that she died.

The belief that Yacyretá brought much sorrow was shared by most of the residents in the affected areas, but only those already relocated seemed to associate it with death. Ramona, a nurse who is now living in the new house compound, thought of Yacyretá as a more devastating force than the floods. She remarked that nobody died with the floods, but that "a lot of neighbors started to die with this thing of Yacyretá." She remembered they had lost Don Rodríguez, just a little time after they left. He died of a heart attack. She mentioned to me that there had been other cases. She, herself, was said to have been sick of melancholy for a whole week after resettlement and that whenever she remembers it:

It feels as if it [the sorrow] wants to come back again, but we must accept and adapt to this, because things cannot always be the same way . . . we all missed the neighborhood a lot. . . . Here, came Mrs. Madrid, shortly after she arrived, she died. I was so sorry, she was my seamstress, such a nice woman. All my neighbors were so helpful, so good. We miss so much. Because over there, we felt at ease. We had the river banks, we would go nearby on a picnic. . . . But now, I can say I adapted to this and I am happy. All I said is the truth of events. We all had gone there, and I had bad luck, because the father of my children passed away and I had to do everything by myself.

Not only the population, but also some of the EBY's social workers related the deaths to relocation. One of them mentioned the case of an old man who came to the Yacyreta's headquarters in Posadas to sign all the agreements the day before moving. The next day, when the EBY sent a van with a driver and a social worker to his house to help him move, his relatives reported that he had suddenly died during the night. She told me she had immediately reported this to the EBY's anthropologist.

Among experts on social-impact assessment, it is universally agreed that population displacement is a disruptive and harmful process which can lead to death. Indeed, many pointed to a close association between compulsory relocation and mortality and morbidity rate increases.[2] Although taking account of the fact that there are more casualties among the old, nobody comments on how the displaced populations interpret the deaths. The belief that connects death with relocation has an effect in that it characterizes Yacyretá as an extremely potent entity and thus enforces the already dominant feeling of helplessness. For the experts, this "mortality effect" is one among the many unintended consequences of projects; for the relocated, it serves as another sign of the might of Yacyretá.

YACYRETA DISPOSES OF THE COMMUNITY'S SOCIAL RELATIONS AND FORCES OF PRODUCTION, AND DOES AS IT WISHES

In previous chapters, I showed how navigation and its riverine economy had been on the decline for decades until it was totally replaced by truck transportation with the opening of the highways. By the 1970s, the majority of the river-related industries, workshops, and other economic activities had either disappeared or were in evident decay. The few that remained were no longer hiring as many men as they had before. However, very few of the lowland residents said they had lost their jobs before Yacyretá's presence in the area. The majority of the interviewed repeated that the EBY brought major changes to the neighborhood by making the Heller factory, the meat-packing plant, and many saw mills go out of business. According to them, before Yacyretá, there was full employment, and many workers lived in the immediate surroundings. After the announcement of the project, there were neither jobs nor people left. According to one informant, "Now, there is nothing left in the neighborhood; you cannot even buy firewood. Before, people would feel all right here, there was plenty of work."

In reality, most of these sources of labor were dependent on factors the residents could neither recognize nor acknowledge. As mentioned before, the regional economy associated with the river had been deteriorating for decades. In addition, the disastrous economic policies of the national government seriously affected local production. Because the exchange rates were so favorable for imports, it was cheaper to buy wood from the United Sates and from Chile than to cut it locally. Therefore, by the time Argentina and Paraguay decided to construct the dam, economic opportunities in the relocation areas were already very scarce. Some of the factories had not acknowledged their situation, either. On the contrary, they were eager to demonstrate that their businesses were prosperous, in order to put them in a position to demand large amounts of money in compensation for the loss of investments. I heard rumors both from Posadeños in general and also from Yacyretá and province officials that compensation negotiations involving some of these industries were shot through with corruption.

Besides being accused of having done away with the sources for salaried work, the EBY was also blamed for the shutdown of most of the groceries. Some, undoubtedly, had to leave the area when their sector was displaced by preparatory works related to the construction of the bridge. Some in this group opted for compensation payments; others moved to the new Yacyretá neighborhood to reopen their stores. Still, the great majority went out of business either because of the acute economic crisis of the 1980s, because they had lost most of their installations and merchandise with the floods of 1983, or both. In 1982, when we were doing a study on means of subsistence at the request of EBY to the National University of Misiones, many of the grocers informed us they had to stop giving credit to their customers because of inflation and the alarming rate of unemployment. Even at that point, it was becoming very hard to maintain the traditional socio-economic arrangements with their accompanying reciprocal obligations. In time, neighbors also changed their buying patterns and shifted to one of the downtown supermarkets that offered discount prices and the possibility of buying on credit.

With regards to grass-roots organizations, such as the neighborhood commissions, neighbors felt that either EBY rendered them useless or that it contributed to their disintegration. In Bajada Vieja, one of my assistants asked whether they had a neighborhood commission and if they had made claims to EBY through it. Doña Juana seemed surprised at the question: "No, the commission cannot be used to deal with Yacyretá, it is not for that. It has another purpose." In this neighborhood, the commission had been organized by the well-to-do living on the paved and nonfloodable parts of the area. It also had the support of the Fatima church on Bajada Vieja Street. Obviously, the interests of the social sectors differed; while those in the lowlands were concerned with getting drinking water and an easy access to their homes, the ones above were interested in maintaining the charm of the historic street and making it into a tourist attraction. The commission organized activities to "help the poor" but did not represent them in their claims.

The situation in the other areas was somewhat different because the neighborhood commissions represent a more homogenous population and members had shared interests. In the late 1970s and early 1980s, most of them ceased to operate, not because of Yacyretá's intentions, but because their activities were banned by the military authorities of the country. Some of the commissions reorganized when the political circumstances changed in 1983 and reopened claims to the provincial authorities and to EBY. The relocated inhabitants did not reject their mediation but seemed to be very skeptical about their possible achievements. In general, they thought these grass-roots organizations were not well equipped to confront a situation like relocation, partly because they tended to get involved in political factional disputes.

Briefly put, most of the neighbors believed that EBY could destroy the basic socio-economic arrangements of the communities. Conversely, they also thought it had the power of creating them. Indeed, during the first years of the project, EBY's social workers promoted technical training courses and promised job opportunities in the dam project and in the complementary works. Many neighbors took the courses with the hope of finding a job and felt disappointed and angry at Yacyretá when their expectations were not met: "They are liars. They had promised us jobs, and we did not get any." Course enrollment could also serve other purposes. More than one of the social workers mentioned to me they were not sure whether people registered for the courses because they were truly interested or because they wanted to please them.

Neighbors thought Yacyretá acted as it wished, without taking into account local needs. To many, the decision to move some people first was just a caprice of EBY. They saw no reasons for the early displacements, basically because they found it hard to determine the rationale involved in such an irregular pattern of relocation policies. They could not understand the mechanisms by which only a few households in a block would receive first priority. Most of the residents were convinced that EBY chose the order of resettlement in accordance to its wishes, favoring those who were well-disposed to the relocation agency. Hence, they regarded relocation as a reward for good behavior. Conversely, they believed that the agency punished troublemakers by postponing their departure from the neighborhood and, also, by making them live under deplorable conditions. Yacyretá neither plotted the best strategy to take advantage of its victims nor did it deliberately require proof of loyalty or take revenge on those who oppose it. Nevertheless, some strategies developed by some members of EBY's staff contributed to this representation of the binational entity. For example, I observed that all the residents from a sector but one were called for a negotiation meeting in which problems with the deeds were to be discussed. The man who was supposedly excluded was an active member of the neighborhood commission. Through comments from neighbors and from some of EBY's employees, through analyzing newspaper articles, and by looking at the dates of relocation, I also verified that in at least one case an active member of a neighborhood commission was neutralized with the offer of a new house sooner than the due date. This, of course, would not be admitted officially as an institutional policy. Furthermore, some say that it was impossible to decide such matters from Posadas because decisions on relocation were made in Buenos Aires and there was no way these could be influenced. Knowledge about procedures is vague. When asked about who had the final word on relevant issues, the social workers told me they were not quite sure, that it could be either the surveyors or the lawyers.

YACYRETA: A STATE WITHIN A STATE

Many informants reported to be just "waiting" until Yacyretá came to do what it had already promised. A lot of them understood there was no need to go to EBY or to any governmental office. Florencio told me: "Why should we, if it is they who are the interested party. When they need the place, I am sure they will come." Similarly, another person from El Chaquito, Braulio Domínguez, asserted: "They will take us from here because they wish to, but this is ours." These statements illustrate a generalized attitude towards Yacyretá which was related to the way EBY was understood.

Doña Marta who is already living in the newly constructed neighborhood, recalled that people did not react in any particular manner when told about the project. Rather, she said most of them were "passive." She added that there was nothing they could do because it was a "thing of the state." And right after that, she commented that they had the "illusion" that they could either get compensation money or a new house and that given the economic conditions, there was no other way they could ever attain ownership of a brick house. In her view, there was no reaction and people accepted everything quietly because they felt they could get something they desired: new homes.

So far, I have shown how Yacyretá was generally identified with the state. The affected population reasoned that EBY, being the state, could dispose of the land at its will and that they could not oppose it. Therefore, they "waited" and were "passive." However, the belief that the state was entitled to do certain things, did not mean that people blindly followed its decisions. They tried to make the best of the situation within given limits. These limits were hard to overcome: "We are under the power of them," more than one person told me. A woman, who had already been relocated, commented that some people missed their previous houses and that they would like to have some improvements made in the new neighborhood, but that they were afraid of asking for them. She attributed this to the fact that with "Yacyretá there is no doctor, there is nobody who may interfere, neither politicians nor anyone else. They are really apart."

Insofar as the relocatees became more acquainted with EBY and maintained more frequent contacts with it—as is the case of those already living in the new housing project— the feeling that they were confronting a very powerful "other" increased. Hopelessness was even greater in the case of those who either had to pay for the house or were uncertain about their legal situation. Ramona, who had a house in the Yacyretá quarter, said that in her sector there was no neighborhood commission and that in a way there was no need for one because:

Ramona: Yacyretá is the one who decides.

Carmen: How does it decide?

Ramona: They come and say: "That thing will be made here and *chau* (bye-bye)." And they decide because, if they say "I want you to take away that bench, it can't be there," we then have to put it away.

Carmen: Yes? Why?

Ramona: Because they have the power, they decide until we finish paying for everything, they are deciding.

This same woman added that there was an office and that "they are there to control what happens with the works." She said that the engineers and licenciadas walked around so as to see " what was done, what they liked, what they did not like."

There was no opposition because the project was indeed shown as something that the state had decided on regardless of what the residents wanted. Analysts have observed that in cases of compulsory relocation caused by hydroelectric projects, people sense that resistance is useless because they are situated in an unfavorable position vis-à-vis the government. They are often poorly organized and do not have the right networks. Most dam projects are presented as faits accomplis and are legitimized with a national ideology which it is difficult to oppose without being considered an enemy of the Motherland.[3]

The affected population of Yacyretá knew and employed the legitimating rhetoric but established a distinction when it came to identify the beneficiaries. They did say that the project was good because it promoted the nation's welfare, brought progress, and would bring many tourists from remote places of the world. Some said that maybe their sons would enjoy the benefits. Most, however, stressed that in their own case, it only brought sorrow and hardship. This was mainly felt by those experiencing the effects of the bridge and water plant construction. Most of the relocatees agreed that they were sacrificing for the benefit of all. They judged that the state was entitled to make such demands on its subjects. In return for their submission, the relocatees expected specific services and benefits. They assumed, for example, that Yacyretá was obliged to solve any problem they encountered, be it legal, financial, or medical. For them, the EBY was a paternalistic authoritarian welfare state, a demanding father who rewarded the obedient children and punished those who defied his authority.

In the previous sections, I have demonstrated how the affected population interpreted Yacyretá within the existing framework of reference and associateed it with familiar concepts. However, Yacyretá was never represented as an exact copy of that which they already knew: It was always seen as if it were charged with a greater potency. Thus, as discussed in a previous section, it was not, for example, "a regular flood" but a "phenomenon, an exceptional flood." This same notion is present when they thought of it as the state. It was the state, but a greater one. As informants said, it was "apart"; the local government had no authority over it. Domingo, from the neighborhood commission of El Chaquito, complained that from the very beginning the province had failed in the defense of its territory's interests. According to him, one of the problems was that the former radical government had not given enough jurisdictional power to the provincial commission for Yacyretá (COPROYA), the provincial agency created to deal with dam related problems. "They did not even have their own seal," he said. He then commented that the new Peronist government was trying to revitalize the COPROYA so as to respond to the Chaquito commission's claims. He added that they could do very little despite their efforts because they had found that "Yacyretá is a state within a state." By the middle of the eighteenth century, the enemies of Jesuits were accusing them of the same thing: of separatism and of "building an empire within an empire."[4] At a press conference, the executive director of COPROYA employed exactly the same expression as Domingo to criticize the power of Yacyretá. This coincidence in meanings and use of speech genres is not surprising; it reveals strategic alliances against the relocation agency.

Once national authorities decided to construct the dam, the inhabitants of the northeastern region explained their situation with regards to the project in terms of their historically subordinate position vis-a-vis the national state. Relocation problems were thus understood as a failure of the local authorities to confront the central government.

Luis María Casagrande, the UCR vice-governor of Misiones until 1987 and former head of COPROYA, compared the EBY to a caste and said that, as such, it was untouchable. He partly traced the independent stance of its technicians and engineers to the fact that the dam project started during the military government. He also compared the functioning of the Binational Entity to that of the army barracks. He felt that at the beginning Yacyretá maintained a cold attitude and that through the years they were able to improve the relations, but never enough.

In 1982, a former Peronist governor, Juan Manuel Oviedo, declared to the press that one of the problems with the provincial government was its lack of interest and subordination to the central power and to the commands of the EBY's Buenos Aires headquarters (*El Territorio*, November 14, 1982). He accused the Buenos Aires decision-makers of being insensitive to the problems of the relocatees. During the military government, criticisms of the centralization of decisions in Buenos Aires were more acute. After elections in 1983, the Peronists advanced claims for greater independence from the capital. In 1986, Oviedo, by then representative to the National House of Congress, submitted a project in which he proposed moving EBY headquarters to Posadas. He argued that those who make the decisions affecting numerous low-income families from the province "had never put their shoes into the red mud."[5] This project outraged the Correntinos who accused the Misioneros of trying to gain too much advantage from something that was being built in their province. They complained that the Misiones press never mentioned that the engineering works were being done in Ituzaingó and that they only said the dam was located "90 km downstream of Posadas." Conversely, the Misioneros accused the Correntinos of being in collusion with the central power. Thus, in discussing matters related to Yacyretá, historical disputes were re-enacted: The Correntinos told the Misioneros that if it were not for their generosity, Posadas would still be a town of Corrientes; the Misioneros replied that they would have never had so many problems with land property had it not been for the greed of their neighbors.

The same system of norms regulating the behavior with the neighbors guided the relationship which the affected population established with Yacyretá as state. It was summarized in the local concept of *molestar*—"to bother." The word connotes a reciprocal behavior involving mutual obligations. It implies making demands of others and through doing so establishing a particular bond through which these others are entitled to make claims in the future.

THE PEOPLE: YACYRETA'S "BENEFICIARIES"

"Uprooted," "dammed," "compulsory" are some of the many words specialists in dam projects use to refer to the population to be resettled. Most of the terms employed connote suffering and impositions from above. The Yacyretá project is an exception to this: None of the most widely known words could be used for many years. Since the times of the military dictatorship, *beneficiario* had been the official name adopted to address the affected population. The choice of a name illustrates a common practice during the years of El Proceso. Authorities did not tolerate the association of any negative effect with government policies. Compulsory relocation could not be acknowledged: An anthropologist at EBY received a penalty for employing such words. There was another word that had to be omitted: *afectado* ("affected"). In Spanish, the verb may mean either to assign or to damage. It is this second sense that they wanted to avoid. One was not allowed to admit that the project could cause any harm. There was a reality created through words, orderly and harmonious, and there was a suppressed, unmentionable one. Through the prohibition of naming dam-generated social damages, power holders negated them.

Although there was a deliberate attempt to create a new individual by renaming it, authorities did not totally succeed. Not a single man or woman we interviewed took this identity of beneficiary as their own. Instead, they called themselves "families with a folder with a right to relocation," "family heads with a folder," or simply "neighbors to be resettled" and on some occasions "compulsorily relocated."[6]

Yacyretá's staff did not include the term "beneficiary" in their everyday speech. They only employed it in written reports or in very formal contexts of communication, such as press conferences, encounters with government officials, and public lectures on relocation. When asked about what terms they used to refer to the relocated population, they would mention the official one, but not a single taped interview shows a staff member employing the term "beneficiary." Two technicians in the social sciences questioned the use of this word because they could not see benefit to the population: "You end up complicating their lives," one said.

Most of the staff members favored a more ambiguous, neutral, and generic term: They generally spoke of *la gente*—"the people." While the use of *la gente* does not imply a value judgement, the expression *esta gente*—"these people"—was imbued with a very derogatory connotation. This latter biased meaning went hand in hand with pejorative judgments, such as "they prefer to live in *ranchos*," "they are very ignorant people," "they are *orillera* ("marginal")[7] people." A Buenos Aires-born lawyer insisted that *esta gente* was very different: "A man, for example, has two houses, each with a woman, and gets the two together on weekends." Then, he added that the problem was that "there are two different cultural levels," exactly the same remark a surveyor made to me. The lawyer thought that even the highest level was rather ignorant (referring to the local upper class). After I allowed myself to be drawn into complicity by behaving as if I belonged to his same *Porteña* social class, he confided that the Misionera lower class was terribly ignorant. "Maybe it is related to the Guaraní influence, maybe it is because they are so much Paraguayans, they do not know the laws of the country." He went on to say that Posadas and the province was an island. He insisted on the differences with the civilized center. There were some details that he seemed to like, though:

They are very respectful, very submissive. Only those who have money complain. But they are so patient. They are used to the paternalism of the state. Most of them trust us a lot. They expect us to solve all their problems. They are not conscious they do have a right. They thank you. They have another way of thanking.

Another lawyer also asserted that "these persons" ignored the most elemental things of life and of culture in general. Both legal experts perceived the population to be relocated as a separate society, not integrated into the national juridical system. They were not alone in this image of the Posadas urban poor. A social worker told me that there was a very special form of social life and that violence was quite common in these areas. "People do not have a form of life committed to the same society."

Some lawyers, surveyors, and social workers reflected that it would probably have been better if EBY had moved the affected population to other huts, because that was "their way of life, their culture." One thought: "Maybe it would be better if we built houses similar to their huts; not with regards to the quality of the materials, but in ambience." The head of COPROYA shared this belief and had a very particular position in this respect. He said that the EBY had broken its word by building "these luxurious houses that have nothing to do with these people's culture." He complained that the Relocation Agency had promised to replace the former dwellings with the same—house by house—and that now people are expected to pay installments for houses that do not correspond to their ways of life. Very often, an essentialist perspective of people's culture and tradition was employed by right-wing conservatives interested in maintaining the inequalities of the dominant social order.

Depictions of the population are based on a combination of the staff's biases and of "objective," scientifically grounded data such as the statistics on income, illiteracy, labor, and other information obtained by the census of 1979. Quantitative anlysis of the population contributed to its objectification. People become things to be counted, registered, scrutinized, and technically manipulated. Instead of being addressed with their family names, men and women to be resettled were treated as units of registration, household heads, and members of domestic units.

Biases might vary slightly according to the social origins of the staff's members. Among the professionals of *porteño* (from Buenos Aires) origin, it was common to see the whole of the regional culture as different, inferior, and not entirely Argentine, as the remarks of one of the lawyers illustrate. Local specialists in the social sciences claimed to be better equipped to understand the people to be relocated, but most of their representations of the poor were as biased as those of the outsiders. Obviously, Misiones-born staff members did not attribute the nondesirable behavior of the population of the lowland areas to an inferior regional culture. Rather, they saw this behavior as an expression of a different class—a migrant peasantry or an urban subproletariat or as due to the presence of Paraguayan elements within the communities— or both of them combined. Both locals and outsiders emphasized ignorance, foreignness, and irrational or wild behavior when describing inhabitants of the areas to be flooded. These were exactly the same attributes which local elites and foreign visitors assigned to the population's ancestors.

EBY's social programs, although said to be rationally and scientifically designed, relied heavily on a priori value judgments of the situation. Social workers developed programs of "social accompaniment," which they defined as actions of "social education."[8] More often than not, social workers inquired very little into people's expectations, and what they called "felt needs" were frequently what they pressuposed should be the group desires.[9]

On rare occasions, social workers encouraged a more active involvement in the identification of problems and needs. When they did, very few were aware of the role they played in the recognition of certain issues as problematic. Indeed, the influence of social technicians can be clearly discerned in the way some of the residents of the neighborhoods to be relocated thought of themselves. Because social workers were the ones involved in the most frequent communicative exchanges, their influence was greater in the process of formation of social identities. However, they were not the sole agents contributing to this; they were simply reinforcing widespread images of the poor already held and expressed by dominant groups. I found many examples of how the relocated population's understanding of the situation was influenced from above. More than one of my informants insisted on the need for being taught how to use the new houses; others believed that some of their neighbors "were so ignorant that they did not know how to get organized and that they needed somebody to tell them what to do." The gradual impoverishment and devaluation of self-identities had overarching implications for the relocation process. It allowed EBY's social workers and other staff members to take on the roles of teachers and guides without encountering resistance.

The affected population did not instantaneously accept the position of "students." There were certain requirements which had to be previously fulfilled. First, as analysts of power relations had long been noting, the EBY had to demolish its adversary—the communities and people it deals with. As Machiavelli wrote: "When those States, that are conquered as it is said, have been accustomed to live under their own Laws, and in liberty, there are three wayes for a man to hold them. The first is to demolish all their strong places" (1953[1532]:18). Similarly, von Clausewitz, the theorist of war, spoke of the "destruction of the enemy or rather, his fighting powers." When saying so, he did not confine this idea to the use of physical violence alone, but pointed to the importance of moral destruction, as well (1968:37). Thus, the people to be relocated became gradually weakened when they started to realize they could no longer use their traditional means of coping with everyday reality. Second, only after devaluation of the own—popular—culture and recognition of the superiority of that of the Other, could the population be allowed to be "gardened, cultivated" (Bauman 1987).

Subordination to the management of their lives was also facilitated by the simultaneous authoritarian policies of a repressive national state which suppressed everything considered a popular expression. Through some exemplary actions in the neighborhoods, authorities could convey the idea that it was useless to take actions against the established order under the threat of being totally destroyed. Military authorities negated the possibilities of politically active subjects by prohibiting every collective action and by physically exterminating some of the citizenry. In comparison to other sectors of the national society, repressive practices were only slightly felt in the Posadas lowland quarters. There were, however, a few grassroots leaders who disappeared or were imprisoned. Explicit references to the *milicos* and to the repression were very scarce during our field interviews. A militant Peronista from El Chaquito once told me his own case, which showed that the actions of the armed forces were felt and had an effect at least among those more politically active. Casimiro recalled that a few years after the military coup a group of armed militiamen came to his house and ordered him to give them his identity document. After he had done so, they told him to repeat his name and while he was obeying to this command, they tore his document into pieces and said: "Who had you said you were? Well, now you are nobody." Such an action had many implications: It meant the likelihood of the physical disappearance of the grass-roots leader in the near future, for anybody who was stopped in the street and caught without a document immediately became a suspect and could be either arrested or killed. With this action they threatened him and his followers with death and voided their rights to be citizens and persons.

During the years of El Proceso, EBY had its own secret security services operating in the areas to be relocated. They controlled the movements of the residents and did not allow outsiders to approach the population without special permission. Thus, the national state and EBY often coincided in the control of the population, in the negation of individual identities, and in the view of community behavior as pathological. As already seen, in the eyes of most of the people to be relocated, EBY and the state were one and the same thing; without doubt, their disciplinary practices were at the origins of the passivity of the population. But a passive behavior does not imply an absence of conflict. There was no active response because the prohibition to organize meetings and the negation of social identity inhibited the generation of a common project with which to fight against the established order.

With the Yacyretá project, identities were greatly affected but not irreversibly damaged. Names, houses, subsistence resources, and forms of social organization became only temporarily suspended. While this discontinuity persisted, people's need of supervision increased. Such was the case of those who already moved to the new houses. Insofar as the majority of them had not yet obtained the deeds of their new residences, Yacyretá continued to be the legal proprietor of all houses. As long as this situation remained unchanged, the subordinate and dependent role of the population would endure.

Yacyretá's practices continued to reinforce the powerlessness of the subject population while it maintained the control of decisive resources. Throughout the years, the EBY reserved for itself the control of strategic resources. The most powerful among those was probably the ability to dispose of people's identities. This is an aspect many analysts of power relations have emphasized: the role played in the struggle for the formation of subjects. Althusser (1971) was the first to propose this with regards to the mechanics of interpellation, through which ideology is said to constitute individuals as subjects (see also, Laclau 1979, de Ipola 1983, Larrain 1983, Smith 1988, Therborn 1980). The EBY became a mediator or grantor of the following:

1. The condition of "relocation beneficiary."
2. The Argentine residence or nationality to the foreign-born residents of the neighborhoods, mainly Paraguayans.
3. The Argentine endorsement of identity through the issuing of personal identity documents.
4. The acqusition of "morally accepted" standards through the legal registration of marital unions.

5. Access to the standardized official culture and language through literacy programs and special labor training.
6. Acquisition of the status of owner.

Besides these institutionalized practices, the EBY's staff members performed other actions that affected the identities of the relocated population. They took away from the population the right to control certain spaces, even those as private as the household domain. The private realm of the house was indeed greatly affected: from the prohibition of the free use of the building itself—including repairs, sale, or moving of the structure—to the establishment of its exchange value. The reproduction of the household was also hindered insofar as Yacyretá would only recognize those registered in the 1979 census. More than fifteen years have passed since then, and the children of yesterday have become adults who have taken mates; many of these couples have children already. Yacyretá calls them *hogares derivados*. For a long time, the name was the only thing they had because Yacyretá refused to recognize them as beneficiaries. Because of local pressures, Yacyretá was compelled to acknowledge these cases and is proposing new solutions.

So far, I have discussed how Yacyretá and the population to be relocated became positioned through their interaction. Asymmetry of the positions in the dialogical set formed by Yacyretá and the people should by now be apparent. Yacyretá was depicted as a provider of goods and as a controller of selves; as an omnipotent entity, capable of disposing of life and of imposing its will even on somebody as grandiose as the Pope. The people, the other component, were seen as ignorant, amoral, abnormal, close-to-nature beings, objects that needed to be regulated and tamed. The extreme asymmetry of the relationship greatly inhibited communication. As objects and as part of nature, the residents of the lowland areas of Posadas were left voiceless.

The positions I have already discussed were not solely determined by Yacyretá (taken as a unit) or by the population. There were other actors who took part, either transitorily or permanently, in the communicative practices of the relocation process and who influenced the acquisition of particular identities. Among them, the various staff members of Yacyretá played the most important roles.

NOTES

1. Rubén employed the verb *to disintegrate* to convey the meaning "to disperse and to separate." This was pointed by most of the informants; they felt that with the floods they were separated from their old neighbors and that their union disappeared.

2. Theoretically this correlation is pointed out in Scudder's multidimentional stress model. There is wide empirical evidence on the increase of the death rate particularly among old people. See, for example, Fahim (1981), Colson (1971), and Cernea (1989).

3. With regards to the presentation of dam projects as *fait accompli*, see, for example: Lawson (1982), and Goldsmith and Hildyard (1984). To see how these projects are promoted as the road to the country's development and well-being see, for example, Fahim (1983), Colson (1971), Chambers (1970), Da Rosa (1983), and Barabás and Bartolomé (1984).

4. Interestingly enough , the governor and some representatives of Misiones have recently used (1988–1989) this same rhetorical device, "the state within the state," to oppose to the

Provincial Law of Indian Rights passed by the former Radical party on the grounds that claims to legally consider the Mbyá Indians as a "people" are unconstitutional because they jeopardize national unity.

5. Misiones is known as the province of the red soil. In Argentina, the expression to put one's shoes in the mud, refers to be in contact with the common people through visiting the places where they live. The mud symbolizes the earthen and floodable roads associated with the dwellings of the poor. The expression alludes to public figures who reject technocratic knowledge and judge the problems through sensing them.

6. This is how neighbors from El Chaquito identified themselves in a letter to Governor Julio César Humada (October 6, 1989) and in various letters to politicians and to the press.

7. People from the outlying districts of a city— from the poorest quarters. It is a synonym of *arrabalero*, also a very pejorative word. Both terms are generally used in tango music and make reference to people who are outlaws and live on the margins of society.

8. To see how social workers at the EBY understood their role, read Schamber (1984). This work includes a discussion of the suggested programs of social action.

9. Nancy Fraser (1988) has shown how needs talk has been institutionalized as a major vocabulary of political discourse. She suggests that the interpretation of needs must be problematized. She contends that discourse on needs is not univocal and that there are various interpretations of them.

CHAPTER 7

Knowledge and Power Struggles in the Relocation Agency

In Chapter Six, I showed how, in their interaction with Yacyretá's professionals and technicians, the neighbors of Posadas positioned both the staff and the development agency. I also showed how development experts variously constructed the people to be relocated. In this chapter, I will consider how Yacyretá's experts became positioned through their daily encounters with other staff members. The positioning within the relocation agency was and still is greatly influenced by those other positions already occupied in the larger society. The relocation agency constituted an arena where previous identities were asserted, although simultaneously contested.

The Entidad Binacional Yacyretá (EBY) was not an homogeneous organization in which members shared the same goals regarding relocation. Differences among members stemmed from their professional and/or technical training, their class ascription, and their previous experience or lack of experience in the region where the hydroelectric dam was under construction. In the following pages, I will describe struggles among staff members and I will analyze how internal conflicts affected communication in the project.

CONTESTING NATIONAL AND REGIONAL IDENTITIES

Not surprisingly, existing conflicts in Misiones society at large—such as those between the locals and outsiders—also existed within EBY. Penchants for such conflicts were part of the baggage people brought with them when they joined the agency. While some professionals were recruited locally, others came from the national center—Buenos Aires—or from other large cities viewed by locals as being nearly as powerful as the capital. As a rule, the professions represented in the group of the *parachutists* were simultaneously the most socially prestigious, traditional, and well established. Law and engineering were two such professions. In the beginning of the project, the status of these specialists at EBY was also economically advantageous, an issue that was the cause of bitter resentment among local employees. For years, the outsiders had been receiving a larger income, which covered moving expenses and rent in Posadas, as well as other fringe benefits. All of this was extended in compensation for what EBY called *uprooting*.[1]

In contrast, most of the specialists working in the PRAS, the Program of Relocation and Social Action, were recruited in Posadas. This was so because the World Bank made the granting of loans conditional upon the implementation of a social program which should include the hiring of social scientists locally. This bank favored those already working in the capital of Misiones because they met the institution's qualifications (proper technical knowledge and working experience in the region). The National University of Misiones and the Department of Planning, at that time a very technocratic and influential governmental office, were also very active in negotiating the participation of local experts.

The PRAS, however, generally identified by other staff members with the vague term of the *social*, was not fully *Misionero*. The social workers generally claimed Misionero identity and argued that only those who were born in the province were capable of understanding "their people." One of them, the supervisor García once told me that, when the PRAS was being formed, he insisted that it should hire local professionals and technicians. A conflicting position was advocated by one of the anthropologists who favored the contracting of personnel with the best qualifications, no matter where they came from. Most of the social workers were born and graduated in the province. The sociologists and the anthropologists were in a more ambiguous situation because nobody recognized them as truly locals, although most of them taught at the National University and had been living in Posadas for years. They lacked the credentials to be Misioneros: They were not sons or daughters of the "land of the red soil" and did not hold degrees granted by a local institution. The anthropologist Guillermo Olivera was an exception to this. He was born in Misiones and was related to many well-known local families. However, even he was not seen as a true Misionero because he had been away from the province for too long. He had left the region as a child, attended school in Buenos Aires, and obtained a doctoral degree abroad.

In the Yacyretá Relocation Agency, distinctions made among staff members in terms of the opposition of the region to the national state generally overlapped with class differences. In fact, many of the lawyers did not see any great difference among members of the various local social classes. They looked upon all Misioneros, and consequently upon all members of EBY's social sector, with the same disdain and condescension. After all, only among people working in that sector could one encounter the anomaly of an employee with the double identity of relocation beneficiary and staff member.

This was indeed the case with a social worker who was born and lived in El Chaquito all her life. Her double ascription made her one of the more controversial figures of the project in the eyes of many former neighbors. One of them once told me while criticizing her: "A monkey dressed in silk is still a monkey."[2] Amazingly, to be able to put her down, he had to employ a rhetorical device used by dominant sectors to refer derogatorily to those trying to climb the ladder.

This social worker's position at EBY had always been a difficult one. Her professional peers felt that EBY's authorities impaired the settlement of her relocation rights. People at EBY explained to me that, to avoid suspicions of favoritism, they thought it better not to give her compensation money until all her neighbors were relocated. According to her fellow workers, this decision had the opposite effect. Neighbors would tell her: "How do you expect us to believe you, if you, who work for them, were unable to get compensation or preferential treatment with relocation." Former neighbors would try to take advantage of their acquaintance with her and would become harsh with her when they realized they would not be favored. She was one of the few of the EBY's staff they could identify by name and also one of the persons receiving the worst criticisms.

I found that this was not the only case of the population making the worst complaints against the professionals they could more clearly identify and with whom they maintained more regular contacts. The most notorious is the case of "El Gringo" García, supervisor of the social workers, after whom a transitory relocation area was named. He recalled how the honor was bestowed:

We had to establish a transitory settlement. We could not call it Heller, after the original owners because they had closed the factory and had collected the compensation payment. So I said: "Call it García." You see, at that time I was sort of a personality. I was seen as the conductor of everything. But this did not last. To the Radicals and to some Peronists, as well, I was an irritant, because I did not want them to be demagogues. . . . First, we decided to call it Sergeant García because it matched with the military era. We made up this long story, that the Sergeant García was my grandfather. We had a lot of fun. There were some people that accused me of having my own neighborhood.

His visibility in the neighborhood (to which he admitted by saying that for some time he was a personality) contradicted what he also claimed to be the ideal role of a supervisor. He maintained that a supervisor in social work should basically stay in his consulting room, know all the field cases, give advice to the colleagues under his guidance, and pass unnoticed among the client population. In fact, he was one of the few staff members every neighbor remembered by name and was also one of the main targets of the population's suspicions and mistrust. This was particularly acute in the area in which he participated most actively, namely, the García transitory settlement. There, most of the residents call him liar; some even believed that he was a thief. He was the object of much local gossip in the relocation areas, in EBY, and in Posadas in general. He was not alone in this— anthropologists also became the targets of many rumors.

There was a symmetry in the way the relocated population and EBY's staff portrayed each other. Each group reciprocally depicted the other as liars. Mutual distrust increased with uncertainty about the completion of the project. The relocated population said the staff members were liars because "they promised us things and then they changed their minds." The major complaints were with regard to changes in the due date for relocation and with the monthly installments on the houses, which, at the beginning, the population thought they would be getting for free. Conversely, at EBY, the anthropologists and lawyers admitted that the population might lie in matters such as their household data or in stating what others supposedly promised to them with the purpose of getting a bigger home or getting relocation in motion faster.

That the population might be involved in cheating and lying was not easily acknowledged by EBY's social workers, for open recognition might hinder their own professional positioning. Such an admission would imply that their expertise was ill-fitted for predicting and preventing transgressions, and this would undoubtedly hamper their professional prestige. For example, when I asked the social workers whether they had found that the relocation beneficiaries might declare more family members or a different income to get a bigger house or lower payments, they assured me that this was very unlikely. However, during my field work I observed various cases where the household composition was different from what the householders had declared and from what was registered in the blue folder.

PLACING EXPERTS

Bureaucratic organizations always define the desired roles of their employees and place them within an institutionalized hierarchical structure. But here as elsewhere, formally assigned positions do not necessarily correspond to the actual power enjoyed by position holders—to their effective ability to mobilize resources or to "shape and modify desires and beliefs in a manner contrary to people's interests."[3] This was apparent with the Yacyretá Relocation Agency. In the early years, lawyers by-passed the head of EBY Posadas, Engineer Pérez, and communicated directly with the Buenos Aires headquarters. More recently, a female social worker controlled most of the decisions regarding social policies, even though her position in the organizational structure did not grant her such power. At EBY, actors used—and were conditioned—by a multiplicity of positioning devices at their disposal. These mechanisms either modified or reinforced the actors' previous identities and the formal status granted by EBY's authorities. The importance of each of these devices varied in accordance with changes occurring in the larger context in which the hydroelectric project was being built.

I will now analyze four of these positioning devices: knowledge, space and time, linguistic resources, and networks.

Knowledge Struggles

While the connections between knowledge and power have been widely addressed in a variety of contexts (Bourdieu 1982, 1984b, 1988; Foucault 1980), the multiple meanings of knowledge have not been sufficiently recognized. The lack of critical thinking regarding the various ways of understanding knowledge is very apparent in analyses of development practice. Most of the recent literature has made important contributions to debates regarding two kinds of knowledge: local knowledge and dominant and/or global knowledge (Kearney 1995, Apffel Marglin and Marglin 1990, Hobart 1993, Fardon 1995). In this chapter, however, I will consider two other different meanings of knowledge. First, I will analyze knowledge as general information. When working with this sense of knowledge, authors generally see it as unproblematic, as a neutral whole of data with a univocal meaning. It is assumed that "information" is transparent and the major problem relies in accessibility. When development specialists advocate communication in development projects, they are mostly concerned with guaranteeing that all relevant data is available to everyone. The challenge is to find new channels to deliver information, new forms of presenting it and expressing it, and new ways of having a more fluid dialogue between senders and receivers (Havelange 1991, Moemeka 1994, Melkote 1991). Only recently, a few development anthropologists have noted that the process of delivering and consuming information is far more complex (Hobart 1993, Long and Long 1992).

Second, I will look at knowledge as a specific ensemble of related notions developed in particular fields of inquiry—for example, the knowledge systems of lawyers, sociologists, anthropologists, surveyors, and social workers. This meaning of knowledge is related to Bourdieu's (1984b, 1993, 1995) notion of field, discussed in Chapter One, and to Messer-Davidow's (1993) "disciplinary knowledge," a historical specific phenomenon which develops in the course of struggles and which is generally concerned with the demarcation of intellectual boundaries (cf. also Foucault 1972, 1980). At the relocation agency, we can observe struggles among the various professional groups involving these two senses of knowledge—struggles to control strategic project information and struggles to assert the authority of particular knowledges.

Knowledge as Information. As far as the first kind of knowledge is concerned, staff members believed that the larger the amount of knowledge, the greater the control of the situation they would have. This belief became apparent to me when I interviewed various staff members. A common complaint among those in the PRAS was that they were being disinformed. On occasions, the social workers told me that even the people to be relocated knew more than they did. More than once, the "Entity" would instruct them to work with a particular sector without explaining the purposes involved. On their arrival at the affected neighborhoods, the household heads would insist that their move was imminent because the building contractor needed the area to be cleared for works related to the bridge or to the railway. At first, the social workers interpreted what the residents had reported as a product of their imagination and an expression of their willingness to leave. But a week later, EBY authorities officially informed PRAS members that they would have to tell the population about the displacement. The PRAS members concluded that a few of the beneficiaries got their "advanced" information through working for the contractors in charge of the construction of complementary works. News spread very rapidly in the local community; as soon as one neighbor heard anything, everyone else would immediately know about it. The social workers agreed that their ignorance of commonly known, relevant information made them lose credibility and affected their work.

Who was in control of the invaluable general information? Why and how was it disseminated or withheld in decision-making? Professionals answered these questions in only the vaguest terms. Lower-level professionals—whether lawyers, social workers, sociologists, or anthropologists—could only identify a vague "they" or the "entity" as the source of decisions and orders.

Felipe Cruz, a former lawyer at EBY, remembered that "they" would ask for legal reports to be submitted immediately to Buenos Aires. He was never told who needed the information or what it was for. He suggested that it was somebody in Posadas who actually required that work. In general, very few EBY employees knew who was responsible for making final decisions related to relocation priorities or who decided which information could be released. Formally, most of the decisions had to be made in the Buenos Aires headquarters by unknown EBY officials. This was the way people in Posadas, both at EBY and in the provincial bureaucracy, interpreted the decision-making procedures during the years of the military dictatorship and the first democratic government. Undoubtedly, the head of EBY Posadas must have played a role in those decisions. However, nobody seemed to be totally aware of how much he could influence the outcomes. Evidently, the boss—playing on the subordinate staff members' ignorance of the full range of his powers— displaced and attributed unwelcome orders to an insensitive and foreign center of which everyone at the agency was a passive victim. Once, Sara, one of the members of the professional staff of *Coproya*, made a distinction between decision-makers in EBY's central headquarters and the Posadas professional groups. She criticized the "callousness and lack of understanding of the situation by authorities determining the policies in the capital city." At the same time, she praised the actions of the local staff because their reading of the "objective" data provided by the census of 1979 and other studies reflected greater awareness of the social realities of the Posadas neighborhoods.

Sara's comments illustrate one problem with the notion of "neutral" information which advocates of the free flow of information like Sara ignore when they see it as a guarantor of a more egalitarian participation of the people and as a means of empowerment. They do not see that any given information is subject to more than one reading and to more than one use. Neither do they realize—as perhaps they should—that information alone does not ensure a more favorable position in the institution. Indeed, the same professionals, as well as their assistants, who complained about being uninformed or misinformed, controlled much information, not all of which could be directly translated into power. Generally, they did not conclude that much information withheld from above might be similarly unempowering.

When the project started, various professionals and technicians of PRAS had a fairly good picture of the boundaries of the neighborhoods, of social networks within them, and of how people used the household space. Notwithstanding, they had no voice when the areas were artificially divided in accordance to engineering needs. They could not say much when lines following technical priorities separated neighbors who were involved in diadic relations. And only with very strategic action could the anthropologists avoid the construction of apartment buildings for relocation proposed by a consulting firm. To succeed in this, they had to carefully screen which of EBY's sectors and individuals could be gained as allies when they argued for the construction of individual house units.

In examining Chile under Pinochet's regime, Lechner noted that in such an authoritarian context, in which secrecy was dominant, the release of more information would not prevent the development of uncertainty. On the contrary, he commented: "The more information gets accumulated, the more suspicions emerge on that which is occult (1986a:132)." The same happened in the Yacyretá case, both with the population and the staff. They generally suspected they were not told the truth and that the others were hiding information.

The population and the staff had good reasons to think in this way. In 1980 and 1981, there were serious doubts about whether the project would ever be finished. EBY authorities decided to reduce the personnel and gradually fired the majority of the social workers. Everybody remembered these years as dramatic in the history of the project. Social workers emphasized how that uncertainty had hindered their work in the field because they had had no answers. What really bothered them, however, was not that they did not know about the future of the project, but rather that they did not know about the future of their own jobs. Social workers and the population shared this uncertainty about their chances of survival. In other words, they wondered whether they would be permitted to become effective constituents of the dialogical set—people and planners—generated by Yacyretá. The problem was not—as is generally stated and as they still express it—a confrontation between already constituted actors struggling for access to strategic information which might facilitate their access to a more dominant position within the institution. What was at stake was their continued existence within the bureaucratic structure.

During the first years, EBY did not hire the personnel directly. The majority of the employees joined the relocation agency through short-term contracts made with Harza, the consultant firm (see Chapter Three). Through this mechanism, no employee was ever sure of continuity in the organization and, hence, of being fully an EBY staff member. This "flexibility" in hiring has recently been re-established to comply with a post-fordist mentality advocated by global financing institutions and embraced by the Argentine national authorities. Uncertainty in the job encourages submissive behavior and discourages solidarity among employees. It also—to return to the heart of my argument—stimulates intrigues and strategic use of information to win the favor of those who might have a say in contract renewals.

Professional Knowledge Struggles. Besides trying to gain the kind of control over the official knowledge of EBY that they believed would solidify them as part of the organization, professionals also got involved in another ongoing struggle. This was related to the specific kinds of knowledge generated and controlled by each profession. Each professional group at EBY claimed to have the right of defining what or who "benefitted" and asserted they possessed the most adequate instruments of knowledge to deal with resettlement.

Three lawyers, Felipe Cruz, Diego Díaz Navarro, and José María Peña, agreed that the "socials" did not use terms properly. Felipe Cruz noted that lawyers and social workers used to define such key terms as *proprietor, intruder*, and *occupant* differently. Lawyers, he said, were concerned with accuracy of terms, whereas social workers were not. According to the lawyers, the proprietor was the one who owned the title deed (*titular de dominio*) of the affected real estate. To a lawyer, only those individuals whose deeds were officially registered might be considered proprietors. The anthropologists at EBY defined proprietors exactly in the same way.

Whereas anthropologists and lawyers adopted an already authorized and codified definition of ownership, the social workers used the concept as employed by the Posadas residents to identify the cases they encountered in their field work. Thus, they registered as owners every individual who self-ascribed himself/herself to that category. To the social worker, it did not matter whether claimants had the deeds or just simply sales contracts, as long as the people identified themselves as owners.

PRAS professionals and technicians also distinguished between owner of the plot and owner of improvements.[4] Lawyers maintained that this distinction was hard to sustain because "the real estate is everything. There is no such a thing as an owner of improvements. If somebody is willing to get a credit on the improvements, they must first be recognized by the owner of the plot." Although lawyers did not acknowledge the legal existence of owners of improvements, they had to go along with that category because EBY was committed to granting some compensation money to those who claimed to own the structure of the house. Unable to impose their concepts on the matter, the lawyers still thought they succeeded in having the last word. They said that it was they who developed the best solution for these problems; they who created a "fiction," as they called it. They decided to act as mediators between land proprietors and the affected population who claimed to own structures. The purpose of these meetings was to convince owners of plots to recognize the rights of the latter.

Besides arguing over the concept of ownership, lawyers and social workers disagreed on what they understood to be an intruder. To the social workers, intruders were everybody who came to live in the relocation areas after the 1979 census; to the lawyers, it was everybody occupying land without the mediation of any legal arrangement with the owner.

At the relocation agency, each participant in the confrontation for the imposition of meanings accused the other of being competitive and of lacking understanding. Each also expressed the need to frame things in a simple way for the other to understand. Finally, each participant considered his/her own profession more necessary than the others.

The lawyer José María Peña thought he managed not to reveal to me his conflicts with the majority of the personnel of PRAS. He confided to another person at EBY that he had hidden those problems from me during the interview. However, his deliberate lack of candor was obvious to me because I had many friends connected to EBY who gave me a different version of relationships among staff members. His statements were immediately transparent and exposed his animosity towards PRAS:

It must be done with those from below (he is referring to PRAS, which was located downstairs). Sometimes it had happened. . . . Things get messed up. . . . Problems of competition may develop. They award the house, but it is we who pass judgment. It is me, the one who says who the owner is. I consider it is very important to have an optimal communication with the sector of urban relocation. I think it is working. It flows better. Differences among us have nothing to do with the main problem.

Mary, a blonde social worker whom everybody called the "Ukrainian," also talked about these professional struggles. According to her colleagues, she had the hardest time with the lawyers. With regards to the relationship with the legal experts, she said:

At the beginning it was very hard to coordinate everything with the legal sector . . . now, we work all right. There are still some problems, like professional jealousy. For example, there was no coordination of activities. They would not call us when they held meetings with the population to reach agreements with regards to expropriation. We came to know afterwards. When they get together to decide the legal issues involving expropriation, they forget to tell us. We did not understand, it was hard. . . . It is this jealousy which develops. We would use a term which was not the proper one. As time passed, they understood. The legal part is extremely difficult. There is no difference in understanding. Maybe they do not like our word. We would say "take" and they would say "possess." We do not have the same language with the legal sector. They thought they could solve everything. Only after some time, they realized that they must work in a team.

Julia, another social worker, said on occasion that she and her colleagues only realized that a beneficiary had ceased to be a beneficiary or had already been paid compensation when they visited the households. She felt that the population looked at them as idiots because they were ignorant of what was going on. Despite this disregard by both the lawyers and the population, the social workers insisted that their knowledge was valuable. Julia and Mary felt that they should be present when compensation was being negotiated because, after all:

We social workers are the ones who really know the composition of the household. They may say they are single and in reality, they are legally married but live in a separate house than their companions. We know those things, we are better informed. We may make them tell the truth.

According to Julia, it was in these encounters with the lawyers, the purpose of which was to reach agreements with the beneficiaries, where the social workers confirmed that there was no communication. She attributed this to the arrogance of the lawyers.

Officially, Yacyretá developed policies on behalf of the so-called beneficiaries. In practice, there was little agreement on who benefited or, even more, on whether Yacyretá was supposed to deal with a thing—a piece of property—or with a collective—a household—or with individuals. Each professional group had its own way of looking at this. Some examples of the various meanings different specialists assign to the notion of beneficiary follow.

Lawyers, quite naturally, saw everything in legal terms. When it came to ownership, they dealt with title holders who might be individuals, families, or other legal entities. In addition, they included *comodatarios* ("individuals with a right of usufruct or comodatum"), and occupants and tenants provided these individuals had already been living in the area when the census of 1979 was taken.

In contrast, sociologists spoke of registration units that corresponded to households. They were not concerned about working with individual cases, but rather with finding regularities among the units so as to characterize the population in general.

Social workers shared the same identification number of each registration unit used by the other professionals of PRAS (sociologists and anthropologists). However, when speaking about their work, they said they dealt with cases pertaining to individual family groups. In their interaction, they generally talked to the family heads. They knew everybody by name and insisted that each case was unique and deserved a particular treatment.

To surveyors what was affected was the plots. They identified affected units which they distinguished in accordance with the cadastral divisions. They proudly said that they worked with spatial units which were invariable with time and could be easily recognized geographically.

Anthropologists used the terms "beneficiary," "units of registry," and "households," which were part of the official language of EBY and PRAS. However, they also employed other terms, borrowed from the conceptual apparatus of their own discipline and of the other social sciences. This was apparent in their reports designed for the exclusive use by EBY and the international banks financing the project and in those addressed to academia. In all their reports, anthropologists referred to beneficiaries as *domestic units*, the *urban poor*, the *marginados* and *urban squatters*.

Undoubtedly, these differences in the conceptualization of the object or subject of the relocation program reflected the theoretical framework of each discipline. The differences also expressed the way each individual professional interacted with the relocated population in accordance with his/her formal status and role expectations within EBY's bureaucracy. Finally, the differences revealed conflicts among professions, many of which existed prior to the dam project. The anthropologists, for example, occupied hierarchical positions requiring the planning, coordinating, and monitoring of the relocation program. They were not expected to go to the field and enter into close contact with the population. This factor became combined with the professional training and orientation preferences within the discipline, emphasizing: theory over practice, the analysis of the "social" over the "individual," a belief in empirically grounded rational science as the basis for policies as opposed to action guided by intuition. As a result, anthropologists at EBY produced a depiction of the affected population which was more abstract and general than the one generated by the social workers. Each of these two professions was supposed to perform different roles in the project. The anthropologists (together with the sociologists) were held responsible for the rational, instrumental handling of the population. Through their expertise, anthropologists and sociologists typified, categorized, and mathematized the population, although sometimes adding qualitative overtones. Once this was accomplished, they predicted possible outcomes and suggested a course of action. It was only then that the social workers were summoned. They were to be the executors of plans produced by the social science theorists. Following Bauman's (1987) metaphor, they were the gardeners of a garden designed, legitimized, and generated by others.

The opposition between theoretically and practically oriented action informed the majority of the mutual criticisms constantly heard in the most diverse settings of Posadeño society. Social workers and anthropologists met each other at the National University of Misiones and in various sectors of the provincial government. Social workers discredited anthropologists by saying they were always theorizing and that they lacked exposure to everyday realities. They maintained that anthropologists were unable to give solutions to practical, concrete problems. But when anthropologists attempted to take an active role in local social problems, social workers accused them of invading territories. Conversely, anthropologists said that the relationship between social work and anthropology ranked equally with that of nursing and medicine. Many anthropologists blamed university training for the poor performance of social workers. They believed that as students progressed in their studies they were increasingly brainwashed, becoming less and less interested in thinking and reading.

Because there existed such a division of labor at EBY and such different views on the role played by theory and practice and by specific kinds of knowledge, we could have expected that anthropologists and sociologists would hold essentially the same views and made alliances to counterbalance the practice of social workers. We could also have expected that those with a more "scientifically" oriented training would have favored expert knowledge and probably encouraged authoritarian models of social intervention and that those with a more "intuitive" approach would have preferred the neopopulist models.

What happened in reality was more complex. Alliances were unstable and greatly varied depending on the issues under discussion and on political changes occurring at a local and national level. During the years of the military dictatorship, when anthropologists, social workers, and sociologists were at constant risk from the repressive regime, the distinctions among the disciplines were not relevant for power holders. The regime regarded everything "social" as subversive. Consequently, in these specific conjunctures, specialists in the social sciences made temporary alliances against their accusers. However, biases against each other's profession remained. Social workers remembered that there had been a time when they had to avoid being noticed by the new councilors and directors coming from Buenos Aires—most of them former armed forces officials or protegeés of the central state military authorities.[5] If any of them had realized there had been still people working in the social area, they would immediately have tried to fire them. Similar stories were recalled by the anthropologists and sociologists who were accused by the secret services of being communists.

With the military in power, the social scientists had to unite, but it became a different story when democracy was restored in Argentina. As soon as civil authorities took office, most of the political parties stated their position with regards to Yacyretá. At EBY, professional staff members started to openly declare their political affiliation and to be active members of the parties. One, the social worker García, was a prominent local figure in the Peronist party. Another one, an anthropologist, became a scientific figure of the ruling Radical party. Thus, the technical and political discourse of individual social scientists increasingly fused. What each advocated was not new, but it acquired a greater political meaning. Although the Peronist development expert had always been in favor of policies emerging from the bottom up—of popular participation and grass-roots groups—he started to praise such policies more strongly with the advent of political times. Rather than being guided by academic concerns on these topics, he did not hesitate to admit that his interest was more pragmatic. He once told me, for example, probably assuming that I was a Peronist sympathizer, that he was encouraging some agreements between the provincial government and EBY to offer various literacy and labor training courses. "You see," he said, "we need the courses to do some political work."

On the other hand, the anthropologist Guillermo Olivera had always seen scientific knowledge as an asset, both with regards to himself and others. He was the only professional at EBY holding a Ph.D. degree from a foreign university. This fact had given him respectability both at a local and at a national level; it had also been the source of much of the animosity toward him. He was probably unique in his ability to draw on his global and local ties to secure his position, which was constantly threatened by power struggles. Unable to compete against his qualifications, a common strategy among the rest of the professionals was to say that foreign higher degrees were of no use when it came to understanding local reality. They also maintained that he produced beautiful writings to please the banks but what his "nice works" proposed was never put into practice. His enviable cultural capital was a key resource he could mobilize when he was under attack. This same cultural capital, however, eventually contributed to his fall from grace in the relocation agency. Shortly after the Justicialista party won national elections, he was forced to opt for early retirement, an elegant way to avoid being fired. The newly appointed officers were local politicians with no formal professional training. They scorned the previous administration for being too intellectual, scientific, and insensitive to the plights of regional interests. Even though they claimed to defend the cause of the Misioneros, they used their office to campaign for the faction of the Justicialista party that their boss and they belonged to. Most of EBY's resources were allocated to back EBY's director, who was running for governor. Although discursively they despised most forms of professional knowledge, they were compelled to employ experts in their dealings with international lending agencies. To my amazement, I found that they were carefully copying the merely "beautiful" earlier reports made by one of the anthropologists with minor alterations (date and other basic data). Neither the few professionals who remained nor the newly hired staff had the expertise required to produce documents that met the requirements of international banks.

The anthropologists' discourse was at odds with a view which claimed to defend people's culture and advocated relocation in simple self-built huts. In public presentations of EBY's social programs and in many of his articles, one of the anthropologists repeatedly insisted that social programs should not "reproduce poverty" and was also critical about participatory views, arguing that people do not always know the best technical and economical solutions. By saying this, he was responding to the commonly employed conservative tactic of praising the "poor" in order to maintain them in their subordinate and dependent position.

As time passed and political factionalism started to impinge upon every sphere of social activity, the opposed views of these two professionals became increasingly meshed with their political affiliation. This was because Argentina's political culture tends to identify disciplinary approaches with politico-ideological orientations. According to a widespread view, the Radicals were said to be technocrats, which is to say they praised science, internationalism, and lacked understanding of the common people. Peronists, on the contrary, were believed to be on the side of the underdog, to be nationalist, and to rely heavily on "life" experience rather than on authoritative expertise. These stereotypes were enhanced to devalue those who subscribed to one or the other perspective in accordance with what became more fashionable at a specific political conjuncture. These constructions of the political parties' agendas did not necessarily coincide with what each of them was currently advocating. In fact, Menem's Justicialismo was promoting neoliberal policies that brought about unemployment and the impoverishment of the working classes. Nobody was truly concerned about the optimal orientation for social action; what was under discussion were the kinds of credentials which would be considered valid to fulfill certain roles at EBY.

To weaken its adversaries, each professional chose a "politically correct" discourse. On each side of the constituent parts of this discourse, the selection was partly deliberate and partly informed by the individual's habitus. When each perspective was enforced, the actions were far from coinciding with what their proponents or detractors claimed. Instead of waiting for grass- roots organizations to form spontaneously and develop their own initiatives once they became organized, the social workers' general supervisor at EBY pressured the staff to motivate the creation of neighborhood commissions. On the other hand, the supposedly insensitive measures devised from the top down by the anthropologist were sometimes more concerned about the welfare of the people than those proclaimed by defendants of the bottom-up perspective. Such was the case of his insistence on providing good housing and encouraging the improvement of the beneficiaries labor situation instead of defending their way of life. The anthropologists at EBY interpreted the cultural traits they observed not as a manifestation of an original culture that people would like to preserve, but as an adaptive response to the conditions of extreme poverty which the prevailing relations of production forced them into. It must be noted that neither of the two professionals totally adhered to a single approach. This is apparent both in their actions and in their statements. The anthropologist might occasionally see the advantages of participation in certain stages of projects and the social worker might praise technical expertise, as he manifested to me in the interviews and wrote in his papers.

In some way or another, every specialist attempted to present not only his/her own field but also his/her own personal action as the most necessary and influential. Lawyers proudly said they had to prepare legal briefs to guide judicial decisions because in dealing with relocation they encountered cases not contemplated in

Argentine jurisprudence, specifically, those related to squatters and the lack of title deeds. The anthropologist Guillermo Olivera was the only one claiming to have higher qualifications than the lawyers. He expressed this by saying that more than once he had to prepare briefs himself to solve complex cases. EBY's lawyers, anthropologists, and surveyors felt more knowledgeable and thus superior to their provincial counterparts. They all commented that they had to explain to provincial bureaucratic officials how to deal with matters related to EBY because these provincial employees totally ignored the basic facts.

Competition between sectors and professional groups at EBY was not only expressed in dialogical disputes over theoretical and practical orientations, planning strategies, styles of social intervention, and the rights to define the object of policies in the last instance; it was also apparent in the attempt to safeguard the material production of each group. Each group produced information on the affected households (or plots) which was kept in individual folders stored in files. The information thus produced was controlled as if it were the private property of the producers. Social workers had their folders in their own offices. The Research and Program Design section kept the census of 1979 records together with subsequent surveys; some of that data was computerized and other was still in the protocols. The lawyers had their own legal written data and so did the surveyors who developed what they had called a "technical folder." When the Office of Information and Claims (OIR) was closed, the head of EBY Posadas retained all the gathered reports which summarized the population's demands and concerns with regards to the project. Engineer Pérez would never share this data with the anthropologist (nor with this researcher), a fact that the latter always resented.

Every group attempted to have access to the other's files. Sometimes this was done compulsively. On one occasion, the head of the lawyers, uncontested and feared within the informal power structure of EBY Posadas, simply ordered the social workers to surrender their files. The social workers had no choice but to give them to him.

Through keeping data about the population in this compartmentalized manner, each group contributed to what in the overall sense was a construction of a fragmented beneficiary. We saw earlier that each group defined what and who was affected with regards to very different attributes and thus seemed to speak about a different object/subject. Here, we see how this fragmented sense was solidified by the reluctance—and often by the refusal—of each group to share its files. It is doubtful that—even with all parties operating openly and generously— a unitarian, a whole beneficiary with a univocal meaning for all, could have been defined. In the existing climate of secrecy and suspicion, such a definition was utterly impossible.

None of this is to suggest that there had not been various attempts to concentrate all the information in one office—to create a common data bank. Most such efforts failed, however, because no group was willing to give away its symbolic capital (see Bourdieu 1982, 1988). While I was doing field work, EBY bought new computers and was ready to try to centralize all the information once more. The original idea of having this sector under the supervision of PRAS had failed. It was apparent that it was soon going to become another semiautonomous area which would also claim the rights over the various EBY records. But, at least during the first months of the existence of this division, its members were unable to ensure free access to files from all sectors. Not surprisingly, they could never get the lawyers to make their files available for processing, something that was by no means a new response from these specialists. Attorneys had always negated access to their documentation with the argument that it was private. An ex-EBY employee commented on this: "They kept everything in secret. They would not disclose anything. I do not know why they did so. After all, everything will be covered by the water."

Space and Time

In the formal organization of EBY, the legal sector of Posadas was independent from the Department of Infrastructure and Urban Relocation. Instead it directly responded to the legal area of EBY in Buenos Aires. The autonomy of the lawyers from the local bureaucracy greatly contributed to their freedom of action and to the relative power they enjoyed throughout the slow relocation process. These professionals were particularly powerful during the military years, when the head of their sector in the central headquarters had greater authority than the general director.[6]

I have already shown how, in Posadas, the lawyers conveyed their "superiority" through their behavior. They also conveyed this spatially. The use of space distanced legal professionals from EBY's staff and from the population and hence contributed to their representation as unreachable. The legal practitioners occupied the upper floor of EBY's building, while PRAS, the administrative and technical staff—in other words, "the rest"—were all underneath. In speaking, attorneys enforced their spatial-professional superiority by referring to "those below." Other professionals experienced this spatial differentiation as symbolic violence. The rest of EBY's staff saw the higher physical position as a symbol that stood for their differences in power within the relocation agency. They commented: "Differences with the ones above are not only limited to a question of having the office on the upper or on the lower floors."

Everybody at EBY accused the lawyers of excessive territoriality. Space in the social sector was so arranged that anybody could reach the personnel without being previously announced. In the legal sector, however, there was a secretary who screened visitors, controlled access, and reserved the right to determine who was worthy of being granted an appointment. Besides this, while the offices downstairs had glass windows and the staff could be seen from the corridor, the lawyers had opaque windows; and therefore, they could not be watched.

By controlling the space where expropriation and compensation was settled and discussed, lawyers enjoyed a favorable position which enabled them to condition the way communicative practices occurred in such setting. They did this in two ways. First, they generally decided when, where, and who might participate in such encounters. Second, they largely determined who was given voice and for what purposes. To counterbalance the lawyers' claims over this space, social workers made use of the space where they reigned: the neighborhoods and the private realm of the households. Only when the importance of knowledge on these latter spaces was acknowledged as strategically useful were social workers admitted into the space dominated by the lawyers. But even on the occasions when they were "invited" to take part in the negotiation meetings, their participation was still regulated by the attorneys.

As with space, lawyers might sometimes deliberately use time as a device to assert authority. Those enjoying a power position controlled the time of appointments and could make people wait as they wished.

The privileged position of the lawyers did not remain uncontested. A new organizational structure was put into place in 1993 when the Posadas Relocation Agency reinitiated operations after the impasse created by budgetary problems, which forced authorities to cancel the social program. The social sector has now moved to the upper floor. This spatial location expresses the greater power that some of the members of this sector, mainly a few social workers, are now enjoying. One in particular, who managed to secure close ties with the head of EBY Posadas, now makes decisions regarding what, where, and when to deliver information. She also determines who among her employees is authorized to speak.

Mastering Linguistic Resources

There are various linguistic resources that certain actors employ at EBY to enforce their position in the institution and to devalue the role of other staff members. Among those mechanisms, I will discuss the way forms of address, nicknaming, speech genres, and specific ownership of meanings were employed for such purposes.

Forms of Address. At EBY, there was an institutionalized way of addressing in which each professional staff member was called by his/her university degree and family name. This was the way the administrative and security personnel referred to the staff members when somebody from the neighborhoods to be relocated came to EBY. This was probably the reason why the beneficiaries spoke of the "licenciadas" and the "engineers," very broad categories that include diverse professionals.

Although sociologists, anthropologists, and social workers participated in professional disputes, they used very colloquial forms of address in their interaction. They called each other by name and used the form *vos* for the second person singular, which in Argentina expresses hierarchical equality and easy access to the person thus addressed. This familiarity revealed that, despite their disagreement, they still constituted a group with certain commonality of interests. At least this was the way the others thought of them when they called them the *sociales* (those dealing with the social). On the contrary, lawyers created and maintained distance by addressing the others very formally and expecting these others to address them in the same way.

Nicknaming. Nicknaming is a common practice in the highly formalized settings that are Argentine bureaucratic organizations. Nicknaming is a form of labelling by which nicknamers grant a person the position they feel he/she truly deserves. In this way, the position officially held is at least partially disqualified. It is, then, an expression of how the person is represented by the other members of the organization. An interesting aspect of this labeling system is that it is not always apparent, and it requires a story to unfold the occult meaning. The social worker García began to be identified as *fresh bread* after the Peronists won the provincial elections and took office. When somebody hears this kind of nicknaming, he must ask the reason why the person is called in such a way. As a reply, the initiated gets another part of the story. In this case: "Fresh bread, because he had come out of the oven."[7] With this they meant: "He had just left." The latter was the answer anybody would get when he was not at work and they were trying to reach him. After elections, he had been an adviser to the secretary of education and was generally away from EBY for many hours.

The unreachable head of the lawyers in Posadas to whom I could never talk was "the feudal lord," because "once he lifted the drawbridge nobody could go across." The anthropologist in charge of PRAS was "the man on the spaceship" because he never landed on earth. During the first years of the project, he and another anthropologist were also called "Batman" and "Robin," more public—and less derogatory—nicknames.

Throughout the long, and so many times postponed, process of relocation, there were other mechanisms of labeling generally generated in what was called the *usina de rumores* ("rumor-producing factory") of the secret services. The main targets were the social scientists of whom they rumored things pertaining both to their private lives and to their political affiliations. The most common labels were "womanizers," "drug addicts," and "organizers of black parties." The favorite of all was, surely, "communists." By using the latter, the producers of rumors marked and isolated the carriers of such label and made them dangerous in the eyes of any possible interlocutor. These derogatory labels discredited the staff and also warned it that somebody was watching. The message was: "Whoever wants to misbehave would immediately be in trouble." Not all these rumors and labels necessarily stemmed from the clandestine law enforcement agents. Various staff members, mainly the lawyers, engineers, and surveyors, would echo or originate these images about the social scientists. When I first arrived in Posadas in 1980, I heard such rumors from a surveyor who no longer worked there. The negative labeling was combined with critical remarks on the practical use of any social study. The discourse of these professionals was—and still is—very similar, if not the same, to that of the paramilitary groups and armed forces in general. This was so because they had all been exposed to the dominant ideology of the military years, had consumed it, and had identified themselves with it. What the "feudal lord" proclaimed provides a good example of the ideological identity of the regime discourse and that of some of the attorneys and technical staff at EBY. I learned his comments through confidences of his adversaries: "He would say without any remorse that all subversives should be killed and he openly supported and justified the repressive practices of the military regime."

The relocated population shared rumors and framed them in the same way. They all insinuated that there is a "black legend" of Yacyretá. When the secret services referred to it, they meant that some of the Posadas and Ituzaingó's EBY employees were involved in contraband, a fact that sometimes also appeared in articles in local newspapers such as El Territorio from Misiones, and El Litoral from Corrientes. (As mentioned in Chapter Two, preoccupation with contraband has always been a reason to call the attention of national authorities so as to encourage a closer surveillance of those living on this national frontier). When they told me about this black legend in El Chaquito and in Heller, residents alluded to corrupt employees getting bribes though promising preferential treatment on the granting of houses. They also referred to staff members getting smuggled goods from Paraguay through the good offices of *paseras* who resided in the affected areas. One of the professionals who hinted the existence of this bad history happened to be the target of many of the population's charges. In his account, the black legend pointed at the persecutions and breaches of trust promoted and executed by clandestine law enforcement agents.

Speech Genres and Specific Ownership of Meaning. Anthropologists have observed that groups intending to distinguish themselves from others sometimes make use of secret languages to maintain their separateness[8] and to enforce their collective identities. In Yacyretá, it was undoubtedly the lawyers who made use of their own, exclusive, private, and yet public language. When speaking about legal cases, they constantly employed Latin words. Nearly always, the addressee ignored the meaning. With these words, they behaved in the same manner that they had been trained to deal with the law: "No common citizen can claim ignorance of the law." But the common citizen neither knew the law nor the Latin words. However, he/she felt too intimidated to ask. Doña Celeste, from San Cayetano, told me: "They speak to us with all those difficult words, and what can we do if we are brutish?" The lawyers situated themselves vis-à-vis their interlocutors by demonstrating the other's ignorance through the manipulation of words. In these communication exchanges there was generally an ongoing struggle for establishing who had the authoritative speech. The advantage of the lawyers was that their speech genre was already socially constructed as legitimate and as normative. To invert this situation was difficult because it was not easy to find an alternative speech genre with which to reply. When I interviewed the attorneys, even those who were my friends, I found myself in the disjunctive of admitting my ignorance of certain words and thus recognizing my "inferiority" or pretending I understood and then risking finishing the interview without knowing what it was about. This is what usually happened when people interacted with the attorneys. Their "secret" language created a sense of complicity among themselves and united them against all others. Through doing this, lawyers intimidated and devalued other employees at EBY, the relocated population, and the politicians they might interact with. They presumed the "stupidity" of all common citizens, but never wondered why they were not understood. Felipe Cruz, one of the lawyers, remembering his encounters with the vice-governor, head of COPROYA, told me how "dumb" he was: "I told him again and again what the problem with the deeds was in El Chaquito. Even if I explained it to him in simple terms, he would never understand. He would insist that it did not matter, that the province would solve everything." Surely enough, Felipe, the same as his professional peers, would never ask himself whether the concepts he used truly had the univocal meaning the law profession claimed for them. His attitude coincided with what Jackson (1985), following Greimas and Landowski, had noted with regards to legislative discourse. This kind of discourse, he said, generally presents words as if they had their origin in natural language, and it conceals the role played by legislators in their construction.[9]

While the attorneys asserted the legitimacy of their discourse and, consequently, of their profession, through presenting them as manifestations of the natural order, other professionals attempted to impose their own discourse as deriving from a more accurate interpretation of the social reality they were working with. The lawyers had the easiest time in this respect. Their goal was not only hard to achieve, it had, in fact, already been attained. The larger society in Posadas, as elsewhere, already recognizes the role of the legal profession in determining right and wrong. Hence, we had a professional group, the attorneys, who imposed meanings on others by recourse to the pre-established authority of their discipline to define virtually any social matter.

Other professionals at EBY employed a disciplinary discourse that was not socially sanctified; some specialists adopted concepts from fields other than their own. Such experts had the ability to show the strength of their own discourse by imposing it on others. Generally, this strength was neither conscious nor intentional. Rather, it revealed the influence of specific positions and the corresponding knowledge that accrued from these positions.

It was my observation that it is not without usefulness to consider the strength as residing as much in the concepts as in the user of the concepts. Such was the case I observed that occurred with some anthropological concepts. When interviewing the PRAS staff, I found that more than one of the social workers and some of the research assistants of the Research and Program Design Section had borrowed terms employed by the anthropologists to characterize the behavior of the squatters to be relocated. The favored words were "adaptive strategy," although they also employed some others such as "marginals" or "domestic units." In parts of the text I obtained in an interview, these two words were used with some irony so as to minimize the strength of the concept and of its original producer, but in other parts of the same text, they would be employed un-self-consciously.

Although occasionally words may carry the power of having an effect over somebody's behavior, in most cases, such power depends on the position held by that one who uses the term and not on the word itself. In fact, word and position mutually determine each other. Thus, on the one hand, the identity held by the speaker grants power to certain words; on the other hand, the fact that others adopt his/her meanings reinforces and is revealing of his/her position. On examining the texts obtained in the field, I have observed that one of the anthropologists influenced EBY's employees, including the most distant ones, such as the surveyors and lawyers, although in their case, his influence appeared slightly blurred. The local press also adopted some of his terms, as well as his characterizations of the population to be relocated.

As we have seen, the social worker García had the power of imposing his family name on a neighborhood, and since then, residents and EBY's staff employed it, even on official papers. Moreover, he also greatly contributed to the imposition of the favorite legitimizing word of the official presentation of the project: as a development program that aims at the social promotion of the population. Engineer Pérez always stated in his public appearances and on press interviews that the relocation program mainly pursued the social promotion of the population's welfare. García and his professional colleagues had also reached the beneficiaries with this justification of the project. In many households, they explained to us that this was a "social" project. Although most of our informants consumed and consequently employed the term, the majority did not seem to know what was meant by it.

Use of Networks. The majority of EBY's staff had been appointed under the good auspices of a godfather. An ex-EBY staff member once described this institution both as the place where everybody sends their protegeés and also as a refuge, a "freezer" where public figures can temporarily retreat until the reason why they withdrew from a state post is forgotten.[10] During the same interview, this ex-staff member said that in Posadas and also at the national level, there was an image of EBY as the great provider, a *vaca lechera* ("a milking cow"). Thus, everybody wanted to get a job there because it was also believed that they paid very well and in dollars. In Misiones, there were very few labor opportunities for certain professions. Quite often, the only possible employer was the provincial government which paid very low wages. Because of this, influential local and national personalities, mainly politicians, sought jobs for their acquaintances. Thus, among the personnel, we found exwives and lovers of politicians, relatives of prominent national political figures whom their famous protectors would like to pass unnoticed because of their sexual preferences, and there are also relatives of former military presidents and military generals. In Yacyretá, we found successive "layers" of employees representing the successive political regimes. The current head of Posadas EBY is a cousin of Argentina's president.

Many of the confrontations among the various staff members were related to the way each member was recruited and also to which were the supporting networks sustaining them. Dialogue with each individual employee was sought or denied in accordance with the power held by those who recommended him/her to the job. Knowledge of who integrated the networks behind somebody might contribute to the exclusion, fear, suspicion, or submission to the individual involved. Relative stability in the position of each group or individual greatly depended on the ability to mobilize external networks to come to their rescue when continuity in EBY was threatened.

Although continuously suspected, the social scientists—mainly the anthropologists—were relatively secure in their jobs and enjoyed considerable influence in policy making. This was because the international banks conditioned financing to the presence of personnel they trusted. One of the two anthropologists originally working at EBY retired at the beginning of 1982; the other one stayed much longer without major inconveniences because it was known that his presence guaranteed the regular flow of money. He was the only one capable of communicating in the language of the financing banks.

Changes in the political alliances at a national and local level impinged upon the distribution of power with which particular individuals and positions within Yacyretá were embedded. Those interested either in maintaining or acquiring power were permanently trying to get external sponsors and to be close to those who, within EBY, already had the right networks. Whoever failed to renew the networks when circumstances changed might fall in disgrace and eventually lose the job. In Yacyretá, there had been notorious cases of this kind. One was a lawyer, who, during the military government, had the "right" contacts both in Buenos Aires and in the local government of Posadas. He even came to hold simultaneous positions in EBY and in Misiones government. Even though this situation was outrageously irregular, he was able to maintain it because people feared his connections (which included clandestine law enforcement agents). While he managed to keep his strategic alliances, he could take advantage of the positionas he wished, from getting rid of people he disliked, to imposing policies, to enjoying monetary benefits. As long as this situation endured, the rest of the staff could do very little to oppose him, especially considering that he had the ability to mobilize members from the armed forces. He reached a point, however, where he was no longer capable of holding his position because his patrons at EBY and in Misiones ceased to back him under the peril of losing their own supporting connections. Something similar happened to a surveyor who once enjoyed a lot of power in the institution. Rumors say the basis of such power was his relation to the secret services and paramilitary groups as an informant. After getting in trouble with EBY, he initiated a suit against it, and his conflict with the relocation agency was written up in the local papers and magazines. This same person later became the head of COPROYA. Ironically, after his notoriety faded, he ended up asking for job recommendations even from those whom he used to attack and despise.

NOTES

1. Posadas is considered to be an unfavorable zone because living expenses are higher than at other locations in Argentina. National agents appointed to this city generally receive the equivalent of what Americans call combat pay.

2. In Spanish: "*La mona, aunque se vista de seda, mona queda.*"

3. This corresponds to Lukes's (1986:10) three dimensional view of power which maintains that power "may operate to shape and modify desires and beliefs in a manner contrary to people's interests."

4. I use the word improvement for the Spanish word *mejoras* which refers to any construction, fence, plant, or tree incorporated to the plot.

5. In 1979, three out of seven members representing Argentina at the Administrative Council of Yacyretá were retired officers of the armed forces. One was a rear admiral; another one was a commodore; and the third one was a colonel.

6. Botana's (1982) book summarizes the first years of the dam project. The book has

plenty of gossip and the author does not disguise his sympathies for one of the groups searching for full control of EBY. The roles played by the financial director and by the juridical director are discussed in detail. Particularly revealing is the discussion of the connections of these characters with the military hierarchy.

7. In Spanish, they say *porque está recién salido*. Speakers play with the meanings of the verb *salir*, which are translatable as "to come out of," and also as "to go, to leave."

8. Bellman notes that for some authors there is a different between secrecy and privacy. While secrecy alludes to the concealment of something negatively valued by the excluded audience, privacy refers to a way of protecting behaviors that are either morally neutral or seen as positive both bythe one who hides and by society as well. He prefers to define secrecy in a way that encompasses both secrecy and privacy, as the calculated concealment of information, whether positive, negative, or neutral (1984:4).

9. It is worth quoting what Jackson says about the use of words in legislation: "Again, the fact that the legislation uses words which have their origin in the natural language, without (for the most part) explicitly defining them, conceals the function of the legislator in constructing the legal lexicon; it reinforces the conventional view (whose background lies in jurisprudential naturalism) that legal language exists prior to and independent of legislation, while legislation merely organizes that language and chooses the specific messages it will convey. Legal language, in reality a cultural construction, is made to appear natural, self-evident.The adoption of "explicit statement" as the arbitrary sign of membership of a legal system (the syntactic rule of the legal grammar) produces the appearance of a system characterized by public knowledge and lack of ambiguity; the grammar of other social semiotic systems, by contrast, remains implicit, underlying the discourse which it produces" (1985:141).

10. A case in point is that of General Suárez Mason, one of the more questioned generals by human rights groups for his participation in torturing and kidnapping. When he left his military appointment, he was about to be named executive director of EBY.

CHAPTER 8

Processes of Communication and Miscommunication

Until now we have examined differences in negotiating power and access to resources enjoyed by participants in the Yacyretá hydroelectric project. Because the positioning process in which they are involved is intersubjective, I have examined various situations in which each participant encounters others and communicates, or attempts to communicate, with them. By this time, readers should have acquired some familiarity with the men and women engaged in communication processes and should also know the various kinds of dialogical sets which were created or recreated once the dam and relocation project was announced. This chapter will further describe communicative practices by showing how some of them emerged, became transformed, and/or were totally abandoned during the many years of the resettlement process. In the first part of the chapter, I will discuss how EBY dealt with communication processes between the agency and the population to be relocated. In the second part, I will examine the case of Doña Azucena and some of her neighbors to illustrate communicative practices at work.

DELIBERATE ATTEMPTS TO DEAL WITH COMMUNICATION: THE BOOMERANG EFFECTS OF ACTION

From the beginning of the relocation program, the anthropologists had been aware that the population from the affected areas felt intimidated by EBY's headquarters and that this constrained their ability to express their doubts and concerns. To overcome such problems, the anthropologists recommended the creation of OIR, the Office of Information and Claims. They had played with the meaning of the initials which in Spanish are the equivalent of the verb to listen. The original idea was to create an office totally separate from the PRAS which would operate in the same neighborhoods. Its main purpose was to listen to people's opinions and doubts and to check the effectiveness of the social programs with the aim of improving communication with the affected population.

Plans for the OIR structure were drawn up and sent to Buenos Aires. Once there, EBY's authorities and the consulting firm interpreted its goals very differently.

When the project returned to Posadas, it had been totally transformed. The "I" in OIR, which originally stood for information, in the sense of listening with the purpose of encouraging feedback, was changed into an "I" which stood for "intelligence." Indeed, EBY's social staff members recalled that the consulting firm defined the OIR as an instrument of intelligence. Thus, instead of being a means to improve communication by knowing where and how it was failing, it was to become a means of controlling both EBY's staff and the affected population by handling secret information about them. The head of public relations, notoriously related to the secret services, was assigned to supervise this task.

Eventually, EBY's authorities decided to appoint two people to the OIR in Posadas, a sociologist and an anthropology student. The office operated in the same building as the PRAS but was independent from it. The OIR had to follow instructions coming from Buenos Aires. A former EBY employee remembered that some of the ideas developed in the capital city were impossible to put into practice because they would not work well with the marginal population of Posadas. One of the failed attempts was the installation of boxes in the neighborhoods where people could leave anonymous letters stating their problems and critiques. This project did not prosper. EBY ended up receiving some insulting critiques and obscenities, and the boxes were promptly removed.

The OIR kept records of the questions and problems most commonly raised. Every month, personnel from this office analyzed the data they obtained when people from the neighborhoods came to EBY to inquire about the project. The analysis of the concerns of the population revealed that the majority of the neighbors were poorly informed and that they misinterpreted what EBY's staff told them. The results of these monthly reports were submitted to the head of Yacyretá Posadas, who never shared them with anybody else at the relocation agency. Although years have passed, and the OIR no longer exists, it is still impossible to examine the records. I could only gain access to one copy which was kindly selected and provided for me by Mr. Pérez (the head of EBY in Posadas). In April 1981, for example, the most commonly asked questions were related to three topics: compensation, regularization of title deeds, and the law of status quo. The majority of the people coming to EBY for consultation were owners who were not living in the area. These people had the right to claim compensation but were not included in the relocation program. Very few among those to be resettled—the beneficiaries—contacted EBY during that period.

Mr. Pérez said that the aim of the office was to take an opinion poll with the purpose of "returning information to the population." But neither the OIR nor EBY ever attempted to ensure the claimed feedback. Indeed, EBY authorities made no serious efforts to overcome the communication problems the OIR and other sectors may have identified. In other words, the OIR was finally set up to hear but not to speak.

A different sector at EBY, the PRAS, was entitled to speak. While the OIR was listening—but not telling what was heard—the social workers were telling—but not always listening.[1] They never knew what neighbors said to employees at the rival office, nor did they ever try to register and analyze the questions and doubts their client population raised. Besides being involved in delivering "oral information" when they visited the relocation areas or when people came to EBY, the social workers also designed some of the written messages. They did so jointly with a local advertising company. This was part of a communication program which did not last long, only through the first two or three years of the dam project. This initial campaign included pamphlets, posters, and press releases for the local radio, TV, and newspapers which advertised the various social programs of EBY (such as vaccination, documentation, and labor training) and informed people about the options—compensation or relocation—that the affected population could choose. One of the social workers told me that they had stopped issuing the pamphlets because very few people could read.[2] Contrary to what she thought, I found various cases where people made direct reference to the pamphlets they had received. They particularly remembered one which contained a map with the possible relocation areas and a division of zones which corresponded to the three stages of the project. This pamphlet is still a source of conflict between the affected population and EBY. People say that Yacyretá lied to them because the pamphlet stated the dates of relocation of each stage, and none of these deadlines have ever been met. EBY Bulletin 1 from July 1980 stated these promised dates of relocation: Stage 1: second semester of 1981, Stage 2: by mid-1982, and Stage 3: from mid-1984 until mid-1985. In one part of the text it said: "And it will be done; and it will be done well . . . and meeting the planned deadlines." In 1996, the houses for stages 2 and 3 were not yet finished.

After these first messages, everything was silenced. Since 1981, there have been no more deliberate attempts to explain the dam project, the characteristics of relocation, and the rights of the population. Moreover, nobody has tried to register the major doubts and concerns of the people involved. Uncertainty about the initiation of the major works was one of the main reasons why there were very few communication exchanges. As far as EBY's employees were concerned, they would have been happy if they had none. The OIR was closed and the sociologist was one of the first to be fired when there were personnel reductions. He later became a congressional adviser to the Peronist representative from Misiones, Mr. Domenech. His case is one more among many illustrating what I have pointed out before: the circulation of professionals within the national and provincial state and EBY.

In 1983, when it appeared that the dam and the relocation housing might finally become a reality, EBY reinitiated more regular contacts with the population and the press. Throughout all these years, most of the interaction with the population was in the hands of the social workers. The head of EBY Posadas said that PRAS was put in charge of communications with the population because its personnel, mainly the social workers, were the ones in closer contact with the affected population. From then on, social workers registered the most commonly raised questions and reported them monthly to the head of the PRAS. When I started my field work, I asked for those records to analyze the characteristics of the people making demands at EBY's offices. To my surprise, the social workers told me that they had thrown away the folders containing such information because it was "old material." This clearly illustrates that they were not interested in checking which were the major communication problems with the population; they had never attempted to examine the nature of the questions people raised. The anthropologist Guillermo Olivera was the only one who studied such information, which was summarized in the reports prepared for the World Bank (see, for example, EBY 1987). Visits to EBY to consult on topics related to relocation and compensation increased gradually from the moment the government announced the initiation of civil engineering projects: 1,308 in 1984; 2,981 in 1985; and 3,733 in 1986 (EBY 1987).

The personnel of the PRAS, primarily a sociologist and the anthropologist, insisted that there should be a specific program in charge of communication with the affected population and with the general public. The sociologist had presented a communications plan which included guidelines to inform about two types of themes: (1) those related to general aspects of the project, such as the relocation program and engineering works, and (2) those related to specific circumstances which require urgent actions. The CECOM (Communications Plan and Liaison with the Community) suggested different actions, according to the kind of public EBY wanted to reach. With regard to communications with the beneficiaries, it suggested "face to face" relations and participatory techniques (see EBY 1985). Authorities never did anything with the plan, arguing that there was no budget to implement it. This contradicts what some people at the World Bank told me informally. They maintain that if the social area demands money for such programs, they might receive it because there is a budget available for such purposes. What in reality is a political decision appears disguised as an economic constraint.

Communication through the media was re-established in the 1990s when popularity of EBY was at one of its weakest points. To respond to widespread concerns with relocation and the environmental damages created with the dam, EBY started an aggressive media campaign highly criticized by those involved in the social movements against the project, who felt the messages distorted reality. These messages, with a subheading saying "Yacyretá, Positive Energy," presented EBY as saying: "To take care of the Paraná is to take care of ourselves. And this, to Yacyretá, is as clear as water." They promised works to guarantee the quality of water, an innovative sewage system, and vegetation clean-up before the flooding.[3] They also asserted that the regional weather and rain system would not change with the dam. Environmental groups and the men and women from the region had a different opinion on these issues but lacked the resources to publicize their views.

Most of the Posadas staff ignored why, where, and by whom many of the initiatives were stopped. However, in the 1980s, many of the recommendations advising that information be controlled and that speaking out be prohibited stemmed from the legal area. For example, in 1988, a new dramatic situation developed. After surveyors took the definitive measurements of the affected area, they determined that some sectors would not be flooded as had been originally presumed. This meant that some residents who had been waiting for more than ten years to be moved were no longer affected by the dam project. Therefore, they were not entitled to compensation money or a new home. Concerned with the humanitarian side of the situation, professionals from the PRAS had written a memo proposing a mechanism to notify the people concerned about these changes.

Nothing was done, however, because the PRAS had received orders to stop these procedures. Although there was no formal explanation for such a decision (there generally was not), some of the staff suspected it had been stopped by lawyers. Apparently, they opposed the suggested line of action on the grounds that releasing such information was inopportune and might damage the interests of EBY. Instead of having somebody from EBY explain the current legal situation with the plots, attorneys advised that neighbors requesting information should be sent to the provincial office of land registration for details. As it affected scattered households, the victims of this new measurement did not unite to protest. Legally, there was very little they could do because they had never received any written statement in which EBY made any commitments regarding relocation and/or compensation. In 1983, for example, the local paper echoed the concerns of the affected population, stating: "The *afectados* ['affected population'] think that nobody speaks to them clearly, nor are they given official documents, proving that the decision communicated to them is the last and definitive one" (*El Territorio*, November 14, 1983).

The problem of the people who were no longer beneficiaries, the so-called "disaffected" population according to some employees at EBY, illustrates one of the many situations in which the relocation agency deliberately obscured facts and hindered communication. In the rest of this chapter, I will examine the case of Azucena Juárez, to show how communication worked throughout the long relocation process.

AZUCENA JUAREZ: HER ORDEALS AND FINAL REWARDS

This Is Not a Relocation, But an Emergency Removal

Azucena Juárez first heard of Yacyretá through the census and the Swap Operation. She did not quite understand what the meaning of relocation was, but after meeting with Mabel, the social worker, she thought it involved the action of taking people from their original homes to others. To her, it was similar to what authorities sometimes did when floods occurred, but instead of being transitory it would be permanent. The idea of having a new house made out of bricks was very appealing, but she did not want to believe in illusions. Throughout the 60 years of her life, she had heard too many promises from the state and politicians. None of them had come true.

One year after they had come to take the census, Mabel stopped by and told her there would be an important meeting in the church of San Cayetano. Azucena wondered what could be so urgent. Once she was there, she saw all the familiar faces of her neighbors of many years. Father Vladimiro and all those people from EBY were also in the room. A man from EBY told them they had to leave the place in a month. Newspapers from Posadas interviewed Guillermo Olivera, the head of the PRAS, on this matter and reported the following statements:

It is necessary to clear an area in a short time to build the access to the construction area of the bridge. These needs, the demand of movement [*sic*], do not derive from the Entity itself, but from the deadlines of the National Highway Department with regards to the construction of the bridge itself. We are not going to start the relocation, because the construction of the houses has not started yet; that does not exist in our own timetable. So as not to create situations of privilege or annoyance, and to avoid falling into the famous "transitory relocations" which end up creating problems, we have found a solution which we believe is the best for these seventeen affected families. The solution we have found is to transfer them, as close as possible to where they now live. This is not a relocation by Yacyretá and does not affect the possible rights of these persons, whom we can say are included in the potential population to be resettled by EBY, with rights to the benefits or to the procedures that would be applied with regard to this. In other words, what we do is to help them move their houses to places where there is some space available, but these people maintain all their possible rights. They are not affected in any way with regard to relocation. In other words, I would like this to be very clear, this is not a relocation or an example of how people would be treated as relocated individuals. It is an emergency solution in available plots, and once there, they will stay as if nothing has ever happened.

Guillermo Olivera continued, saying that nobody should be naive and expect that situations such as this would never develop in a process of such complexity. He then repeated something he had said before during the interview: "But this is not a conflict. It is rather a problem of confusion" (see *El Territorio*, February 1, 1980; cf. also *El Libertador*, February 1, 1980).

Azucena was indeed confused with what she heard at the meeting and with what was later published in the local paper. Although she could not afford to buy the paper daily, she and her family found a way of keeping informed. Everyday they would go to the railway station to pick up the papers and magazines passengers had left behind. She examined the interview carefully with the help of one of her granddaughters, Cecilia, who, with great sacrifice, was studying social work at the local university. There were reasons to feel disoriented. She asked herself how it could be that people from EBY were telling them to go and simultaneously kept repeating that it was not "their relocation." She wondered what this movement was to be if it were not a relocation.

"Confusion" and "wrong interpretations" were attributed to the way the news was released in previous newspaper articles, but the reasons for confusion can be easily found in the text just transcribed, which reproduces what Guillermo Olivera from EBY said. The anthropologist from EBY presented the problem of the construction of the bridge as something independent from Yacyretá. He was referring to something EBY has always maintained officially—that the dam and the bridge were separate undertakings. He said so in a way which suggested he presupposed that the listener was aware of such distinctions and, therefore, that he did not need to elaborate. His statements reflected the ambiguities regarding the two works. He did not explain why Yacyretá would intervene in the "emergency transfer," considering—as he indeed stated—that the Entity had nothing to do with the bridge. He presented EBY as a mediator in this issue, as somebody trying to find solutions for an inconvenience created by others. His statements also reflected his own uncertainties, which he shared with everybody at EBY. In one part of the text, he admitted that Yacyretá had not yet started to build the resettlement homes. Moreover, he was careful not to assert that relocation was an unquestionable and certain fact. Instead, he spoke of "possible" and "potential" resettlement.

Obviously, neighbors felt disoriented and uncertain when they heard this ambiguous discourse. Azucena thought they were hiding information from her but was sure about one thing: Very soon, she and her neighbors would have to leave. Olivera's words did not meet the conditions of credibility, but some words were signs indicating the authority of the speaker and, therefore, carried the power of commands.[4] Thus, Azucena and her neighbors felt that they had to obey even though they did not believe in the reasons people from EBY had given to them. Felipe Cruz, one of the lawyers, speculated that the fact that many of Azucena's neighbors preferred to get compensation money, instead of waiting in the area until the relocation homes were completed, proved that very few believed that Yacyretá would ever construct the new settlements.

Although Azucena was very skeptical about what they could do, she did go to the meeting Father Vladimiro organized at the church of San Cayetano. They protested against the measure for some days but in vain. Finally, Azucena decided to ask to be moved temporarily because she still hoped that one day she would get the promised house. After all, EBY had told her that, when she reported that she was an owner, she would get a house in exchange for her own. She was not going to do as her neighbors, who preferred to have the money. That is what Doña Asunción had asked for, and they gave her so much money that she could buy that nice little house near the hospital.

Some days later, they came to Azucena's with a truck and took everything, including the parts of the house, into an area next to the old Heller factory. They put a metal plate on the door which had a number and said EBY. She felt as if she was marked and also wondered why EBY had said they had no involvement and then had put this sign outside. She was very upset with this. The frequent visits of the social workers also annoyed her: "They always come, but one day they say one thing, and another day, they say another thing." But what annoyed her the most was what happened to her in 1985, the year when she found out that she was not an owner.

From Owner to Squatter

Azucena recalled that, in 1985, somebody from EBY stopped by and announced to her that there would be a meeting at the Posadas office of the relocation agency. She was told that she had to take her personal documents, her blue folder, and the property's documents with her. They recommended that she bring a lawyer, but she could not afford one. As a washerwoman, she was barely making enough money to feed her family. Luckily, her granddaughter had gotten a job with the municipality and was contributing some money to the household budget, but it was not enough. She decided to go without an attorney to see what they wanted. She took her folder and the sales contract and headed for the Entity. Once there, she was asked to wait in the street until the other neighbors arrived and EBY's staff was ready to see them. She felt intimidated. After a prolonged wait outside the building, where they could feel the burning summer's heat, they were finally allowed inside. One of the guards at the entrance took them up to the second floor. There were three men sitting at a large table, all dressed in dark suits. Azucena only knew one of them, Mr. Pérez, the engineer—the *dirigente* ("leader"), as she called him. One of the other two men was particularly serious. He was tall, blonde, and blue eyed and spoke with all those hard words. He had a very strong *Porteño* accent. Azucena was afraid to ask him anything. The man made some comments about the deeds that she did not quite understand. Meanwhile, Mabel, the social worker, came in and sat next to the neighbors. Although she was the only friendly face in the room, she was not behaving in the same way she did when she visited their home. Every time Mabel tried to utter something, Mr. Mariano Arroyo Costas, the biggest lawyer, interrupted her. Maybe, Azucena thought, she is also afraid of him. He must be her boss.

Mr. Arroyo Costas wanted to see everything they had brought. Doña Azucena showed him the folder she had saved so carefully throughout all those years, even when the flood had covered her home. She had also taken the sales contract from the plastic bag where she had put it after her husband died. The big lawyer had put his glasses on and looked at the papers for an interminable time. Then he asked with a commanding voice: "Where is Mr. López? You say he is dead? Where are the papers proving that? Where is the succession? We cannot proceed with your case unless that is done." He continued looking at the documents and suddenly he asked disdainfully: "What is this paper? It is illegible in some parts. . . . It looks as if you had washed it." Azucena tried to explain: "It was in 1983, with the big floods." She was interrupted, and Mr. Arroyo Costas continued telling her that her sales contract had no legal value. Then, he added: "Unless you get the title deed, you will technically be an intruder." Soon after that he asked the others what they had brought. He told them that most of their documents were useless. He explained that EBY was a state institution, and therefore, every operation in which it participated had to conform to the National Law of Accounting and to other legal instruments.[5]

Azucena thought she might have misunderstood him. It could not be true. She and her neighbors had been paying taxes for years as if they were owners, and now EBY was telling them that the papers they had did not prove their ownership. "How could it be, "she asked herself," if the other neighbors got compensation when the bridge construction started only through presenting the same kind of papers." She told me: "It is unfair, they do one thing with some and a different one with others." She was right. This was confirmed by people at COPROYA and by some of the EBY's staff. When EBY intervened in the urgent displacement of the 17 families and, even later, when they moved some more because of other complementary works, they had paid compensation to residents without the proper deeds. To avoid conflicts at that time and having no homes to offer, EBY opted for a solution which people could not understand because of its complexity. Yacyretá purchased from the population their sales contracts and, through this, the right to legally claim the title deeds. It did not really buy the plots themselves. This procedure was not clear to any of the neighbors, and until now, they are convinced that EBY's behavior was capricious.

Felipe Cruz, who was also there, felt very upset. Something was wrong in EBY's procedures. They should have never given those famous blue folders. The problem with them was that people who only had a sales contract were registered as owners.

For years, people like that poor woman, Azucena, had thought that they would get a house without paying. Only when they met with the lawyers did they realize there might be some problems. Cruz remembers:

For us, somebody with a sales contract was not a proprietor. We had to explain the situation with the title deed. We spoke different codes. They closed themselves, they were biased against us. Because they had always heard another thing about relocation. There were so many problems. Sometimes they would come with papers that were legally "non-existent." Some had bought their place in the wrong way in various senses: (1) From somebody that was not an owner, (2) With a document which was not suitable. They think that just through the act of paying, they become owners. They do not know they have to see a notary and get the title deed. They consider these things with absolute omission of the official sector. They do not take into account that an instrument has to be opposable to third parties. For them, it is only important that it has value among their group.

The legal situation with the deeds was indeed chaotic. It was partly due to the particular history of Misiones, which was first a part of Corrientes, then a national territory, and finally a province. Because of this, land registration was extremely disorganized. The legal situation was also related to the way people understood property. In Argentine law, a house and the land on which it stands are considered a whole, unless otherwise stated. For many of the neighbors affected by Yacyretá, the houses are movable property which can be taken and installed in various places, preferably on public land. They do know, however, that land may be privately owned and that it can be either purchased or occupied with the permission of the owner. What they do not understand is that all transactions must be legally sanctioned and registered. To most of them, it is enough that the others recognize their claims of ownership of a specific house or plot. They distinguish between those who presumably own the land and those who do not, and they hierarchically position the residents with regards to these criteria. To people like Azucena, who had always looked a little down on the neighbors who were not owners, it was a total shock to hear that, according to EBY and the state, she was also propertyless.

After finding out about the problem with her title deed, she felt so angry that she got together with some neighbors and hired a lawyer. She had to work extra hours to pay for his legal assistance. Besides this, she also attended meetings organized by people from COPROYA and EBY. EBY had told them that they were trying to find the person who had originally sold them the land. EBY's employees had to trace some of these owners in all parts of the republic and even in foreign countries. Azucena and her neighbors had bought the land from Mr. Rolón, the grandson of one of the first Posadas residents. But Mr. Rolón had died years before. EBY had to invite his widow to recognize the sale of the plots. She agreed to do so in some cases, but not in all of them. In the case of Doña Azucena and Don Ruiz, she would not acknowledge the purchase of the land, but instead she admitted their right to make a claim for the structures of their houses. As a result, Doña Azucena and Don Ruiz were from then on considered EBY's beneficiaries with the right to the new houses. They would no longer get them free but would have to pay monthly installments on them. EBY would deduct the value of their current house from the total they were expected to pay.

In 1985, after envoys from Buenos Aires established the final value of the property, Doña Azucena and Don Ruiz were called once again to EBY to sign a final agreement. Juárez, another neighbor, was also invited to go. He was luckier than they because Mrs. Rolón recognized his dealings with her former husband. Consequently, EBY considered him an owner.

During the meeting, EBY told them the sum each neighbor would get for his/her home. A few were unhappy with the amount. Don Juárez remembers the meeting bitterly:

Don Juárez: The other time we went to a meeting at EBY and we made many demands. . . . First, there appeared a guy who looked like Jaroslawski (a national representative), and he said, "O.K. gentlemen."

Gustavo: Don't you remember who the man was?

Don Juárez: It was an old fellow, thin, tall and bald. He said, "Those who are proprietors, who will sign, here are the papers." You may read and you may sign here. If there is anybody . . . a problem, that is no longer my problem, because I am doing my own things. I am doing my own work and it is my duty. Whoever likes the deal, he should sign and we give him the house and *chau* ("bye, bye"). And if somebody doesn't like it, he may remain here, and if water comes, that will be his business. And then, all of us felt astonished. We were like 20, we were all there. He wanted to make us sign, nearly by force.

Gustavo: You were all together?

Don Juárez: Of course, we went together. That is what killed us. He made all of us keep our mouths shut. Because he convinced us. In other words, they had pressed us.

Gustavo: And when was that?

Don Juárez: Last month. We had been arguing since 4 to 8 p.m., four hours. In the end, he made us sign everything. They all fought because they give little money for your plot. They wanted to give you 9,000 or 10,000 australes (Argentine currency in the late 1980s) for the house and the plot to those of us who were owners. But there are two others on the same block (Doña Azucena and Don Ruiz) who were told they were not owners and they were given the same amount. And I do not understand. What are you going to do with that money? You cannot even buy public land. There's nothing you can buy. We all fought against it.

Don Juárez was still unable to distinguish the differences in rights between the owners of plots and houses and those who only got some credit on the improvements. He did not realize that even though the former might get an estimated value, which was roughly the same as the one given to nonowners of the plots, their rights were totally different. In their case, they would not pay any money for the new home. Nonowners, however, would have to pay monthly until the cost of the house was covered. I have found that most of the people who were living in the new settlement areas did not know exactly which definition applied. Many residents still did not know whether they were owners, occupants, or tenants.

In the next and last section, I will examine the reasons why they were unable to say what their current status was.

Interdictions, Contradictions, and Myths about the Poor

Before moving to the new Yacyreta housing project, Azucena had heard various rumors from her neighbors. She felt very anxious at some of the things they had said to her. Don Juárez said he had heard that once the owners gave EBY the title deed from the old house, they would have to wait for more than three years to get the deed of the new home. Moreover, he was also told that he would probably have to pay installments, even if EBY considered him an owner. Azucena knew that this did not fit her case because by then she was aware that she would have to pay, but what worried her was the amount they would charge her. At the beginning, she remembered, they had promised that residents would be charged so little that even a maid who received hourly wages could easily pay. Now, she was hearing that the poorest of those who had already been resettled would be evicted because they could not afford the homes.

Another thing that worried Azucena was what she called the *status quo* law. Some former neighbors had told her it was forbidden to build fences or to make improvements in the houses. EBY, she explained to me, would only allow changes which meet certain construction requirements. "They want us to do everything with bricks or concrete and there is no way we can afford those materials."

When I asked professionals at EBY about these fears, one of them told me it was part of the myths people make. Then he asked me: "Have you been to the neighborhood?" He meant: "Have you seen all the changes they had made?" He was right, or at least, partly right. The fences were among the first things the new residents had built after the move.

The concern with the construction of fences illustrates some of the misconceptions about the poor, even among social scientists. When the houses were in the planning stages, EBY's staff said that the design should respect their own ways. They thought, for example, that a woman would want to see her neighbors and her children while she was washing clothes in the backyard, and hence they recommended that all houses should communicate with the others. This idea proved to be false. Residents wanted to have fences to keep some distance from their neighbors (neither to bother them, nor to be bothered). They were very concerned about their privacy, something most of the social scientists did not expect as a behavior among the poor, since they assumed a sense of community among them (cf. Ferradás 1997). There was indeed a feeling of closeness and cooperation with neighbors, but simultaneously there was a need of separation from them. They justified this through concepts such as "envy." "There is so much envy," Doña Porota once whispered to me," that if you buy a new pair of shoes, everybody criticizes you. That is why I do not want to see them." Fences were also related to a peasant way of life which was revealed both in those who migrated from the countryside to Posadas and among the ones who had lived in the city since they were born. They needed fences, they told me, not to have animals getting into their yards because they might destroy their vegetables and flowers (cf. Ferradás 1997).

The fact that the new residents of the Yacyretá neighborhood had built fences and made improvements did not prove that there were not any prohibitions or restrictions. What it showed, was that even if those rules existed, most of the residents were not afraid of breaking them. In fact, at least until recently, when people were receiving the houses from EBY, they had to sign a contract of *comodatum,* where the comodatario—the person and his/her household with the right of usufruct of the house—agreed:

1. To return the unit at the request of EBY as it is established in Article 2285 of the Civil Law.
2. To verify that the house is given in good condition.
3. Not to introduce any changes and/or to raise any demands for compensation.

EBY did not really enforce the construction requirements, and in general, residents made most of the changes they wished. A lot of the people to be relocated thought that the provincial law of *status quo* which was passed in 1974 and declared unconstitutional in 1983, was still valid. Once people moved into the new homes, they interpreted the conditions stated in the contract as part of such law.

The comodatum also confirmed another fear expressed by most of the people I interviewed: That owners did not get a title deed for the new homes. While we were interviewing proprietors who had been resettled, none of them had a deed, and they were very upset about this. Yacyretá got caught into its own trap. After years of insisting that nobody was an owner unless the person could present a title deed, and after repeating again and again that people should never accept a transaction unless they were given the corresponding proof of property, they were now expecting that people should feel content with contracts of comodatum. EBY justified the situation by saying that, in some cases, the definitive houses were not yet ready, or that, in others, they were waiting to have some legal problems solved. The agency also stated that there was very little personnel to deal with the complexity of most cases. But most of the residents had learned their lesson and wanted what Yacyretá had so well taught them to demand: a legal instrument proving that Yacyretá had not lied to them. Not until they saw the deeds would any of the neighbors stop mistrusting the Entity.

NOTES

1. Everybody in Yacyretá recalled the separation between the two sectors. The pamphlets distributed among the population also revealed such division of labor: "If you still have doubts and if you wish to ask questions: Go to the Office of Attention to the Public of the Entity [Rioja 1640]. Or consult the social worker." (EBY 1980) To make things even more confusing, posters and papers did not refer to OIR but rather to "*La Oficina de Atención al Público de la Entidad*" (Office of Attention to the Public of the Entity).

2. As the results of the 1979 census show, 11percent of the total population to be relocated is illiterate. The most critical group is the age group of 50 year old people or older, which registers 24 percent of the total as illiterate.

3. See Yacyretá's news releases *Crecidas,* "River Floods" (*El Territorio,* June 23, 1993) and *Cuidando al Paraná,* "Taking Care of the Paraná" (*El Territorio,* August 18, 1993).

4. I am following Greimas's (1983:103) concept of the *vraisemblable* (credible) which

refers to the conditions under which people take a discourse as true. I have taken from Bourdieu (1982:59) the notion that discourses are not only signs to be deciphered but that they are also signs denoting authority and wealth.

5. For detailed comments on the legal constraints, see for example, *El Territorio*, August 6, 1985.

CHAPTER 9

Mediating on the People's Behalf?

Nearly twenty years have passed since the first announcement of the construction of Yacyretá and the consequent population displacement was first made in the affected neighborhoods of Posadas. Reactions of the population had varied according to a multiplicity of ever-shifting factors. These factors included the national and local political situation, the advancement of the engineering works, the level of certainty about the completion of the dam and the attitudes toward relocation. As long as the factors changed, the inhabitants of the areas to be flooded were compelled to change their coping strategies. Many of the population to be displaced came to realize, for example, that personalities who had previously been of invaluable help in reaching the authorities within EBY or the local political system proved ineffective once a new provincial government was installed. Choice of mediators has thus been influenced by the recognition that in different conjunctures different positions (and position holders) might be useful in the negotiation process with Yacyretá.

During the military regime, there were few alternatives to dealing with problems created by compulsory relocation. There were also few people and organizations that could act on behalf of the displaced population without risking their own personal security, as well as that of the population. Church representatives furnished this limited group of people because church institutions were favored with some freedom of action. Thus, priests became spokespersons for the concerns of the uprooted neighbors. Such was the case of the priest of San Cayetano church, Vladimiro Lichowski.

With the advent of renewed democratic politics, instances of negotiation multiplied and so did prospective mediators. Neighbors had an array of choices which included a range of political personalities, political brokers living in the affected areas, human-right groups, grass-roots organizations, labor unions, and provincial and municipal institutions. While representatives of some of these visited the neighbors to offer their good auspices, others were sought out actively by community members. Specific persons and organizations were particularly favored and trusted. Nonetheless, no possible mediator was ever totally rejected. As long as they could, the relocated made use of all the available mediators to whom they had access.

In this chapter, I analyze how various mediators were positioned by the other participants in the communicative practices of the relocation process. The existence of these mediators has been hinted at or pointed to in previous chapters. They appeared among those "others," against whom the population, Yacyretá as an entity, and EBY's staff members acquired their own identities. I will now bring them into the foreground and show the obverse side of the coin: how church representatives, politicians, provincial and municipal functionaries and their departmental domains, as well as neighborhood grass-roots organizations became involved and came to participate in the long process of resettlement.

CHURCH AND PEOPLE

I have already described the role played by the church of San Cayetano in the neighborhood where it was built, as well as in the adjacent neighborhoods of Heller and El Chaquito. The church influenced community events and everyday routines in matters as public as soccer games and festivals and as private as marital unions and family size and composition.

The majority of my informants agreed that Father Vladimiro was the driving force behind when they organized the celebration of special holidays and also when they decided to build the chapel, the pride of all the community. He was regarded as an organizer; most neighbors followed him. However, a few of the neighbors we interviewed praised the efforts of the community "to build a church which was the envy of those in the center," but minimized the role played by the priests, for whom they expressed little sympathy.

Even though all the neighbors did not think of Vladimiro in the same manner, he considered that he was entitled to represent them. When, in 1980, Yacyretá announced that 17 families had to be transferred to another sector because it was necessary to clear a site to construct the workshop for the Posadas-Encarnación bridge, he led the protest against this measure. He went to see the governor of Misiones in the company of a group of neighbors. According to the local papers, the priest headed the delegation (see *El Territorio,* January 31, 1980, and *El Libertador,* January 31, 1980). On that occasion, he declared to the journalists: "With regards to this [he refers to EBY's announcement], there had been uneasiness in the neighborhood, which is also mine, as long as I am in charge of them in ecclesiastical matters. I took these families claim as if it were mine. I think we are abandoned" (*El Territorio,* January 31, 1980). Father Vladimiro simultaneously distinguished himself from the neighbors by saying "these families" and "these neighbors," and identified himself with them by using "we" and by saying the neighborhood was his. At the same time, the residents spoke of him as "our father," thus recognizing him as an integral part of the community, and yet different from the rest. They expected from him what they expect from a father— protection and help in critical moments. By this double process of distancing and identification, he could then become the mediator for the population. He continued to play this role as long as the neighbors acknowledged him as a valid interlocutor with authorities.

When the church building was endangered, the father was a mediator and, obviously, at the same time an interested party. As mediator, he was the spokesperson for the residents who had built their own chapel at great sacrifice. As an interested party, he was defending the basis of his power within the community. He tried all the alternatives at his disposal to attract the attention of authorities, from holding mass to processions. As shown in previous chapters, he failed in all his attempts. As a result, not only did he lose the church building, but he also lost the trust of the residents. The neighbors have never made claims through the priests since then, although mass was not suspended with the demolition of the chapel and priests continued visiting the area to celebrate the ceremony in private homes. Everybody agrees that nothing is like it used to be: "We are all dispersed. We were left alone. Then, all people started to change. We could not do anything else. A lot of people left the church. Priests come only on Sundays, but they are always different ones."

The priest was one of the few who could mediate on behalf of the community when all meetings were prohibited under the state of siege declared during the years of El Proceso. Nonetheless, Father Vladimiro's failure in representing the community did not leave it unprotected. Very soon, the demise of the military regime would open new alternative channels for making demands.

Besides the priest, Sister Mariana was another religious figure who, on occasions, would act as a mediator. Doña María admired her: "The *hermanita* (little sister) struggled so much. She helped the poor— those who needed her most." The nun made sure that there was always a priest to hold mass: "I don't know where she brings them from. It must be one that is not busy, because there are so many." She was said to be the one who found the solution to a bitter dispute between the neighbors from San Cayetano who were first resettled in the new Yacyretá houses and those who stayed behind. The conflict erupted because those moving wanted to carry the image of San Cayetano with them. The ones who stayed, greatly resented their exneighbors intentions. Not content with leaving them alone to go to the so-much-desired new homes, they also wanted to take the symbol of the neighborhood. It was like taking a part of their selves. To put an end to the competition for the possession of the saint, Sister Mariana managed to obtain a new image. For some time, there were two San Cayetanos: One *grande* and one *chico* (a big and a small image), the biggest was in the new neighborhood, and the smallest was kept in the homes of the residents of the old quarter; harmony was back among the old neighbors. They visited each other, and when floods occurred, they gave shelter in the new settlement to the ones still living in the affected areas.

LOCAL POWER: THE PROVINCE AND THE MUNICIPALITY

The population thought of the provincial and municipal organizations in the same manner as they did of Yacyretá. To them, "the province" and "the municipality" were also entities, but they lacked the overwhelming power of EBY. Nevertheless, quite often, they were approached for help to find solutions to problems created by the relocation process.

With regard to communication in the relocation process, most professionals I interviewed at EBY did not see any significant changes after the restoration of democracy in Argentina. Nevertheless, communication strategies did vary. While residents barely visited governmental offices during the military years, they increasingly did so with the advent of democracy. This was in part related to the particular stages of the project, and the difficulties each of them generated. It was also due to the way residents of the lowlands of Posadas appraised the military and politicians.

From 1979, the year of the census, until 1982, contacts with government representatives had been rare. After the intense activity of EBY's staff during the first two years, everything slowed down because of personnel reductions and uncertainty about the future of the project. Neighbors went on their own to EBY to ask what was happening, but they had not organized collectively to protest against the delays. Nobody saw the military as potential allies in the negotiations with Yacyretá. In general, members of the armed forces never figured in the people's narratives. On the rare occasions when they did, they were depicted as repressive and as responsible for the successive postponements of the initiation of the engineering works.

In fact, it seems that neighbors were right in not trusting those in government because many of them were said to be involved in corrupt dealings with condemnation settlements—in collusion with some EBY's functionaries.[1] Moreover, the inhabitants of the affected areas knew very well that to the military, the poor were only a nuisance. Indeed, papers and TV news continuously showed how the national government was committed to the "eradication" of slums. The message was always the same: Society had to "extirpate this malaise through surgical treatment."[2] In Posadas, most of the local bureaucrats appointed by the military shared this view of the poor and did not think they deserved new homes. On the occasions when they met with EBY's staff members under pretext of reaching agreements on behalf of the province and the Misioneros, what they were really expecting was that EBY would take care of most of the Posadas squatters. At least, this is how the members of the EBY's staff saw it.

Provincial and municipal authorities and their technical personnel had always claimed to be concerned with the problem of intruders, both the ones living in affected areas with no relocation rights and also other individuals occupying fiscal land. Yacyretá maintained that it had given the municipality a large sum of dollars to find a solution for that sector of the population and that they had not done anything. The sole exception to this was a neighborhood with uninhabitable dwellings constructed through self-help. Even today, the municipality of Posadas cannot satisfactorily explain what happened with the money. In sum, local representatives were more interested in obtaining personal and monetary advantages for one particular sector of the regional society rather than defending the interests of the dispossessed. They were not willing to act as advocates on behalf of the men and women against whom they were very biased. On the contrary, more than once they pursued policies that damaged the individual freedoms of the poor. Social specialists from EBY remember that in the early days, for example, provincial functionaries insisted that prostitutes and single mothers should not be given new houses.

Descriptions of modern states generally see the functioning of bureaucracies as independent from the political actions of the executive and parliamentary branches of the state. In contemporary, "democratic" Misiones province in particular, as well as in Argentina in general, it is hard, if not impossible, to draw a line between bureaucratic and political actions, even if only for analytical purposes. The neighbors from the areas to be flooded themselves found no difference between state bureaucrats and politicians. To them, they were all *políticos*. This phrasing expressesed their disbelief and resentment. They were aware of the manipulation exerted by politicians. They said that before elections they were visited by leaders from all parties: "They tell us: There will be no problem, you will have a house. There were promises for elections which they never keep. Elections passed. We are still waiting." Domingo, a member of the neighborhood commission of El Chaquito, commented that they had invited the governor to see with his own eyes the terrible conditions they were living in and to ask him to do something on their behalf. Then, he added: "We are still waiting."

The case of Alberto "Polo" Gutiérrez is very illustrative of the mistrust and confusion created by the multiple roles of certain individuals identified with the encompassing category of politicians. Polo had become a councilor to EBY's Administrative Council in Buenos Aires through the offices of the former Radical governor of Misiones. Nearly everybody spoke of him as the province representative to Yacyretá. The local newspaper, incidentally owned by Alberto Gutiérrez, referred to him as the Misiones councilor to EBY (see *El Territorio,* October 4, 1988). But at EBY, staff members explained to me that there is no such thing as a provincial representative: Polo was simply a member of the administrative council. In 1987, he was also the Radical candidate for mayor of the city. Obviously, when visiting the affected areas, he was playing with the ambiguity of his position. Obviously, too, he was caught in the contradiction of being simultaneously a member of a contesting Radical party (as a candidate for mayor), the province (as presumed representative to EBY), and EBY (as councilor).

Instead of giving him more power, Polo's varied roles hindered his possibility of interceding on people's behalf. While one social worker acknowledged him as a mediator by identifying him as the province's councilor, as a kind of ombudsman, another social worker denied him such a public identity. Rosa told me the case of two women who came to EBY expecting to get preferential treatment because they were recommended by Polo. She pretended not to know him by saying "Polo, who is he?" The women felt offended and left, slamming the door behind them. Lucía had a different attitude in this matter. When doing field work, she found many cases of people with letters of recommendation written by politicians who had told neighbors they could intercede. Lucía reported to me: "I had to explain to them that these personages had no power to do anything on their behalf, and tell them 'Your councilor is Polo'."

The ambiguities and false expectations created by the politicians upset the EBY's social workers who were in close contact with the population. They complained to me that, when these political figures offered their mediation, they unwittingly caused a lot of harm because they gave wrong advice and raised expectations that were impossible to fulfill. In El Chaquito, Heller, San Cayetano, and in the new Yacyretá neighborhood, some of the areas where the social workers had been more active, I could easily identify the politicians' influence by the way neighbors spoke of them. In some cases, neighbors were explicit about the source of their opinions:

Dorotea: The politicians who came here, like the Governor and Polo would tell us that we would move soon. But the licenciada told us that those were things that politicians say. They, Yacyretá, will tell us when to leave.

The one thing that all Yacyretá staff members agreed on was their disdain and annoyance with politicians and government officials. García complained that a lot of the local political leaders went to the neighborhoods and distorted information because they were badly informed and did not make a great effort to obtain the correct data. Rosa remembered that during the electoral campaign government officials would pressure EBY's employees and decision-makers to move some specific areas first. On one occasion, they succeeded in their request. But at another time, the social workers accompanied authorities while touring the affected areas to demonstrate that conditions were much worse in other sectors not favored by the government's mediation. Rosa was convinced that through doing this they managed to make authorities change their minds. Nearly every professional I interviewed at Yacyretá had an anecdote about the inefficiency and ignorance of politicians. They had the same negative opinion about the more technical offices set by the local municipality and by the provincial government to deal specifically with problems related to Yacyretá.

Supposedly, the municipality of Posadas had always had a commission, the COMUYA (Municipal Commission for Yacyretá), created for the purpose of negotiating issues related to the dam. When I started my field work, I went to the information desk of the municipality to locate this commission. Nobody was aware it existed. After consulting with various employees, they finally sent me to another building where there were other municipal offices. Again, no one in this second building knew about the commission with the exception of an employee who said that there was an architect who sometimes went to meetings involving Yacyretá. I tried to see this person several times, but his office was generally closed. Evidently, very few neighbors would attempt to get the help of the local city government if it was nearly impossible to identify who was in charge of EBY matters. This situation changed considerably in the 1990s, when the municipality created the position of ombudsman to mediate on the citizens' behalf. In the next chapter, I describe how some municipal officials encouraged and supported popular action against EBY.

Although COPROYA had existed for nearly ten years, it was not until the restoration of democracy that it began to take a more active role with regards to relocation problems. The vice-governor of Misiones became the new head of COPROYA after it was reorganized during the Radical administration. At one time, the staff included one social worker, three architects, and a lawyer. The staff composition reflected a common pattern in the recruitment of professionals in the province: They circulated through posts in the national agencies, local administration, the national university, and, more recently the NGOs. A social worker and the recently appointed executive director of COPROYA had previously worked at EBY. An architect, who was a COPROYA technician, was later employed by EBY. One of the social workers at EBY later became an advisor to the governor on hydrolectric projects. This phenomenon had an effect on the way the commission operated.

Since EBY's salaries were significantly higher than those offered by the province, some COPROYA staff members might try to be on good terms with the relocation agency in the hope of getting a contract at EBY. Instead of confronting EBY and trying to find solutions for the relocation problems, they let EBY indicate what they should do. In other words, they were—or allowed themselves to be—co-opted. What is sometimes interpreted by analysts as inefficiency and irrationality in a bureaucrat's behavior may actually be efficient and rational in regards to the aims of the organization. A state functionary may be more interested in getting a job in the private sector than in controlling outcomes in the name of his current employer.

On the other hand, former EBY employees might be resentful and biased against the relocation agency in a way that kept them from seeing the best solutions and from negotiating on behalf of the province and the population. This is what occurred in the case of Horacio Paz, COPROYA's executive director in the late 1980s. When he spoke of EBY's staff members he disparaged them professionally and morally. A few of his remarks made me feel uncomfortable. His allegations were the same made by the secret services about EBY's staff. He also appropriated the discourse of human rights activists, which—coming from him—sounded frighteningly out of place. I could not help taking his statements as a personal threat: "Yacyretá is a violation of human rights; it violated their rights with its arrogance." He insisted on this throughout the interview in a way that sounded more like a warning than a commentary on EBY. He then asked me who I was writing this for and when I told him it was for a study to be published in the United States, he said: "It is important that you do this, because Americans really appreciate the truth!"

Conversely, EBY's staff thought of Paz as negatively as he did of them. Before I interviewed him, some of my acquaintances at EBY told me that when he worked there he was very authoritarian, that he was a misogynist, a *cursillista*,[3] and a friend of the military. Obviously, given this mutual dislike, it is unimaginable to expect a dialogue with the purpose of reaching an understanding between the head of COPROYA and Yacyretá employees.

Paz was in close contact with delegates of some of the neighborhood commissions. I realized this through comparing the texts I obtained when I interviewed each of them. What he said was strikingly similar to what one of the members of a neighborhood commission told me. The resemblances revealed the exchange of information and the sharing of bias. The two were very critical of the social sector and employed exactly the same adjectives to characterize those they despised, namely the social workers García (the supervisor) and Mabel (who used to live in

El Chaquito). The two social workers were accused of dividing the neighbors and of favoring some in particular. Both Paz and the delegate Domingo reveal their biases in the way they addresed the population: "these people," "they are better off in a hut," "they need to be educated to use the new houses." The two men also employed the same expression that established an analogy between the functioning of the Jesuit empire of the eighteenth century and that of the EBY. A document of the *Justicialista* party made public shortly before provincial elections for governor conveyed the same opinion of EBY:

Until now, this Entity has been for the Misioneros like *a state within a state*, a separate republic, the reign of the consultants, where any mediocre foreign or native functionary has planned and decided with a greater power than any of the sectors of the government which razed Misiones during these seven years of this "process of national destruction." (*El Territorio*, October 15, 1987)

This document was written before Paz became head of COPROYA but after he left EBY. Another part of the newspaper article revealed that he participated in the writing of the declaration:

We wish to state to the *conductores* (administrators) of that Entity some questions about issues that go beyond the high walls of that bastion of La Rioja street [EBY's address], despite prohibitions of access imposed on some former functionary who is concerned for the abandonment and submision of the local administration, mainly in the area of relocation. (*El Territorio*, October 15, 1987)

Paz argued that EBY infringed the original guidelines for relocation which established "functional replacement in accordance with inventory."[4] He interpreted that this meant that EBY should return to the population a house which was the exact equivalent to the one they had before. Thus, according to him, a hut should be replaced with another one. He maintained that, by constructing houses of a much better quality than the *ranchos* of "those people," EBY was not keeping the promises stated in the guidelines and was forcing the relocated population to pay monthly installments they could not afford. He suggested that the affected population should ask for the houses in *comodatum*. EBY's staff opposed this on the grounds that such a legal formula left the population in a vulnerable situation because it only granted the usufruct of the property. The technical staff of COPROYA shared this opinion.

Professionals at COPROYA complained about the same things as their counterparts at EBY: "Politicians are a burden. They do not understand anything and give the wrong advice with only the purpose of gaining political support." Victoria López told me that she disagreed with the provincial authorities because they suggested to the people already resettled that they not pay for the installments on the new homes. She recommended to neighbors in the new Yacyretá quarter that they continue paying until a law that changes the conditions was passed. Victoria complained that the functionaries are immoral, they only want to get votes:

They promise that they will get a *comodatum* for a hundred years. They think everything is easy. But there is no legal instrument. Because I respect the people, I cannot create false expectations. Then, just because I confront them [authorities at COPROYA], they tell me I am a Radical [member of the Radical party].

I do not know how, thinking so differently than her boss, Victoria managed to continue in her job. She was very aware of the gap between professional expertise and politicians and was also very critical of the role played by the provincial government. She believed that the province could not do much with regards to EBY because the local government lacked a clear project for regional development. As they could not define their own alternatives, they made demands and questions which were out of place. When authorities from EBY asked local authorities to tell them what they wanted and needed, they did not know what to answer. She felt that COPROYA's professionals were better informed by reading the papers than by talking to their bosses and complained that there was no dialogue between the politicians in charge of decision-making and the technicians. She was convinced that the provincial government would be in a better position to negotiate with EBY if authorities consulted with the technicians.

In contrast to what is generally believed by followers of the Weberian model of bureaucracy, in Misiones (as in the rest of Argentina) no position is wholly stable. Indeed, nearly all the bureaucratic positions that do have some decision-making power are both vulnerable and insecure. They are reserved to those loyal to the ruling political party. The ruling party cannot "risk" placing anyone from the opposition or a neutral individual in an office charged with interacting directly with common citizens, especially if this interaction is related to social-welfare services. Every government office is seen as a strategic resource to be used with political purposes. Each unit of government is marked by a permanent tension between "technical" considerations and "political" interests as has just been illustrated.

COPROYA changed its organization, goals, location, and even communication styles following changes in the executive branch of the provincial government. With the Radical administration, it moved its offices a number of times. When I first interviewed the staff, they were sharing the building with other departments. Employees did not see their boss, the vice-governor, very often but, instead, they enjoyed a great freedom of action. The technicians could design their working strategies in the neighborhoods and coordinate lines of action with other areas of government. However, they lacked resources and had limited access to higher levels of decision-making.

After Peronists won the local elections in 1987, they modified the 1984 Decree 1369 through which COPROYA was officialy created. They passed a new decree (463) which provided COPROYA with a hierarchical structure. It was composed of the provincial ministers, the mayor of Posadas, and the newly created post of executive director. The vice-governor continued presiding over the commission (see Boletín Oficial 7294, May 4, 1988). The executive director had his office next to that of the vice-governor and shared the secretaries with him. He received the neighbors who wanted to make claims. He told his staff that he was also the only person in COPROYA authorized to give information to outsiders, unless he gave special permission to do otherwise. This rupture with a more fluid and egalitarian access between the population and COPROYA's staff was legitimized by arguing that the new government had granted this office with the "hierarchy" it deserved.

The technicians were not very far away from their boss, just one block from the house of government, where their offices were located on an upper floor of an apartment building. On the street level, there was no visible indication of its location. I visited this office on various occasions. The room was very spacious with only three desks. In its barrenness, the office looked even larger. I have never seen any neighbor in this office. They did not seem to go there very regularly.

COPROYA's staff sometimes went to the neighborhoods to offer help. They were particularly interested in those beneficiaries without *capacidad de pago* (credit worthiness), terms which are interpreted in a different manner than at EBY. At COPROYA, they alluded to the individuals who could not afford to pay for a lawyer, taxes, or installments. To COPROYA, it did not matter whether these were property owners or not. To EBY's staff, the term referred to a very specific category of beneficiaries: Those who did not own the property where they lived and whose income was so low that they would not be able to pay for the monthly installments. In general, COPROYA did not take individual cases because it lacked the resources to do so. COPROYA's lawyers and social workers tried to solve collective problems, like those shared by most of the neighbors in EL Chaquito, who lacked title deeds for the plots they thought they had acquired through paying monthly installments for years. Negotiations for these issues were very difficult and costly, and residents did not have either the knowledge to deal with the complex bureaucratic paper work nor the money to pay for seals, photocopies, certifications, and legal advice.

Silvia Juárez, the lawyer, told me of numerous dramatic cases for which she could do little. When there were legal problems, Yacyretá attorneys told the beneficiaries to come back with a lawyer. As they were unable to hire one, they asked province authorities for advice and ended up in COPROYA. The only thing she could do was to tell them how to do the paper work and give them directions on where to go to get all the documentation needed. But there were problems which were beyond her capabilities.

COPROYA's professionals said that residents complained to them that they did not understand what EBY told them. Members of the provincial commission wondered why they were understood while people at EBY were not. Luisa, an architect, thought: "Maybe they need an external affirmation." Irene, another architect, added:

It is possible they do not understand because of the image they have of EBY. They are afraid of it and that [fear] inhibits communication. When people from Yacyretá go [to the neighborhoods], they all say that everything is all right. Afterwards, problems start. They do not tell anything to the Entity. Probably, it is because there is a paternalistic relationship.

As already mentioned, COPROYA was basically set to mediate on behalf of the province and its inhabitants, but its membership interpreted the goals very differently depending on the positions occupied within the agency. Those holding higher positions in the hierarchical structure and with greater decision-making power were more likely to respond or to define such goals politically. Conversely, those in lower positions tended to defend a "technical and neutral approach." Yet in such a highly politicized environment, it was hard, if not impossible, to claim neutrality. Even if the professional tried to keep herself/himself apart from partisan politics, his/her suggested lines of actions would receive a political reading. Despite partisan pressures stemming from the higher levels of government, professionals insisted on maintaining the independence of technical knowledge. In part, this constituted a strategy to survive in such a context. The technical staff claimed that they filled a dual role as translators at COPROYA. They had to explain to the population what Yacyretá had already communicated to them, and they had to convince decision-makers of the advantages of various policies and programs.

GETTING POLITICAL CLIENTS

The population to be relocated and the Misioneros in general regarded government actions, including those from the state bureaucratic sector, as an expression of the ruling political party. Indeed, as the previous section shows, the influence of the party in power might be felt in every sector of the local administration. However, when people talked about politicians, they did not only think of those in government, they also had members of the political parties in mind. Although not in very high esteem, political parties were seen as a necessary evil. EBY's beneficiaries counted on them as a source of counseling, mediation, and special benefits. Benefits included things as diverse as free mail, telephone calls, bus and airplane tickets, and the use of political party facilities for meetings. These benefits were, undoubtedly, invaluable resources for a population with a meager income and with no direct access to such services. No offer from any party was rejected as long as it contributed to meeting some of their needs. Political preferences, however, were basically distributed between the two major parties. And of the two, the majority favored the *Justicialista* because as more than one informant commented "they worry more about the *pobrerío* (poor people)."

Shortly before democratic elections, all parties became active in the areas to be resettled and made public their position regarding Yacyretá. Nobody opposed the project. On the contrary, they pressed authorities to hurry the negotiations with Paraguay so as to definitely start the engineering works. The return of political parties to public life was allowed during the days of the Malvinas War[5] (1982). It was made possible because the military regime needed the support of the whole citizenry. Mr. Domenech, currently a Misiones representative to the National Congress, resumed his involvement in Yacyretá's issues as soon as political activity was permitted. He was leading one of the factions in which Peronism was divided at that time. To some, Domenech's group was the most "intellectual." Apart from his political activity, this leader was a member of the *Junta* of Historical Studies of Misiones, which was composed of Misioneros concerned with finding an identity through studying their past. Imbued with a Misionero ideology, he had always represented the interests of Misiones against the "insensitive central power of EBY Buenos Aires" (see *El Territorio*, November 14, 1982). As most of Misioneros, he believed that the "center" ignored the local human resources, including the local (but national) university which he considered of the "highest level." He used to say that what happened with Yacyretá "was the result of dependency and of federalism which is praised but not practiced." With regards to relocation, he maintained that people did not understand many issues because nobody tried to explain anything to them. Domenech postulated that development should be humanistically oriented and include the active participation of the population (*El Territorio,* November 14, 1982). Nevertheless, he knew that limitations to this existed which were inherent in the characteristics of the project. He told us that EBY's goal, the relocation, was compulsory and consequently authoritarian. And then he added that it could not be otherwise.

As a politician and as a national representative, Domenech had presented various projects to congress on the Yacyretá dam. The most controversial was one passed in 1986 which suggested that Yacyretá's headquarters be moved to Posadas, arguing that the city would be suffering the greatest social impact. This proposal outraged the Correntinos who protested by saying that the dam would be located in their territory. Probably remembering how Misiones took the city of Posadas from Corrientes at the turn of last century, a Correntino paper said: "In Misiones, political parties, and not only the ruling one, are determined to take from Corrientes what belongs to it" (see *El Litoral*, September 3, 1986). Although the argument to move the headquarters was made on behalf of the population to be relocated, the move was sought for other reasons. It would serve as a symbol of the power of Misiones over its previous "mother province," and it would contribute to the assertion of the local identity, a major concern of the Misioneros.

Political parties started to play a more active and radical role in opposing the nation-state's decisions regarding Yacyretá when it became apparent that the Argentine president was determined to sell it at a "vile price" without public consent, and when there was no clear indication about the completion of relocation and environmental programs. As we will see in the next chapter, at times politicians acted in association with the affected population; at other times; they interacted in other arenas, obtaining considerable success.

GRASS-ROOTS MEDIATIONS: NEIGHBORHOOD ORGANIZATIONS

Neighborhood commissions are supposedly nonpartisan. Their statutes generally state that members should abstain from political proselytizing. Despite their own regulations, most of these commissions furnish arenas of struggle in which different political parties and factions compete for control. Occasionally, attempts to control them politically are led by the local government by setting a special office to coordinate the relations between Posadas quarters and the municipality (the Office of Neighborhood Affairs). Neighbors are aware of the political manipulations of various members of the commission and comment: "They are only active before elections."

Politics is not the only source of conflict within these commissions. A common complaint against these grass-roots organizations is that they operate "for the benefit of some of the members' pockets." Doña Tomasa, from Bajada Vieja, once told me: "You know how these things are, they fix everything for their own benefit. And they do not take care of the others. Everything is arranged between *compadres*, and *comadres,* as the saying goes."

In every neighborhood where we did field work we heard the same remarks. We found people who said they would never sacrifice for others because nobody cooperates: "The only thing they do is to accuse us, who work, of being thieves." We also found those who said that the commissions organize social gatherings and sell food, "but nobody knows where the money goes."

Mistrust, suspicions, and political in-fighting did not contribute to the stability of these organizations. Because of these continual conflicts, very few could maintain a large following. However, when problems became very acute, neighbors would temporarily forget their disputes and unite to make collective claims. The commissions from El Chaquito and San Cayetano used to be the most active in articulating their claims. The reason why neighbors sought the mediation of these commissions might in part derive from the fact that they were faced with the disastrous living conditions created by the floods of 1983 and with the construction of the complementary engineering works. But the explanation for a greater involvement of these organizations on behalf of the residents must be sought in the history and in the strong identity of these two communities.

Major problems created or associated with the dam project brought the neighbors together in order to make collective demands. First, in 1982, neighbors from San Cayetano went to the government house and to the local newspaper to explain the situation created with 17 families who were asked to leave but were only offered compensation money because EBY had not yet started to build the new homes. On that occasion, as discussed earlier in this chapter, they had to negotiate with the help of their priest, as this was the only safe way to protest during those days. A year later, commissions from all the areas to be relocated demanded immediate resettlement because all the affected areas were suffering one of the greatest floods of the century. Ever since the great flood of 1983, the grass-roots organizations from San Cayetano and El Chaquito had been writing letters and visiting authorities, politicians, and various local organizations to explain their situation and ask for support. To make claims, they adopted the methods they had learned from the "social" area of EBY and from government sectors. They took a census of the affected families, gave the number of each household folder, and also estimated the number of intruders.

Unlike the COPROYA, the neighborhood commission from El Chaquito did have a seal. It also had a hierarchical structure. All their letters were signed at least by their president and their vice-president. Since 1983, they had been sending numerous letters to the authorities. They sent copies of each letter addressed to any authority to the rest of the local personalities. Demands included exemption from taxes in view of the fact that they were no longer getting any public services, resolution of legal problems regarding their title deeds, and immediate relocation both for the EBY's beneficiaries and for the intruders to whom they extended their solidarity but from whom they distinguished themselves.

Members of the executive council of these commissions presumed that COPROYA was created because of their mediation and they also said that many neighbors were finally resettled as a result of the organization's struggles. The rest of the neighbors, local authorities, and EBY employees did not acknowledge these claims of power.

Many social scientists and politicians romanticize grass-roots organizations and think that they always represent an expression of popular resistance and class consciousness. Others take them as an index of the successful integration of the community. Their absence is seen as an anomaly, as a sign of anomie or poor consciousness. It has always puzzled me why middle-class intellectuals and politicians expect the poor to act collectively whereas they simultaneously defend privacy and individuality for themselves (or at least they do not force their social equals into participatory enterprises). In the Yacyretá relocation process the action of the neighborhood commissions and the participation of the community had not always developed as a spontaneous response. On the contrary, more than once it had been pursued by social planners rather than neighbors.

The Yacyretá beneficiaries who had already been resettled were not willing to be involved in commissions or to participate in other forms of organization. Most of them said they had no time to go to meetings and that they needed those hours to make money to buy staples for their household. Although they were still concerned with specific issues, such as the monthly installments and the issuance of deeds, the majority of them were very satisfied and happy with their new houses. They saw no reason to get organized, mainly because every problem they had with regards to the houses or the neighborhood was solved by Yacyretá. However, the social workers insisted that they should have a commission and encouraged them to have elections to form them. For example, Susana asked Antonia:

Susana: And when you have a problem, where do you go to?

Antonia: There is a commission that they had elected, a commission to speak with the people.

Susana: Who chose it?

Antonia: They had given us some leaflets to choose the commission. They had called us to the plaza to choose the commission, and they had explained to us what it was for.

In some cases, the social workers succeeded and a few commissions were formed. Most did not last long. Many residents still did not see why they should have them and expected EBY to tell them what to do with them. EBY was caught in its own contradictions. It had set a paternalistic *modus operandi* which reinforced the traditional mode of relating to authorities, but it expected people to demonstrate their ability to organize and act autonomously because that was a sign of the success of the social programs. As reality did not operate in the desired way, they tried to modify it to make it fit into their ideal model. People ended up participating not by choice, but rather by command.

NOTES

1. A newspaper article commented sarcastically that it was strange that members of the *Tribunal Nacional de Tasaciones* (National Tribunal of Valuation) were simultaneously holding jobs at EBY. Both positions, the paper said, were full time. With this, corrupt behavior was implied, as there was incompatibility of functions (see *Convicción*, June 10, 1980). It was also suggested that this corruption was apparent in the sums paid for Heller and for the meat processing plant: 27 million and 4.5 million U.S. dollars, respectively (see *El Territorio*, February 27, May 7, June 15, October 18, October 21, December 12, 1980).

2. Hermitte and Boivin (1985) discussed the policies of forced population displacement and eradication during the years of El Proceso in the city Buenos Aires. Eradication was distinguished from relocation because the former did not include any provisions to place the people in new settlements. In Posadas, authorities and the press employed the same terminology. An article in *El Territorio* announced: "The Province has received an important subsidy. It will be used for eradication of *viviendas de emergencia* (emergency houses; the euphemistic way to refer to the houses of the poor) in Posadas and Oberá" (June 6, 1980).

3. *Cursillistas* are Catholics who participate in "courses of Christianity." To call somebody a *cursillista* also identifies that person as politically oriented to the extreme right wing. With regards to Paz, some informants also said he was de colores" (of colors), an extreme rightist church group which functions as a sect. This group, together with the Opus Dei, enjoyed great ascendancy over the military government.

4. In Spanish: *Reposición funcional a nivel de inventario*. It means that all the infrastructure affected by the hydroelectric project should be replaced with new infrastructure which fulfills the same function.

5. The war between Argentina and Great Britain over sovereignity on the Malvinas islands (known in Great Britain as Falklands).

CHAPTER 10

People Resist at Last

Years ago, speaking about Yacyretá, a social scientist from the World Bank commented to me that this project was one of the few that successfully handled relocation because it did not encounter major opposition from the population. He attributed this to an effective social planning. I responded that irrespective of the social planning—which was not always followed because of lack of funding and often lack of commitment from EBY—the major reason why there was not much resistance in the first years of the project should be attributed to the desire to obtain the promised quaint resettlement homes. People stoically underwent postponements and the worsening of their living conditions in the hope of becoming owners of red-tile-roofed houses located in areas free from floods. I doubt that the World Bank's expert would dare to judge Yacyretá as a success story nowadays. As discussed in previous chapters, the binational agency lacks the resources to build the homes for relocation and even attempted, unsuccessfully, to avoid constructing them altogether. Not surprisingly, it is precisely the failure to satisfy the expectations regarding the houses that has triggered the resistance and bitterness of the population.

This chapter discusses the emergence of movements both in Paraguay and Argentina, the escalation of resistance against the project, and the incomplete (albeit at one point quite effective) transnationalization of the movement of the people affected by the dam.

Critics of development and the establishment of the new social order suggest that we should seek greater communication and transnational and transcultural strategies to challenge them (Escobar and Alvarez 1992, see also Kearney 1996). In the same vein, others stress that we should more thoroughly examine the role played by global agents in fostering these connections (Mato 1996). This chapter is concerned with both issues as they pertain to the Yacyretá case. I highlight the conditions under which popular action became transnationalized, I look at the role played by various actors in mediating relations in the global arenas, and I examine the factors which hindered, as well as the ones which facilitated, positive outcomes.

Although studies concerned with situating social action in space have proliferated recently, very few have examined the role played by place in the development of social movements. Routledge's (1993) study of "terrains of resistance" in India is probably one of the few works attempting to explore the contestation of space in social struggles. Like Routledge's study, in this analysis of the population's actions regarding Yacyretá, I look both at the physical place where people's responses are enacted and the process by which people assign meanings to particular spaces. As I will demonstrate, choice of particular places of action expresses people's perception of the changing nature of power within the project. Also, because the project occurs in the borderlands of two nation-states, we will observe a variety of spatial identities at work. Structures of feeling (Williams 1973, Appadurai 1996b) related to locality are mobilized in the confrontations with the two nation-states. Sometimes, locality is understood in an inclusive way that ignores national borders, in that case distinctions such as Posadeños and Encarnacenos become irrelevant, and the affected men and women perceive themselves as regional victims with a shared history. At other times, the prevailing identities are those that identify the struggles as those of residents of cities or provinces but within a national territory. However, despite deliberate efforts by diverse actors to minimize national boundaries, grievances made as citizens of a nation-state still prevail, mainly in Paraguay, for reasons I will attempt to identify. I also seek to show that ironically, when global forces try to erase national boundaries through integrating the regional economies into common markets and shared resources, such as the production of energy, they revitalize and/or produce local forms in unexpected ways, mainly among those who are excluded.

THE PLIGHT OF THE ENCARNACENOS

When I started studying Yacyretá, I could only research the Argentine side because foreign researchers, especially from Argentina, were not welcome under Stroessner's regime in Paraguay. Yacyretá was a sensitive national issue, and the key information regarding relocation was carefully guarded, not only from me, but also from EBY's Argentine partners. Since the beginning of the project, there was an agreement that every investment on one side had to be replicated on the other side of the border, in what was customarily called "mirror effect." However, Argentines always complained that although they were providing the resources, they could never confirm whether they were invested properly. Animosity against Argentina increased during Alfonsín's government because he strongly advocated human rights and had friendly relations with the opposition parties.

After the fall of Stroessner in 1989, following similar processes in the Southern Cone, Paraguay announced that it would have free elections. In 1993, with democratization processes underway, I decided that time was ripe to venture into the analysis of the Paraguayan experience with Yacyretá. I was not the only one who delved into the neighborhoods to be flooded in Paraguay; that same year, the renewed Posadeño grass-roots organization also contacted their Paraguayan "brothers."

My attempts to interview Yacyretá's staff both in Asunción and Encarnación failed. In the latter city, my brief encounter with the head of the local program convinced me that times had not changed as much as I had presumed. I was interrogated and "subtly" threatened with the same intimidating techniques I knew so well from living under an authoritarian and repressive regime in my own country. Although frustrating, the experience was instructive. It showed me the kind of institutional structure the population confronted. Indeed, a priest working among the affected families commented that Yacyretá's executives acted like the Colorado party: "They want to conceal everything, they do not want anybody to poke their noses, they do not want anybody to see anything, and afterwards they say they had transparent elections. Yacyretá has hidden the reality from everybody. Nobody knows anything."

Unlike in Posadas, where the areas to be flooded are predominantly populated by the poor, in Encarnación the areas to be flooded include some of the most dynamic commercial and industrial sections of the city. Most of the economic prosperity of the low areas is based on the particular frontier economy which developed throughout the years. In the vicinity of the port, which until recently was the only entry point for people coming from Posadas, hundreds of shops mushroomed to offer the goods that Argentines could not afford in their own territory because of striking differences in their taxation system. Even today after the adoption of free market policies and the MERCOSUR agreements that pursue a uniform taxing system for imported goods, Posadas merchants cannot compete with their neighbors' prices for certain goods (including smuggled ones and Argentine products which are sold at a lower price). Rather than dying slowly while waiting for relocation, this section of the city has boomed in the last decade. It has also attracted impoverished peasants from elsewhere and former laborers of the Itaipú dam who had been left jobless after the completion of the project, many of whom joined the busy commercial activity by becoming street vendors of the most varied commodities. Because of these different realities, Yacyretá has faced a much more complex relocation challenge. In addition to finding homes for squatters, who also inhabit some of the riverine neighborhoods, the binational agency has to develop solutions to resettle or compensate for the various business that occupy the floodable sectors. The greatest difficulty, from the perspective of EBY's interests, is that, contrary to the Posadas case, in Encarnación a large group of the displaced are well connected to the decision-making levels and possess the economic resources for taking legal action. Since the beginning, the *Centro de Comercio e Industria* (Center of Commerce and Industry) actively negotiated with EBY and with municipal and national authorities. In the late 1980s, they were already coordinating their activities with other groups: the *Asociación de Comerciantes e Inquilinos* (Association of Merchants and Tenants), *Asociación de Comerciantes Propietarios* (Association of Commercial Business Owners), *Asociación de Industriales Ceramistas* (Association of Ceramics Industrialists), and representatives from only two neighborhoods.[1] These groups represent an array of sectorial and class interests which were not always compatible. In the original organization, they reproduced the hierarchical, authoritarian, and paternalistic style dominant in the larger society. They spoke in the name of the poorer sectors to whom they denied participation.

Overall, they made claims well in tune with their sectorial interests. The merchants, who generally led the negotiations, were concerned with property assessments, which included a "fair" consideration of their profits and possible losses, and with obtaining a strategic location for resettling their commercial activities. Through time, a more inclusive *Comisión Intersectorial de Afectados por la Represa de Yacyretá* (Intersectoral Commission of Peoples Affected by the Dam of Yacyretá) developed, and at times, they coordinated collective action. In April 1992, for example, they marched along the downtown streets of Encarnación. That same year, they traveled to Asunción and concentrated in front of congress to push for legislation, finally approved, that guaranteed the participation of the affected population in the appraisal of damages and property values. Their actions were actively supported, and even encouraged, by the mayor of Encarnación, who obviously had a vested interest in the outcome. He presumed that the law would also favor the city which had been investing in many improvements, even after the announcement of dam construction.

The Intersectorial Commission formed by various local organizations, including the municipality, was quite similar to another multisectorial commission operating in Posadas. Both had regular meetings with EBY representatives. In the two cases, these commissions are remembered as relatively successful attempts at bridging the communication gap between EBY and local groups.

Some sectors did not feel satisfied with those more powerful who said they represented their interests. Tenants, and poor residents, both intruders and occupants of land with relocation rights, held goals which conflicted with those of the well-to-do. In 1986, for example, the mayor of Encarnación opposed the relocation program, arguing that the neighborhoods were different. She reasoned that because people's activities, needs, and socio-economic backgrounds were so distinct, they should be resettled in separate spaces. She disagreed with the proposed houses because there were no substantial differences among them. Assuming the representation of the poorest residents, to whom she euphemistically referred as rural men, she maintained that to them, radical changes in their lives did not mean progress. In sum, she voiced the concern of the richer families who did not want to mix themselves with a social sector traditionally despised and excluded. Yacyretá was a threat to the existing system of class relations (cf. *HOY*, August 20, 1986; *Ultima Hora*, August 25, 1986).

In 1993, residents from the poorer areas, discontent with what in their judgment were "bureaucratic" organizations, decided to form a new commission, the *Coordinadora de Barrios y Sectores Afectados por el Embalse de Yacyretá* (Coordinating Committee of Neighborhoods and Sectors Affected by the Yacyretá Dam), to represent the interests of the neighborhoods which until then had been ignored in the negotiations. One of the members attributed its beginnings to the visit of a group of ecologists: A Canadian, a German, a Uruguayan, and a Paraguayan sociologist. The Posadeños experienced a similar encouragement from an NGO which I will discuss later. Also, the two groups received advice from, as well as had some members active in, the rural movements. At the time of my initial interviews during that year, 13 neighborhoods integrated the commission.

Concerned with the lack of response and the imminence of the raising of the river level with the operation of the first turbines, the *coordinadora* secretly organized its first massive demonstration. It is interesting to note the sites considered to manifest dissatisfaction with the current state of affairs: (1) the closing of Route 1, which connects Encarnación and Asunción; (2) the closing of the newly constructed bridge, which connects Encarnación and Posadas; (3) a gigantic demonstration within the community.

About 2,000 residents finally cut off the highway which connects their city to the capital and said they would not leave unless the newly elected president came to see them. Members of this group consistently repeated they were tired of technicians who were charlatans and demanded that they be heard by those who held the real power. They stopped their blockade at the promise of an audience with the new president.

Juan Salgado, one of the members who had strong ties with the Paraguayan peasant movement and who had been a militant of the left for years, praised the democratic and participatory nature of the organization and insisted that it did not want upper-class peoples: "This should be in the hands of the popular sector." He was also proud of the massive attendance of delegates at meetings, between fifty and sixty, which I had the opportunity to witness. He also emphasized the nonpartisan spirit of the new coordinadora. He insisted on the differences between the modest brickmakers and the ceramics industrialists (tile producers) and suggested that the coordinadora was more interested in the former. The organization took a census and established that some of the affected peoples demanded compensation and provision of clay in the case of the brickmakers; those who owned the land expressed that they wanted new land for their activities. It also required solutions for the families who had not been registered in the last EBY census from 1989.

In 1993, its motto was "No filling of the reservoir, no starting of the turbines, until the relocation and environmental problems were solved." Imbued with the fashionable discourse of corruption, the organization employed it to include those who first articulated it. National authorities and EBY's administrators were the corrupt ones: the followers of Stroessner, because they managed to change the rural zones into urban to obtain greater and early compensation; and EBY's administrators, because they appropriated so much money that "even one of them celebrated his daughter's sweet fifteen by putting cake ribbons with a key to a brand-new Volvo." Members of the coordinadora felt that the early compensations were an injustice. To amend this, they asked that the government modify a new law which classified their land as rural. Antonio Ramírez insisted that property valuations should be done with fairness, as in Argentina.

THE PLIGHT OF THE POSADEÑOS

Shortly after Argentina returned to democracy in 1983, human rights organizations such as *Paz y Justicia* started to discuss their goals under the new conditions.

In Posadas, local intellectuals, including university professors and students predominantly connected to the anthropology department, joined this group, bringing their baggage of fashionable watchwords in the transformed discursive formation. Some of the favorite watchwords were "participatory democracy," "communication," and "citizenship." Imbued with Paulo Freire's idea of popular critical consciousness, they wanted to facilitate the creation of networks of groups from popular sectors. One of the major objectives was to redefine their understanding of human rights once the repressive dictatorship was on the wane. According to a former member, they wanted "to know who were the social actors, what the major social problems were, where was the locus of political action." They started to define rights in a broader sense. The group identified the right of development as one of the goals to pursue under the new democratic conditions. It was organized as an NGO.

This did not occur in isolation. Similar trends were occurring on a global scale. In 1986, the United Nations defined development as a right. Also at that time, unlikely actors such as the International Monetary Fund (IMF) and the World Bank advocated democracy and praised the role played by NGOs in guaranteeing a more democratic and effective participation of the people in development.

It was in this context that *Paz y Justicia* (SERPAJ, Peace and Justice) began working to facilitate grass-roots organizations among the people affected by dams. It established networks with various local ecological and rural organizations, including the Brazilian *Sem Terra* (landless peasant movements), the *Atingidos por Barragens* (affected by dams), and women movements. Working with participatory techniques, they organized meetings to discuss the social and ecological impact of the projects. They concentrated most of their efforts on the Yacyretá dam.

Two men, one from SERPAJ, and one from a neighborhood commission became key actors in the early years of what later became the *Coordinadora de Comisiones Vecinales Afectadas por Yacyretá* (Coordinating Agency of Neighborhood Commissions Affected by Yacyretá). Tomás Díaz, from SERPAJ, was not new in grass-roots organizing. Before coming to Posadas, he had participated in land seizures in Buenos Aires. Don Jiménez, on the other hand, had years of involvement in neighborhood commissions. One of his concerns was the number of people living in the affected areas without relocation rights. The coordinadora decided to take a census and found that around 1,500 households did not have any relocation rights. Under Don Jiménez's leadership, community delegates began to discuss common strategies to negotiate their resettlement rights. It was at this time that they started to hold periodic meetings with municipal and provincial representatives and EBY's staff. At one point, they felt they were not going anywhere, especially with EBY, which in the early 1990s was experiencing one of its many crises. Indeed, this coincided with pressures to rationalize personnel and to close the Posadas and Encarnación EBY branches. Obviously, the social scientists sitting at the negotiation table could not say much, if they were uncertain about their own fate. As a result of this, the local coordinadora decided to demand the support of the local government.

In the early 1990s, Don Jiménez's popularity waned because he became embroiled in the political factional struggles of the Justicialista party, by then divided in various blocs seeking to take control of the municipal and provincial governments. Mr. Jiménez was appointed advisor to the mayor of Posadas, who would later become EBY's executive director. At that point, he lost the support of many of his followers. However, his unexpected death, the day Yacyretá was about to resettle him, made him a symbol of the victims' struggles against the binational agency.

A conflict for succession ensued. Mainly two factions confronted each other for the control of the organization and for the use of Don Jiménez's name to identify their group. Each contending group was also said to be backed by various political coalitions within the Justicialista party. At this point political parties were well aware that Yacyretá was a highly sensitive issue and wanted to co-opt a movement which they presumed would make an impact in the region. This "cynical manipulation" (Routledge 1993) of political parties is not new; it is a quite common feature of social movements. It needs to be noted that the manipulation goes both ways. People take advantage of the parties' offers (often times every party offer) to meet their organizational needs. Even more, in a society used to clientelistic relations, they feel entitled to this and help, quite frequently, they complain that it is not enough. Help encompasses multiple resources necessary for the functioning of the grass-roots organization: gasoline coupons, telephone calls, photocopying, transportation costs, typing and computer facilities, and legal advice. They also obtain food and medical attention, including free prescription drugs.

Ultimately, one of the two groups gained control of popular mobilization. The new leader, "Toti" Gómez, was a relative of Don Jiménez and had worked closely with him for years. His networks included former activists in the more radical movements of the 1960s and 1970s, some of whom had experienced exile or imprisonment during the military dictatorship. Although the role played by continued left-wing activism has already been noted (Schneider 1992), the transformation of the militants' discourse and practice still requires closer examination. A few authors, however, have noted the transformation of the radical discourse of former militants and the adoption of more liberal or social-democratic orientations—what some see as the adoption of "possible utopias" through a peculiar Gramscian reading (see, for example, Angel 1992, Rozitchner 1992, Viñas 1992). I will return to the influences on the transformation of the movements discourse when I analyze contemporary discursive strategies. One of the problems in most of the studies is that either they see the activation of the movements as a result of the work of organic intellectuals, as spontaneous and autonomous protest, or as the result of a common history of political activism (Schneider 1992). The problem is that each of these factors is analyzed in isolation. In practice, things work quite differently. Movements, such as the one studied here, do not exist in a vacuum. Their membership simultaneously participates in multiple social fields (political parties, university activism, local cultural groups). Also, the organic intellectuals, often analyzed as outsiders, might have a history intimately linked to that of the movement members. For example, the Coordinadora of Posadas participated in various meetings to discuss the ecological and social problems of hydroelectric projects with other interest groups. Participants included members of the *Movimiento Agrario Misionero* (Agrarian Movement of Misiones), the *Centro Para la Participación Popular*, CPPYD (Center for Popular Participation), and an evangelical church. One of the members of the CPPYD formerly lived in one of the affected neighborhoods, was related to Toti, had suffered imprisonment during the dictatorship, and briefly studied anthropology. Moreover, we will see him participating once again; this time as an NGO consultant hired to suggest solutions for the brickmakers.

Both in Posadas and Encarnación, I heard these types of comments: "We only get a response when we actively participate in demonstrations. Only at that point, money and concrete proposals suddenly appear." "We are tired of writing notes." "Mobilization is our only hope." Certainly, they had got the most positive results whenever they protested in some public space. One of the first collective actions widely covered by the media was the peaceful occupation of a Yacyretá relocation housing compound still under construction.[2] More than 300 families occupied the houses both in June and later in September of the same year. They were coming from transitory neighborhoods where they were resettled after the floods of 1983. They had been living in precarious conditions for ten years waiting for their dream houses. Their houses were damaged with some serious hail and rain storms, and a few of them complained about the law of *status quo* that maintained their lives in limbo for so long. A great number of them were early "beneficiaries" (a word no longer used) in the possession of the powerful blue folder. Others had been registered in the new census of 1989 and were promised some kind of solution. As in every case I followed, the majority misunderstood their rights, and the press and the politicians seemed to be just as confused. Municipal representatives mediated the negotiations and finally built another transitory neighborhood to host the families until EBY awarded them the homes. The coordinadora oversaw the agreements between EBY and the occupants, but the families voiced their frustration and skepticism.

THE INCOMPLETE TRANSNATIONALIZATION OF THE MOVEMENTS OF THE AFECTADOS

At least since the late 1980s, representatives from the Coordinadora of Posadas had attended meetings of the grass-roots organizations and NGOs with the purpose of discussing regional problems. In some cases, the meetings included Brazilian organizations. Initially, discussions centered around the impact of hydroelectric dams on various populations: peasants, Indians, and the urban poor. As time passed, the MERCOSUR agreements became another focus of their discussions. The discussion of the MERCOSUR brought a larger group of participants from northeast Argentina, Brazil, and Paraguay. Labor unions also joined the discussions. Promoters of these meetings invited experts to discuss what would happen with the regional economy, with the environment, with their organizations. For the Quincentennial of the Conquest there was a gathering in a town on the Brazilian and Argentine border to counter official ceremonies. Overall, discussions of dams and trade agreements summoned a broad grass-roots base. They made posters saying "let integration be ours" and opposed dam construction by using ecological arguments. Many of these debates coincided with the Earth Summit in Río, which some of the organizations attended.

Paraguayans and Argentines intensified their interaction in 1993. To analyze this development it is useful to consider Tarrow's concept of "political opportunity structure"—the field of opportunities and constraints that delimits the actions of collective actors (Mellucci 1996:200). In the case of Yacyretá, a combination of factors contributed to the short-lived transnationalization of the conflict: (1) impending partial filling of the reservoir, (2) regionalization, and ecologization of the conflict, (3) democratization of civil society, and (4) change in the perception of the locus of power—the role of the Banks.

Impending Partial Filling of the Reservoir

In 1993, roughly 15 percent of the relocation works was finished. With the burden of a serious fiscal crisis and lack of external financing for relocation, Argentina decided to start by partially filling the reservoir in 1994 to defer the relocation of most of the families until they could find a solution. One of the alternatives suggested was to offer lots with basic services (water, electricity) and the materials to build houses through self-help. This option was mainly designed for the cases identified in the 1989 census (mainly the married offspring of the families registered in 1979 and newcomers to the area). What truly infuriated many of the prospective relocatees was the change in the design of the houses. Instead of the nice red tile-roofed-houses with white stucco walls, they were now speaking of cheaper constructions commonly known as "shell homes" to convey the fragility of the structures. While the original ones had a cost of approximately 24,000 dollars, these would cost 4,000.

Also, in 1993 it became apparent that the situation of the brickmakers in both countries had been overlooked. They claimed that while some of their homes would not yet be flooded in 1994, the clay deposits essential for their productive activities would be irremediably lost.

Regionalization and Ecologization of the Project

The re-emergence of regionalism and localism has puzzled analysts of globalization who sometimes thought that this process encouraged homogenization. Globalization, however, is marked by a paradox, the politics of difference, intimately tied to the spatial fragmentation produced by processes of capital accumulation and time-space compression, is increasingly informing social identity and action (Harvey 1989, 1996; Smith 1984). Globalization, in fact, revitalizes or valorizes notions associated with locality (Watts 1996, cf. also Ferradás 1996, Laclau and Mouffe 1992, Appadurai 1996b, Fardon 1995, Mato 1994).

The decision to build Yacyretá was made by two nation-states without consulting the provincial and municipal constituencies. While the ecological and social burden of this development project affected a region which, especially for Argentina, was seen as marginal, it was apparent that the benefits would be basically enjoyed by the richer, central regions. "Regional discursive formations" (Pcct and Watts 1996:15) have gained momentum with the growth of awareness of geographical inequalities—such as the one generated with Yacyretá—produced by the central governments. Indeed, in the 1990s, both in Paraguay and in Argentina, municipal authorities, and to a lesser degree provincial governments began to perceive Yacyretá as a project that damages the region without offering a fair compensation. The discourse of these politicians emphasized the historical roots that tied together the fate of Encarnacenos and Posadeños as victims of Buenos Aires centralism since the times of the Virreinato del Río de la Plata and early years of independence. As with the grass-roots organizations, they organized meetings with mayors from the two countries to discuss common problems—mainly those related to the construction of dams. With the MERCOSUR agreements, they also gathered with Brazilians to define the position of regional actors vis-à-vis the central states.[3] Some of the regional claims included the payment of royalties in compensation for the loss of land, construction of basic infrastructure to prevent ecological damage (such as sewage systems, protection of river banks, quality control of water, the piping and/or drainage of streams. In Misiones, they also pressed to be interconnected to the national energy system to get electricity from Yacyretá. In 1996, it looked like this controversial issue would finally have a satisfactory solution. Lack of housing alarmed authorities in both border cities. They were well aware that if Yacyretá did not offer a satisfactory solution for the thousands of families inhabiting the urban lowlands, local governments would be compelled to seek alternatives.

In 1993, the mayor of Posadas told me that municipal authorities were planning to meet with the presidents of Paraguay and Argentina to make their demands. "We have a common position," he said. "We do not speak exclusively for Posadas or for Encarnación, we are going to defend our environment through legal, political, and social means. So far, the benefits are only for outsiders." He complained that EBY behaved as if it were "a game preserve," and added that it had systematically ignored the municipality and the affected population for more than fifteen years. He insisted that the Posadeños wanted to have a leading role.

Municipal authorities pondered the seriousness and maturity of the community. Although they emphasized the responsibility of the coordinadora, they repeatedly stressed the possibility of a social outbreak if EBY did not find immediate solutions. Obviously, this argument was used as a warning to national authorities who had been facing social upheavals in various economically depressed areas burdened with structural adjustment measures. The praising of the movements also revealed the strategic alliance they had established with the population to exert pressures on the centers of power in the capital cities of the two countries and in other remote capitals, such as Washington, D.C., where the World Bank is located. The ombudsman commented to me: "The bank is aware of the possible social conflicts. In a recent report, it warns that they might increase in intensity. Meanwhile, EBY is incapable of producing an appropriate response."

While observing a massive meeting of the Coordinadora of Posadas, I was surprised to hear the motto *por la vida* (for life) employed by the participants. In my interviews with municipal authorities, the concern with life was expressed repeatedly. Speaking about Yacyretá, one of the functionaries told me, "This is taking away life from us." The mayor also mentioned to me that they had been working in a commission for the life of Misiones. During the grass-roots meetings, people referred to Yacyretá as a monster which brings death and disease. The use of the watchword "life" to frame claims regarding the project intrigued me because it had been originally identified with the struggles for human rights during the military dictatorship. But while in the past people campaigned for the return of the *desaparecidos*—the disappeared ones—demanding they appear *con vida*—with life, the people affected by the dam were claiming *por la vida*—for life. The same motto was used in 1996, in demonstrations led by church groups, rural organization such as MAM, and grass-roots organizations that gathered on the day of San Cayetano, the patron saint of workers. On this occasion they were asking for "*Paz, Pan y Trabajo*" and criticizing MERCOSUR agreements and free-market policies that were devastating the regional economy. Some of these groups have also been meeting with the movements of people affected by dams. How did this fusion of meanings alluding to very different realities occured? In one case, the request was that people were brought back alive; in the other, that quality of life be ensured. This word association is not gratuitous; the ambiguity in the use of the word "life" has a particular disturbing effect on those participating in these communication exchanges. To understand how and why human rights talk enters the field of a development project, we have to identify the particular contexts in which these discursive forms were produced and transformed. Certainly, the role played by SERPAJ in the revitalization of the coordinadora provides us with one of the clues. As we have seen, once this human rights group became an NGO, it transformed its raison d'être, and began working with a strongly ecological agenda. With the renovated agenda focused on the environment, they targeted development policies as the focus of contestation.

Ecology occupies a center stage in the dominant discourses of the 1990s. It has displaced development concerns based exclusively on economic growth and started to frame issues in terms of ecological sustainability (Escobar 1996, Peet and Watts 1996). In Misiones, this is reflected institutionally with the dismantling of the department of planning and the creation of a ministry of ecology (the first one in the country, Misioneros claim). Both in Posadas and in Encarnación, the ecological component dominates the discussion of Yacyretá. While in this case we cannot speak of the "ethnicization of ecological destruction" (Parajuli 1996), we can surely speak of the regionalization of ecological destruction. At least, this is the way regional actors are framing the effects of dam construction. A common regional identity had been highlighted at the time some of the collective action became transnationalized.

Ethnicity is not completely present in these struggles and it is not deliberately manipulated. A former SERPAJ member framed some of the commonalities of the inhabitants of these Southern Cone borderlands in terms of the use of Guaraní language among the displaced. Members of the movement also mentioned their common ancestry and noted that many of them had kin ties on both sides of the Paraná.

Democratization of Civil Society

In 1992, EBY's style of social intervention changed, reflecting guidelines imposed by the World Bank. At this point, they adopted what I had called a neo-populist model of social intervention. The redesigned relocation and ecological programs suggested by international consultants was presented to environmental groups, university professors, professional associations, municipal and provincial representatives, and representatives from the coordinadoras from the two countries. Consultants expressed their concern with the top-down social strategies employed until then and encouraged participatory approaches. The meetings held in Paraguay and Encarnación to discuss the consultants' reports were meant to be a first step in this direction.

With the discovery of civil society of the 1990s, participation, often mediated by NGOs, was endorsed by international agencies (such as the World Bank and the Interamerican Development Bank), political parties, and professional groups.[4] This project is a good example of how participation was incorporated rhetorically but failed to be fully exercised in practice. Representatives of the neighborhoods perceived the limitations of this idealized model. After attending these meetings, they presented a document to the World Bank to complain that they had been invited to listen but not to speak. What was expected from them was their compliance with the proposed changes in the programs, not their input (cf. *El Territorio*, September 7, 1992). The meetings, however, had unintended effects, because they contributed to the convergence of various interests groups who would become actively involved in the demonstrations to oppose the filling of the reservoir. Also, some of the NGOs present at these events had been instrumental in intensifying, and even generating, transnational connections which challenged and threatened the continuity of the project.

The praising of the role of NGOs in development in the 1990s was not innocent. It coincided with the dismantling of the social-welfare state, austerity measures, and privatization imposed by the multilateral lending banks. These organizations were expected to fill the vacuum left by the retreat of the nation-state. What made them so attractive to institutions such as the United Nations or the World Bank? One of the keys to their appeal is found in low cost operation: It is argued that they provide services more efficiently than the state—a goal which undoubtedly fits very well in the agendas of the international agencies and the debt-ridden local governments.[5]

The economic dimension, however, is not what those championing NGOs highlight. It is often argued that these groups are egalitarian, promote participation, defend local issues, are environmentally sensitive, facilitate the expression of subaltern groups, and support emancipatory projects. Although this is true in many cases, as I have asserted elsewhere (Ferradás 1996), what is sometimes overlooked in these depictions is the NGO potential for neutralizing the transformative and critical capacity of subordinate groups. The universalist discourses of human rights, democracy, sustainable development, and participation, in which the practice of NGOs is embedded, are a historical product and, as such, are manipulated by multiple actors with often contradictory agendas. Local municipal authorities in the early 1990s regarded NGOs as allies in their goal of reaching the poor to guarantee their populist agenda, while maintaining a hierarchical structure through which the potential of contestation could be carefully monitored. Unlike what is generally claimed, most of the local NGOs—especially in Misiones—were not autonomous; most of them had strong links with the various political factions of the Justicialista party. Municipal and provincial authorities had vested interests in NGOs and the grass-roots organizations which they expected to maintain within their traditional clientelism. Their strategies clashed with those of Yacyretá as they were competing for the allegiance of the affected population. Although EBY claimed to adopt participatory approaches, both municipal authorities and members of the coordinadora felt that most of their actions were truly pursuing the co-optation and neutralization of the resettled population. As one of the municipal functionaries told me, "everything is political." EBY is not exempt from this; the head of EBY Posadas is a relative of the Argentine president, and he is well aware of the explosive political effect of Yacyretá both in regional and national politics. Thus, Yacyretá, regional authorities, and political parties competed for the allegiance of popular sectors of the population. This process was occurring simultaneously in the two countries.

Even though manipulation, co-optation, and neutralization are generally involved when bringing together participants with very different cultural capital, subaltern groups are not easy prey for those who intentionally or unintentionally wish to capitalize on the asymmetries of power in these encounters. In fact, they operate within the contradictions of the existing systems of social relationships and try to profit from them. According to the characteristics of each specific conjuncture, they become clients of key players, might establish alliances with the powerful, and take advantage of the material and symbolic resources put at their disposal. In spite of deliberate or unconscious efforts to hegemonize the control of the subaltern, nobody can anticipate outcomes when social forces are unleashed. Even limited and carefully controlled participation can trigger social action which subverts the existing order.

Change in the Perception of the Locus of Power: The Role of the Banks

As we have seen, with democratization the range of strategic alliances, the number of actors taking the role of mediators, and the spaces of contestation available to confront the project multiplied. In the early years, the privileged interlocutor in the negotiations for rights was Yacyretá, constructed in the collective imaginary as an omnipotent entity. Nowadays, the Bank (the World Bank) has acquired the doubtful privilege of being depicted as the most powerful actor. With this transformation in the perception of the location of power, strategies have also changed as the various participants in this project realize that in order to be successful they also have to operate in a global arena.

With the inability of the Argentine treasury to face relocation and environmental costs, the multilateral banks started to play a more visible role in decision-making processes. They conditioned the granting of fresh loans to the compliance with their own resettlement and environmental guidelines (which encourage consultation and participation of affected populations),[6] they pressed for privatization to obtain the resources necessary to finish engineering and infrastructure works; they suggested the restructuring of EBY; and they reserved some say in the choice of consulting firms. Politicians and the media highlighted the role played by the lending banks by saying that these institutions "dictate," "impose," "oppose," "refuse"—a language that clearly suggests where power resides.

The Bank is also held as an arbiter in the nationalistic confrontations with which the project had been fraught since its inception. On more than one occasion, World Bank representatives played a key role in introducing "neutral actors," after becoming aware of how history matters in this project—such as the rivalry between Argentina and Paraguay even before the Triple Alliance war. For example, they opposed the hiring of Paraguayan or Argentine firms to avoid accusations of national favoritism. Also, when the relocation departments were restructured, they suggested that EBY appoint a supervisor from a third country to administer the program in the two border cities.

The members of the coordinadoras were well aware of the veto powers of the Bank. In the early 1990s, Tomás Díaz from SERPAJ, actively involved in the Coordinadora of Posadas, traveled to Washington D.C. to discuss the concerns of the affected population. On my first contacts with leaders and members of the movements of the countries, they wondered whether I could help them reach the Bank because "they have to know what is happening to us." Some of them speculated that if the Bank "knew" that proposed timetables had not been met, they would press for a rapid solution before filling the reservoir. Julio Delgado, an *olero* (brickmaker), expressed a common feeling among the victims of dam construction: "We want the Bank to come and talk to us, not to EBY."

The feeling that their nation-states were conditioned by supranational powers led leaders of the movements to think that, to face the new challenges, they should organize into a broader movement which went beyond national boundaries. They also chose a specific site of contestation that symbolizes the new spatialization of the global order—the bridge connecting the two countries that contributes to breaking the boundedness of the nation-states. The boundedness, however, is not so easily broken.

VANQUISHING BORDERS OR BORDERS OF ANXIETY?

When the movements of the two countries came together in 1993, they agreed to organize a joint demonstration on the bridge connecting Posadas and Encarnación. As opposed to other forms of popular mobilization in which they had been involved in the past, with this public event they lured the solidarity of a broad spectrum of the local societies. Also, unlike other collective actions, this event was not secretly planned.

Initially, the demonstrators wanted to converge in the middle of the bridge and from this space call national and international attention. Although the integrationist climate generated with MERCOSUR rendered this form of expression possible, the sectors of the nation-state apparatus created to guard territorial boundedness imperiled the symbolic erasure of boundaries. The armed forces responsible for the protection of national frontiers jeopardized the unification of Encarnacenos and Posadeños. They said that they could not gather on the bridge by invoking a prohibition to pedestrian transit. The Encarnacenos, who obviously counted on greater support from the powerful, went across the bridge by car and other vehicles. The Posadeños, who failed to obtain the number of promised buses to reach the bridge marched on foot to the vicinity of the customs buildings. The two groups were led by men and women carrying their national flags. At one point, they exchanged their flags. This act, which was interpreted by some of the press as a sign of fraternity and sisterhood, was in fact an attempt to challenge the controls set by the guardians of sovereignty. One of the Argentines leaders told me that they decided to give their flags to the Paraguayans as a subterfuge to avoid the restrictions to circulation.

Despite attempts to curtail this massive demonstration, overall it was very effective in obtaining the public exposure that they were pursuing. However, they never accomplished what they claimed was their major goal at that time: to stop the filling of the reservoir. Talking about this demand a few years later, the leaders from Encarnación and Posadas admitted that they knew that this was not possible. They had used this demand to press for solutions to the relocation and environmental problems. The more inclusive movement of Encarnacenos and Posadeños did not work as closely a year later, when the plight of the *oleros* became the more contentious issue.

BACK TO THE NATION: THE STRUGGLES OF THE *OLEROS*

In 1994, the situation of the *oleros* in the two cities became dramatic. Their houses and clay deposits were under water with the flooding of the Paraná and its tributaries. The population believed that the behavior of the river was now unpredictable, and they blamed this on Yacyretá. EBY maintained that the waters rose because of torrential rainfall. The flooding affected brick production in areas which theoretically would not be affected by the operation of the first turbines. Unable to work and to sustain their families, the *oleros* urgently demanded solutions. Negotiations with Yacyretá concentrated exclusively on the *oleros*. Concerns with relocations of other households and solution of environmental questions dwindled.

By then, the unified movement of the two cities was quite inactive. Participants felt that it was mainly due to their lack of resources. Support from NGOs had been withdrawn because these organizations were also suffering an economic crunch. With the retreat of organizations such as SERPAJ, which was very instrumental in establishing global and regional networks, popular mobilization concentrated once again on negotiating with different actors within the nation.

Also during that year, antagonism between the two countries increased, partly because of the negotiations regarding privatization, which Argentina handled arrogantly without consulting her binational partner. Another factor affecting the relationship between the two nations was specifically related to this border region. Responding to pressures from local merchants, who felt they were losing business to merchants from Encarnación favored by the imbalances generated by differences in the taxation system, Argentine customs enforced rigid controls to goods and people coming from Paraguay. This infuriated Paraguayans; the press echoed their discontent by reminding its readership of Argentina's behavior during the War of the Triple Alliance. Both the privatization and the customs issue stimulated discourses emphasizing nationalist feelings, as both events were constructed as threatening Paraguayan sovereignty.

The *oleros* from Paraguay shared this nationalist fervor and some of them did not even trust the Colombian EBY functionary appointed to supervise relocation in the two countries. Because she was living in Posadas, they suspected that she favored the Argentine side. The climax of their strategy, which based their struggle on national antagonisms, was reached on occasion of the visit of EBY's experts from Argentina to one of the neighborhoods of the *oleros*. In that opportunity, they expressed their discontent with EBY by turning upside down one of the vehicles of the visitors. This act was accompanied by allusions to the Mitrismo (an Argentine president during the War of the Triple Alliance) of their neighbors and other comments expressing nationalist sentiments. This created a serious diplomatic confrontation.

Men and women from the affected areas of Posadas were quite ambivalent about the loyalties of their Paraguayan allies. Even though they endorsed many documents criticizing the geopolitical arguments initially used by Argentina to justify dam construction—documents which warned about the damages Paraguayans and Brazilians could cause downstream with the construction of Itaipú—in 1996 they were still convinced that their neighbor countries could "kill us all if they wished." Those NGOs that obviously produced the statements to which the members of the *coordinadora* subscribed envisaged an integration of oppressed peoples beyond national borders to challenge the alliance of the central governments with multinational interests. Although they aimed at developing a critical consciousness among popular sectors, following Paulo Freire's methodologies, their message did not come across. Once they stopped their involvement, some of their integrationist goals vanished. Not everything was lost, however, as Posadeños still sought counseling from Paraguayans to negotiate with EBY. Another interesting outcome from attempts of unification beyond borders was not intentionally planned by anybody. The Posadeño *oleros*, who were using very traditional techniques to produce their bricks, learned a great deal from the more profitable business of some of their Encarnaceno neighbors and were eager to incorporate these innovations into their own production.

The Paraguayan *oleros* negotiated compensation for the loss of profits while they waited for relocation, and a fairly large sum for the loss of their business if they opted for compensation, an agreement that their Argentine counterparts wanted to reach. Although I do not know the details of how the negotiations proceeded, I suspect that the Paraguayan *oleros* benefited from the eagerness of Argentina to please their neighbor and therefore facilitate consent for privatization.

The *oleros* of Posadas felt that the *oleros* of Encarnación succeeded because they had the support of local authorities. In Misiones, "we took advantage of some situations, we had to push municipal and provincial authorities to fight against EBY," Miguel Sánchez from the coordinadora remarked. Don González, a very active *olero,* also stressed how they "went to the government to demand that it confront EBY, but nothing happened. I do not know what kind of arrangement they have." To press the government to become more involved in supporting their claims, they camped in tents on the plaza across from the house of the provincial government. To press Yacyretá, they occupied the Posadas building. Praising the effectiveness of their mobilization, Miguel Sánchez said, "What we could not obtain in more than fifteen years, we obtained in one day." He added that although they kept saying that there was no money for relocation or compensation, all of a sudden they found resources.

While some *oleros* were provided with a house, lots to continue with their brick activity, and clay deposits that might guarantee production for some years in an area that would have all basic services, others opted for compensation. Yet another group of the *oleros*, tired of waiting for solutions, occupied some land, now optimistically called "the Future," which a provincial minister once told them would be given to them. This latter group received a small compensation and signed papers renouncing any other claims. When I visited them, they were convinced that they were still entitled to other benefits from Yacyretá. Their situation is very precarious. The provincial government has left them on their own, and Yacyretá says they have no further obligations. The land where they settled is now in private hands, and they lack the most basic services. They showed me with pride how they had rebuilt their productive units and told me they were determined to stay there no matter what. A leader from the coordinadora, and some EBY staff members very sympathetic to their claims regretted that they had accepted this settlement. They saw them as losers in this struggle which unexpectedly resulted in impressive benefits to some of the other *olero* players.

Different responses seem to be tied to the political alliances and expert counseling that each group secured. When I was visiting the former leader of the coordinadora in his new office as a town councillor, Don González, from the Future, stopped by to ask for help. The councillor promised he would look into the matter, and when he left he commented to me that he would give him a hand even though he knew he did not vote for him. Political strife divided and weakened the movement which was finally achieving positive results. In 1996, the leaders of the coordinadoras of Posadas and Encarnación had been elected city councillors. According to many, this confirmed the success of the political machinery to co-opt leadership of the social movements. According to the leaders, this new position would allow them to bring the voice of the people to local government. Time will tell.

Leaders lamented that co-optation and pressures from EBY debilitated their organization. They said that various residents were warned that they would not receive a home if they insisted on making trouble. Both members of the coordinadora and EBY's staff agree that once money was set on the negotiation table, tensions eased. This, however, is a solution that would only bring more nightmares in the near future. Once the money is gone, the cities will be facing the problem of thousands of homeless households threatened by the completion of the dam. The multilateral banks are aware that this might happen. For this reason, they have always favored relocation instead of compensation. When the conflict re-emerges, the accusations will backfire to these powerful entities. In fact, they are already seriously challenged by the same organizations they started to support in the last years: the NGOs.

CHALLENGE IN CYBERSPACE AND IN THE GLOBAL CENTERS OF POWER

Sobrevivencia, Amigos de la Tierra (Survival, Friends of the Earth) is a Paraguayan NGO connected with others of a more global nature. It is one of the hundreds of Paraguayan NGOs which have mushroomed in recent years. Some of their membership includes professionals who had been unable to find a niche in the shrinking structure of the state apparatus, individuals who felt they should maintain autonomy from the state, and former political exiles from Stroessner's regime who came back with democratization. As in Argentina, the returnees came back with higher degrees from European, North American, or Latin American universities and with a broad range of networks and fashionable discourses from the north, mainly associated with democratization and environmentalism.[7] They also know how to lobby globally, a valuable resource in an age in which information has a center stage in the allocation of power.

Sobrevivencia targeted Yacyretá as one major issue in their environmental and social agenda. They are now accusing the World Bank and the Interamerican Development Bank of not respecting their own guidelines on resettlement and environmental issues and of guaranteeing loans exclusively for civil works. They claim the banks have violated their own policies regarding environmental and social impacts, have neglected indigenous populations, and oversaw the protection of endangered species.[8] They also assert that they have not adequately monitored how their loans were invested. Their documents have reached congress members in the United States, Great Britain, and Italy—three countries which have business interests in Yacyretá. They have also reached environmental groups through discussion groups on the Internet.[9] These groups in turn, are exerting pressures on the banks. The banks have been discussing whether they should approve an inspection panel to look into the matter. A Paraguayan paper says that this would be the second time that the Bank would undergo such an evaluation since they created this mechanism in 1993 (*Noticias*, March 25, 1997). In recent years, accountability has become a major concern in development circles.[10] The banks have to respond to the same contradictory and ambivalent structure they helped to create: on one hand, endorsing free-market policies, privatization, and the dismantling of the social welfare state; on the other hand, claiming that their major goals are to alleviate poverty and promote people's involvement (cf. Horowitz 1997). The first goals presuppose exclusion; the latter, presupposes inclusion. The banks now have to confront a country like Argentina which has complied with the demands set by their economic agenda. Argentina has opposed any investigation with the argument that it would be an attack on a sovereign state. It is backed by many developing countries. An attack on Argentina would mean chastize one of the most obedient pupils in the structural adjustment plans. By not taking action, however, the banks would in effect, acknowledge the questioning from NGOs they allegedly support.

I cannot not take sides in this more recent confrontation, not having researched either of these two actors. Instead, I will focus on how a small NGO, assuming the representation of people's (and nature's) interests, has had such an impact. Elías Díaz Peña, from *Sobrevivencia,* said: "The claims demonstrate that people's concerns can reach decision-making levels within the banks. It also reinforces our hope that the financial organizations will abandon support for massive socially and environmentally destructive projects, such as Yacyretá" (Link 74. FOEINT 1997). As Melucci (1996:185) notes, sometimes changes are produced by "small symbolic multipliers, through action carried by what Moscovici calls "active minorities." The power of these small groups depends on their accessibility to key spaces of power and on their ability to speak the language of power that has recently adopted the environment as the dominant discourse.

NOTES

1. For example, in a document presented to congressmen to make demands regarding the impact of the dam, only residents from two neighbors participated: barrio Obrero, and barrio San José (*El Diario,* September 28, 1989).

2. For a detailed analysis of the occupation of the Yacyretá neighborhoods, see the following 1992 issues of *El Territorio*: June 16, September 2, 4, 5, 10, 11, 19, and December 23.

3. In 1993, six provinces from the Argentine littoral forming the CRECENEA (Regional Council for the Economic and Cultural Development of the Northeast), and four Brazilian states integrating CODESUL (Committee for the Economic Development of the South) also gathered to speak about the "other" MERCOSUR. They demanded a greater participation of their regions in decisions regarding integration and MERCOSUR issues.

4. In the 1996 Task Group Report on Social Development, World Bank social experts stressed the social issues to be covered by its institution: poverty reduction, gender, indigenous peoples, resettlement, participation, country assistance programs, social assessments, social capital, and civil society. Acknowledging the increasing importance of civil society, it is reported, the bank added NGO coordinators to its missions (World Bank 1996).

5. Cernea (1988), a World Bank social scientist endorses the role of NGOs in development by emphasizing their ability to mobilize people to become self-reliant. He stresses their

success in promoting local participation and notes that they operate at low cost.

6. Projects funded with World Bank loans must comply to guidelines set in the following documents: Involuntary Resettlement in Development Projects (World Bank 1988), and the Operational Directive (World Bank 1990). There is also a Resettlement Planning Guidance (World Bank 1997), prepared for privately funded projects.

7. Another discourse also dominant among returnees is gender, a topic which I have not addressed because the project excluded the consideration of women from the ouset. I have partially addressed this issue elsewhere (Ferradás 1997).

8. When I started my research, still during Stroessner's dictatorship, I was told that a few Paraguayan experts were aware that indigenous groups inhabited some of the Paraná islands to be flooded. They decided to register them as peasants because they feared that if they acknowledged their identity, they could suffer discrimination. At that time, I was only researching the Argentine side and I could never verify this information. Nowadays, it is publicly acknowledged that some of the isleños are indigenous peoples.

9. See for example, Links 74 and 77 of Friends of Earth International (FOEINT). Link 77 "Green Light for Yacyretá Inspection Panel" comments on the request filled by Sobrevivencia (http:/www.xs4.nl/~foeint/077_2202 html).

10. The World Bank Task Force document on Social Development and Results on the Ground was divided with regards to the Copenhagen Declaration on Social Development approved during the World Summit for Social Development in 1995. This document refers to people-centered approaches and supports "accountability and transparency in government" (World Bank 1996).

CHAPTER 11

Power: The Dam and the People

To delve into the misfortunes of the Yacyretá hydroelectric dam project is to delve into the controversial journey of development discourses and practices of the last two decades. It is also to explore the consumption, resignification, appropriation, and reproduction of such discourses and practices in a very particular arena: the borderlands of Argentina and Paraguay. My major concern has been with unveiling the complexities of the social relations which unfolded with the decision to construct a major engineering work in a region historically marginalized by the national centers of power.

Power has been a central theme of this book. I have examined it in the multiple ways and places where it is exercised. First, I looked at energy power, which represents the power of technology to mobilize collective constructions of well-being and progress. Dam power with its gigantism and sophisticated engineering has been a key component in the development ideology, which triumphally presented humankind in control of nature. Today, in a world prone to apocalyptic depictions of the future, where the consciousness of risk (Beck 1996, Giddens 1996, Melucci 1996) has been incorporated in the global imaginary, we are witnessing a transformation in the constructions of the power of dams. Imbued with the catastrophism of much of the current discourses on the environment, most actors involved in disputes around dams no longer perceive them as among the ultimate examples of men's (surely never women's) ability to harness nature. Yacyretá has now become an "ecological bomb." It has been paired with Hiroshima in its destructiveness.

If dams no longer promise well-being, what, if anything, would? Those holding power now make that claim for market forces. They paint a rosy picture of market integration, a topic I will discuss in these concluding pages.

This brings us back to the other forms of power I have touched upon throughout my analysis: the power of naming and controling discourse, the power of controling settings of interaction, the power of allocating resources. Rather than looking exclusively at the way discourses are deployed, which is the focus of most of the contemporary critiques of development, I have looked at how various actors strategize, resist, and are co-opted in response to the shifting regional, national, and global contexts in which they operate. Because I have played multiple roles—related to my multiple identities—in the process I have analyzed, I was particularly interested in showing how anthropologists and other planners participate in the field of development. I was concerned with disclosing the extent to which our own professional and personal positioning within a given reality influences the way we construct it and contribute to the way it is transformed. In other words, I wanted to show our own intellectual mystifications. Let me now discuss some of the problematic points in which we are implicated as social scientists and development practitioners.

THE UNEASY RELATIONSHIP OF ANTHROPOLOGY AND DEVELOPMENT

Years ago, when discussing my research plans among some North American colleagues, I was outraged at the reaction of a few of my associates. I told them that when relocation was announced, there was practically no resistance from the people to be displaced. Without knowing the specific context in which the relocation was proposed, many immediately remarked that "people do resist." Their comments were informed by two assumptions that often dominate most of the development critiques: first, development is inherently negative; it is an imposition from outside which aims at the destruction of local cultures. Second (and this follows from the first), people vehemently refuse any changes in their way of life and always actively react against them.

Surely, these assumptions have some validity. I often subscribed to and even engaged in challenging certain dominant views of development. What troubled me was the oversimplification of the working of development. Ideas of development have become hegemonic precisely because they have enjoyed the ability to capture both the imagination of the powerful and also of many among the subaltern groups.[1] They are associated with goals of progress and well-being which have been part and parcel of various discourses contributing to the formation of a national identity. Among them, the educational discourse played a decisive role. The pervasiveness of these ideas is attested to by the names popular sectors have chosen to call their businesses and their neighborhoods, such as the recently formed settlement called "The Future" which I discussed in the previous chapter.

My friends also ignored the fact that a great part of the relocation process took place under an extremely repressive regime. Lack of response is not an indicator of the passivity (as some of my associates probably presumed I implied) of the people, but the result of a careful appraisal of the costs and benefits of popular protest under conditions of extreme state violence and surveillence.

Moreover, in the case of Yacyretá, most people initially expected a much valued reward: beautiful stucco homes in nonfloodable areas which symbolically would place them among the middle classes (Ferradás 1997). While the promise remained a viable outcome, they endured numerous hardships. As soon as they realized that it would never become a reality because decision-makers changed the designs to adapt to new economic constraints, grass-roots organizations started to mobilize.

I have also been influenced by dominant discussions of democratization in the social sciences. I first hypothesized that communicative practices in the Yacyretá project might have changed with the advent of a democratic government. My underlying assumptions were that social relations are generally asymmetric and that systems tend to be rigid and constraining under authoritarian regimes. Conversely, I was expecting that in a democracy boundaries would loosen and multiple channels of participation and communication would emerge, thus enabling actors to relate to each other in a more egalitarian manner.

By the time I started field work in 1987, Argentina had already been under the rule of a freely elected president for four years. Contrary to my initial expectations, very little had changed in the Yacyretá relocation process since that political transformation. Shortly after my first interviews and field observations, I realized that most of my assumptions expressed my desires and my romanticized version of democracy rather than representing a regular behavior of human groups in processes of political change. During my first years of observing the Yacyretá processes, I was always amazed to observe the frequency with which various professionals associated the process of democratization with greater participation and communication.[2] For example, a sociologist working as a consultant on hydroelectric projects asserted at a workshop on methodologies for assessing social and environmental impacts that "participation and communication increased with democracy and thus transformed development policies of hydroelectric projects." This view reflects the recovery and resignification of the concept of democracy by Latin American social scientists after decades of military dictatorship. The same authors who talked about "formal democracy" in a derogatory way during the 1960s and early 1970s and promoted revolution as a means to gain control of the political apparatus now promote a democratic form of government based on a collective order achieved through permanent negotiation over the rules of the game, respect for individual and group differences, and through defense of a "utopian horizon" geared to attain popular sovereignty and consensus (see Lechner 1986).

After critically examining the "democratic syndrome" that impinged upon the way many of my colleagues and I interpreted postauthoritarian phenomena, I started to regard communication and participation as phenomena in which politicians and social scientists are very often implicated, since they are in part the architects of that which they seek to describe. Indeed, in the Yacyretá relocation project, it was the social scientists who suggested the introduction of participatory forms, who designed communication programs, and who insisted that social workers should encourage the organization of grass-roots groups into neighborhood commissions, in the understanding that, if this goal were achieved, it would be a positive indicator of a successful—and democratic—development project. This was also the procedure followed by NGOs when they worked with the movement of the affected population. Thus, this desirable behavior did not grow spontaneously out of democratic conditions but was stimulated, cultivated, and modeled by social science.

Obviously, these efforts did not suffice because they stemmed from wrong assumptions about social processes and social practices. These action strategies—an example of the neopopulist model of social intervention discussed in the second chapter—generally fail because they do not acknowledge power differentials. The Yacyretá project has followed neither a fully authoritarian nor a neopopulist model of social intervention. Throughout EBY's history, different members of the relocation agency tried to enforce both forms of action, although in practice the authoritarian model prevailed. The planning bureaucracy and its experts controlled most of the relocation process during the military dictatorship and during the democratic government of Alfonsín. This fact made EBY's staff and the affected population think that nothing had changed since the installation of a freely elected president. To them, the initial structure of EBY continued to be as rigid as before, and they maintained that there had been no significant changes in decision-making procedures. Despite pressures from the banks to be more participatory, neither within the agency nor between the agency and the population do we see a significant change in this respect. The staff still works under rigid systems of internal surveillance to prevent leakages of information that could reach politicians and the general public. This has been intensified with the escalating of popular protest and political attacks.

The widespread belief that EBY remained the same despite the political changes was instrumental to the purposes of the agency's decision-makers, as it helped dissuade attempts to influence policies or to confront authorities. However, changes in the perception of the location of power in decision-making processes have recently affected the way EBY is constructed and the way people relate to it. As we have seen, Yacyretá has been increasingly forced to accommodate itself to the increase of mediating options and interlocutors. Challenges to its power have come both from global and local actors who have got to the point of negotiating without seeking EBY's input, an outcome that would have been hard to imagine in the early years of the project.

Certainly, what occurred was neither a total rupture with the past nor a profound transformation. Thus, although democracy does not inevitably and even magically bring about a transformation of these projects, it does open up possibilities and choices. It enables the emergence of a greater range of forces that struggle to impose their own project. With Yacyretá, it gave room to the competition of various groups that attempted to gain control—and representation—of the population's demands. But the increase of options does not necessarily guarantee more transparent procedures. It may, as it did, multiply rumors and distort messages as each agency comes to negotiation with its own hidden—and sometimes overt—agenda.

Besides romanticizing democracy and popular participation, contemporary academic debates have also discovered and became fascinated with the interactions between the global and the local. It has been noted that anthropologists are prone to support populist ideals (Robertson 1984, Kitching 1982); advocacy of the local and indigenous and traditional societies are often defended by anthropologists critical of development. In debating globalization processes, many colleagues have tended to picture the local and social movements that purportedly sustain alternative projects as moral reservoirs that challenge the project of modernity (Friedman 1992; Kothari 1989, 1993). Others have questioned the authenticity of indigenous movements (see, for example, Rogers 1996, Jackson 1995, Linnekin 1991) and have noted the existence of internal divisions. Current debates are now tending to show that notions such as the "region" or the "local" are categories mobilized by various actors who do not necessarily share the same political agenda and identity. The Yacyretá case illustrates how contentious the arena of the local is. Some of those who advance the cause of the region do not always represent the interests of the oppressed minorities. Rather, they want to maintain the prevailing system of inequalities. The defense of a way of life and of popular culture sometimes is used to reproduce an extremely hierarchical system of social relations. As Gupta and Ferguson (1992) noticed, anthropological concepts sometimes are appropriated by the repressive apparatus. This obviously happened with the use of the culture concept to justify leaving the poor with their original poor huts.

Many of the efforts to create a sense of regional unity also stemmed from social scientists working at NGOs and at the local university, who combined their old academic interests on dependency models with new discourses on the environment, empowerment, and participation. Their ideas were not put to work in a vacuum. Rather, they were introduced in a context where the tradition of populism and clientelism has been dominated by the Justicialista party. Participation in this context has been implemented very differently from the way it is envisaged by the World Bank and other more global agents. The local version emphasizes a collective behavior in which people feel entitled to make demands on the state— a behavior which is highly politicized and rather hierarchical. The World Bank version, on the other hand, is tied to a more liberal ideology and pursues more individualistic, autonomous, self-initiative behavior. The World Bank opposes partisan politics.

Our anthropological and social science fashions have contributed to the choice of meanings to be mobilized in the confrontations and communication exchanges of the diverse actors in the Yacyretá relocation process. Earlier in the project, an anthropologist used the concept of survival strategies to define the behavior of the poor of Posadas. His relative power enjoyed at one point in the relocation agency of Yacyretá is attested by the adoption of this concept by other professionals and even the press. Now that he is no longer at EBY and now that the development discourse has changed, other concepts and methodologies have been adopted. Other anthropologists, social experts, and environmental professionals are now introducing their own discursive strategies to address the problems of Yacyretá and influence the way members of the movements frame their claims. Does this reveal their power over the movements? Are NGOs simply political buffers and patronizing agencies (Arellano-López and Petras 1994, Gardner and Lewis 1996)? Obviously this is the role local authorities and multilateral banks would like them to play, particularly now that the government is unable to meet people's needs and unemployment is threatening social stability.

In Argentina, the NGOs working in connection with Yacyretá were not the autonomous agencies that the academic literature describes. Most of their members were closely associated with the political machinery and were eventually co-opted. In Paraguay, they seemed to act more independently, and as we have seen, they became a serious challenge to both Yacyretá and the multilateral banks. It remains to be seen whether they have not been or will be co-opted by the Paraguayan government to exert greater pressures over the Argentine government, mainly regarding the negotiation of compensation.

Interestingly, by highlighting certain issues in the struggles of Yacyretá, certain identities and spaces of confrontation have come to the fore. Regional identities have generally been emphasized. Regional meanings have been mobilized in various ways—sometimes, in terms of the opposition between the region and the central state. This sense has been employed in both countries. The use of region here mainly connotes provincial interests, and it refers to an understanding of problems circumscribed to a national space. Another sense of region refers to a more recent way of spatializing conflicts, which reflects the changing nature of the role of the state in an era of globalization. It involves an understanding of region in a more inclusive way, transcending national borders. Those who manipulate this meaning often make reference to the historical opposition between the Paraná region and Buenos Aires. The region here evokes a common past as an earlier autonomous space with people with a distinct culture that became a threatening borderland when national boundaries were imposed. The region in this case is the victim of global forces associated with insensitive national centers of power. These depictions obscure and neglect other identities, such as those based on gender and class, which have been recurrently used by the affected population during my interviews but ignored by those who speak on their behalf. What Juana Rodríguez told me about the betrayal of the Argentine president of the historical role of Peronism regarding the defense of the national patrimony and the advocacy of the interests of the working class illustrates very well my point about aspects of popular identity that have been overlooked. Speaking about privatization, including Yacyretá, she said: "Menem does not sell his underwear, because he needs it. *El pobrerío* (the poor) is what he wants to eliminate. Where is Argentina going to end, in a civil war?"

In recent years, many analysts interested in globalization have stressed the emergence of deterritorialized identities. Borders in these interpretations are a privileged site to observe the emergence of hybridized identities (Kearney 1995, Gupta and Ferguson 1992, Refslund Sorensen 1997, Escobar 1995). They are also places where national identities are fiercely defended by the guardians of national sovereignity. Certainly borderlands such as the Paraguayan-Argentine have a history of integration, continuous crossings, and ambiguous national identities, despite efforts of the nation-states to maintain national integrity and rigid boundaries. The trajectory of the movement of the affected peoples by the Yacyretá dam reflects both the resilience of national imaginings and a common history of exclusion and exploitation. The two nation-states enforce the ambiguities. The Argentine state attempts to legitimize the construction of the new Corpus dam to provide energy to Brazil and the sale of Yacyretá surplus of energy in terms of the new integration created by MERCOSUR. Simultaneously, when threatened by riots and massive demonstrations triggered by unemployment and the impoverishment of regions excluded from the new open market economy, they resort to xenophobic arguments by blaming the lack of jobs on the unfair competition of illegal immigrants. By doing this, they jeopardize the unity of the self-proclaimed *pobrerío* who see their neighbors as competitors. Likewise, in Paraguay, they warn Argentina that if it does not solve the situation of the displaced promptly they will have to face the invasion of thousands of homeless and jobless Paraguayans.

As social scientists, we follow processes as they unfold, and we also help to produce and transform them by selecting and prioritizing certain phenomena over others. When I tried to contact an Argentine researcher who for years has monitored hydroelectric projects, he bluntly told me that he no longer studied dams because governments were no longer interested and they would stop investments. Therefore, funding was unavailable. He then added that his research efforts have moved to MERCOSUR. Indeed, MERCOSUR has replaced dams in the official constructions of promising futures. The Paraná River still plays a strategic role in the new strategy devised by the Southern Cone countries. But while two decades ago the Paraná was a contested space where dams were built as shields against neighbors, it is now seen as the MERCOVIA, the hydroway that will connect Buenos Aires and Sao Paulo.

As with Yacyretá, the benefits are promised for all but will be enjoyed by few. The excluded will still be the same.

NOTES

1. For a discussion of how development is not necessarily a monolithic discourse imposed from outside, but a process in which Latin American political elites have been engaged even before Rostow's discussions on the stages of economic growth, see Sikkink, 1991.

2. Numerous articles discuss the relationships among democratic governments, communication, and the emergence of participatory forms of organizing (see, for example, Lechner 1986a, and Nun 1987). For discussions on the participation of intellectuals in processes of redemocratization, see Brunner and Barrios 1987.

References

NEWSPAPERS

ABC Color
Clarín
El Cronista Comercial
El Diario
Hoy
El Libertador
El Litoral
Mayoría
La Nación
Noticias
La Opinión
El Territorio
Ultima Hora

MAGAZINES

Convicción
La Ingeniería
Revista Cambio

BOOKS AND ARTICLES

Abente, Diego. 1987. The War of the Triple Alliance: Three Explanatory Models. *Latin American Research Review* 22(2): 47–69.
Abínzano, Roberto C. 1985. Procesos de Integración en una Sociedad Multiétnica. Unpublished Dissertation. Sevilla: Universidad de Sevilla.
———— 1993. *Mercosur. Un Modelo de Integración*. Misiones: Editorial Universitaria. Universidad Nacional de Misiones.
Adams, Richard Newbold. 1988. *The Eighth Day*. Austin: University of Texas Press.
Althusser, Louis. 1971. *Lenin and Philosophy and Other Essays*, pp. 121–173. New York: Monthly Review Press.
Alvares, Claude. 1992. *Science, Development and Violence*. Delhi, New York: Oxford University Press.
Ambrosetti, Juan B. 1892.*Viaje a las Misiones Argentinas y Brasileras por el Alto Uruguay*. La Plata, Argentina: Revista del Museo de la Plata, vol. 3.

Angel, Raquel. 1992. El Ocaso del Intelectual Crítico. De Prometeo a Narciso. In *Rebeldes y Domesticados. Los Intelectuales Frente al Poder*, Raquel Angel, ed. pp. 9–26. Buenos Aires: Ediciones el Cielo por Asalto.

Anzaldúa, Gloria. 1987. *Borderlands/La Frontera*. San Francisco: Spinsters/Aunt Lute.

Apffel Marglin, Frédérique, and Stephen Marglin. 1990. *Dominating Knowledge. Development, Culture, and Resistance*. Oxford: Clarendon Press.

Appadurai, Arjun. 1996a. Sovereignity without Territoriality. In *The Geography of Identity*, Patricia Yaeger, ed. pp. 40–58. Ann Arbor: University of Michigan Press.

———— 1996b. *Modernity at Large*. Minneapolis: University of Minnesota Press.

Arce, Alberto, and Norman Long. 1992. The Dynamics of Knowledge. Interfaces Betweeen Bureaucrats and Peasants. In *Battlefields of Knowledge. The Interlocking of Theory and Practice in Social Research and Development*, Norman Long and Ann Long, eds. pp. 211–246. New York: Routledge.

Arellano-López, S., and J. F. Petras 1994. Non-Governmental Organizations and Poverty Alleviation in Bolivia. *Development and Change* 25(3): 555–568.

Asad, Talal. 1973. *Anthropology and the Colonial Encounter*. New York: Humanities Press.

Bakhtin, M. M. 1986. *Speech Genres and Other Late Essays*. Austin: University of Texas Press.

———— 1996[1981]. *The Dialogic Imagination by M. M. Bakhtin*. Austin: Texas.

Bamberger, Michael. 1986. *The Role of Community Participation in Development Planning and Project Management*. Washington, D.C.: World Bank.

Banuri,Tariq. 1990. Modernization and Its Discontents: A Cultural Perspective on Theories of Development. In *Dominating Knowledge*, Frédérique Apffel Marglin and Stephen A. Marglin, eds. Oxford: Clarendon Press.

Barabás, Alicia, and Miguel Bartolomé. 1973. *Hydraulic Development and Ethnocide: The Mazatec and Chinatec People of Oaxaca, Mexico*. Document 15. Copenhagen: International Work Group for Indigenous Affairs.

———— 1984. Apóstoles del Etnocidio: Réplica a Partridge y Brown. *América Indígena* 44: 201–211.

Baranger, Dionisio. 1978. *Análisis de Algunos Aspectos de la Estructura Agraria de Misiones*. Posadas: Universidad Nacional de Misiones, Instituto de Investigación.

Bartolomé, Leopoldo. 1975. Colonos, Plantadores y Agroindustrias: La Explotación Agrícola Familiar en el Sudeste de Misiones. *Desarrollo Económico* 15(58): 239–264.

———— 1982. Base Social e Ideología en las Movilizaciones Agrarias de Misiones entre 1971 y 1975. Emergencia de un Populismo Agrario. *Desarrollo Económico* 22(87): 409–420.

———— 1984a. Aspectos Sociales de la Relocalización de la Población Afectada por la Construcción de Grandes Represas. In *Efectos Sociales de las Grandes Represas en América Latina*, F. Suárez, R. Franco and E. Cohen, eds. pp. 115–150. Buenos Aires: Centro Interamericano para el Desarrollo Económico y Social.

———— 1984b. Forced Resettlement and the Survival Systems of the Urban Poor. *Ethnology* 23: 177–192.

———— 1985. Introducción: Las Relocalizaciones Masivas como Fenómeno Social Multi-dimensional. In *Relocalizados: Antropología Social de las Poblaciones Desplazadas*, Leopoldo Bartolomé, ed. pp. 7–22. Buenos Aires: Instituto del Desarollo Económico y Social.

———— 1987. Social Aspects of Population Resettlement in Latin America: The Urban Dimensions. Paper presented at the Seminar on Involuntary Resettlement in Bank-Financed Projects. Washington, D.C.: World Bank.

—— 1988. The Yacyretá Experience with Urban Resettlement: Some Lessons and Insights. Paper presented at the International Congress of Anthropological and Ethnological Sciences, Zagreb, Yugoslavia.

Basch, Linda, Nina Glick Schiller, and Cristina Szanton Blanc. 1994. *Nations Unbound. Transnational Projects, Postcolonial Predicaments, and Deterritorialized Nation-States.* Langhorne, PA: Gordon and Breach.

Bastide, Roger. 1973. *Applied Anthropology.* New York: Harper and Row.

Bauman, Zygmunt. 1987. *Legislators and Interpreters: On Modernity, Post-Modernity and Intellectuals.* Ithaca, N.Y.: Cornell University Press.

—— 1992. *Intimations of Postmodernity.* London and New York: Routledge.

Beck, Ulrich. 1995. Ecological Enlightment. Essays on the Politics of the Risk Society. Atlantic Highlands, N.J.: Humanities Press.

—— 1996. Teoría de la Sociedad del Riesgo. In *Las Consecuencias Perversas de la Modernidad,* Josetxo Beriain, ed. pp. 201–222. Barcelona, España: Anthropos.

Bekerman, Marta. 1995. Las Ventajas Económicas Potenciales del Mercosur para la Economía Brasileña. In *Integración y Sociedad en el Cono Sur. Las Relaciones con el Mercosur y Chile,* Marta Bekerman and Alejandro Rofman, eds. pp. 37–60. Buenos Aires: Espacio Editorial.

Bellman, Beryl L. 1984. *The Language of Secrecy: Symbols and Metaphors in Poro Ritual.* New Brunswick, N.J.: Rutgers University Press.

Belshaw, Cyril. 1976. *The Sorcerer's Apprentice: An Anthropology of Public Policy.* New York: Pergamon Press.

Benda, Julien. 1955[1928]. *The Betrayal of the Intellectuals.* Boston: The Beacon Press.

Berger, Peter, and Thomas Luckmann. 1966. *The Social Construction of Reality.* Garden City, N.Y.: Doubleday.

Bethell, Leslie. 1996. *The Paraguayan War (1864–1870).* Research Papers 46. London: Institute of Latin American Studies. University of London.

Bhabha, Homi. 1990. DissemiNation: Time, Narrative, and the Margins of the Modern Nation. In *Nation and Narration,* Homi K. Bhabha, ed. pp. 291–322. London: Routledge.

Blau, P. 1973[1955]. *The Dynamics of Bureaucracy.* Chicago: University of Chicago Press.

Boleda, Mario. 1983. El Proceso Emigratorio Misionero en las Ultimas Décadas. *Desarrollo Económico* 23(90): 287–298.

Botana, Helvio. 1982. *El Caldero de Yacyretá.* Buenos Aires: Peña Lillo Editor.

Bourdieu, Pierre. 1977. *Outline of a Theory of Practice.* Cambridge: Cambridge University Press.

—— 1982. *Ce que Parler Veut Dire.* L'Economie des Echanges Linguistiques. Paris: Fayard.

—— 1984a. *Distinction: A Social Critique of the Judgment of Taste.* Cambridge, MA: Harvard University Press.

—— 1984b. *Homo Academicus.* Paris: Les Editions de Minuit.

—— 1988. *Cosas Dichas.* Buenos Aires: Gedisa.

Bourdieu, Pierre, and Loic J. D. Wacquant. 1995. *Respuestas por una Antropología Reflexiva.* Madrid: Grijalbo.

Bove, Giacomo. 1923. *Note di un Viaggio Nelle Missioni ed Alto Parana. Settembre 1884–Febraio 1885.* Luca: Tip. Edit. G. Giusti.

Britan, Gerald, and Ronald Cohen. 1980. Toward an Anthropology of Formal Organizations. In *Hierarchy and Society. Anthropological Perspectives on Bureaucracy,* Gerald Britan and Ronald Cohen, eds. pp. 9–30. Philadelphia: Institute for the Study of Human Issues.

Brittan, Arthur. 1973. *Meanings and Situations*. London: Routledge and Kegan Paul.

Brunner, José, and Alicia Barrios. 1987. *Inquisición, Mercado y Filantropía. Ciencias Sociales y Autoritarismo en Argentina, Brasil, Chile y Uruguay*. Santiago de Chile: Facultad Latinoamericana de Ciencias Sociales.

Burton, Frank, and Pat Carlen. 1979. *Official Discourse: On Discourse Analysis, Government Publications, Ideology and the State*. London: Routledge and Kegan Paul.

Carrier, James. 1995. Introduction. In *Occidentalism. Images of the West*, James Carrier, ed. pp. 1–32. Oxford: Clarendon Press.

Cavazzutti, Esteban. 1923. *Naturaleza. Labor Humana. Crímenes*. La Plata: Talleres Gráficos Olivieri y Domínguez.

Cernea, Michael. 1988. *Non-Governmental Organizations and Local Development*. World Bank Discussion Paper #40. Washington, D.C.: World Bank.

———— 1989. *Relocalizaciones Involuntarias en Proyectos de Desarrollo*. Washington, D.C.: World Bank.

———— 1996. *Social Organizaton and Development Anthropology: The 1995 Malinowski Award Lecture*. Environmentally Sustainable Development. Studies and Monograph Series no 6. Washington, D.C.: The World Bank.

Cernea, Michael, ed. 1991. *Putting People First: Sociological Variables in Rural Development*. 2nd ed. New York: Published for The World Bank by Oxford University Press.

Chambers, Erve. 1977. Public Policy and Anthropology. *Reviews in Anthropology* 4(6): 543–554.

Chambers, Robert. 1983. *Rural Development. Putting the Last First*. London: Longman.

———— 1989. *The State and Rural Development: Ideologies and an Agenda for the 1990s*. Discussion Paper 269. Brighton, England: Institute of Development Studies.

———— 1993. *Challenging the Professions: Frontiers for Rural Development*. London: Intermediate Technology Publications.

————, ed. 1970. *The Volta Resettlement Experience*. New York: Praeger.

Charsley, S. 1982. *Culture and Sericulture: Social Anthropology and Development in a South Indian Livestock Industry*. London: Academic Press.

Cochrane, Glynn. 1971. *Development Anthropology*. New York: Oxford University Press.

———— 1980. Policy Studies and Anthropology. *Current Anthropology* 21(4): 445–458; 21(5): 682–684.

Cohen Imach, Victoria. 1994. *De Utopías y Desencantos. Campo Intelectual y Periferia en la Argentina de los Sesenta*. Tucumán: Universidad Nacional de Tucumán. Facultad de Filosofía y Letras. Instituto Interdisciplinario de Estudios Latinoamericanos.

Colson, Elizabeth. 1971. *The Social Consequences of Resettlement. The Impact of Resettlement Upon the Gwembe Tonga*. Kariba Studies IV. Manchester, England: Manchester University Press.

———— 1976. Culture and Progress. *American Anthropologist* 78: 261–271.

Colson, Elizabeth, and Thayer Scudder. 1988. *For Prayer and Profit: The Ritual, Economic and Social Importance of Beer in Gwembe District, Zambia 1950–1982*. Stanford, CA: Stanford University Press.

Comisión Técnica Mixta Paraguayo Argentina. 1977. *Necesidades Habitacionales de la Población Afectada por el Embalse en Posadas*. Unpublished report.

Conlin, S. 1985. Anthropological Advice in a Government Context. In *Social Anthropology and Development Policy*, Ralph Grillo and A. Rew, eds. pp. 73–77. London: Tavistock Publications.

Crozier, Michel. 1964. *The Bureaucratic Phenomenon*. Chicago: Chicago University Press

Curtis, Donald. 1985. Anthropology in Project Management: On Being Useful to Those who

Must Design and Operate Rural Water Supplies. In *Social Anthropology and Development Policy,* Ralph Grillo and A. Rew, eds. pp. 102–116. New York: Tavistock Publications.

Dahl, G., and A. Rabo, eds. 1992. *Kam-Ap or Take-Off: Local Notions of Development.* Stockholm: Stockholm Studies in Social Anthropology.

D'Andrade, Roy, and Nancy Scheper-Hughes. 1995. Objectivity and Militancy: A Debate. *Current Anthropology* 36(3): 399–440.

Da Rosa, Eliseo J. 1983. Economics, Politics and Hydroelectric Power. The Paraná River Basin. *Latin American Research Review* 18(3): 77–107.

De Ipola, Emilio. 1983. *Ideología y Discurso Populista.* Buenos Aires: Folios Ediciones.

De Janvry, Alain. 1981. *The Agrarian Question and Reformism in Latin America.* Baltimore, MD: Johns Hopkins University Press.

Dijkink, Gertjan. 1996. *National Identity and Geopolitical Visions. Maps of Pride and Pain.* New York: Routledge.

Donzelot, Jacques. 1979. *The Policing of Families.* New York: Pantheon Books.

EBY (Entidad Binacional Yacyretá). 1975. *Estudios de la Población en el Area Afectada por las Obras del Proyecto Yacyretá Apipé, Lado Argentino.* Posadas: Entidad Binacional Yacyretá.

———— 1978. *Síntesis del Registro de Población y Vivienda Afectadas por el Embalse, Lado Argentino.* Posadas: Entidad Binacional Yacyretá.

———— 1980. *Bulletin 1, July 1980.* Posadas: Entidad Binacional Yacyretá.

———— 1981a. *Memoria y Balance. Posadas:* Entidad Binacional Yacyretá.

———— 1981b. *Informe Analítico del Censo 1979 de Población y Viviendas Urbanas Comprendidas en el Proyecto Yacyretá, en la Ciudad de Posadas, Misiones, Argentina.* Posadas: Entidad Binacional Yacyretá, Programa de Relocalizaciones y Acción Social Urbano.

———— 1985. *Verificación de Asentamientos Urbanos.* Posadas: Entidad Binacional Yacyretá, Programa Urbano de Relocalización y Acción Social.

———— 1987. *Memoria sobre el Programa de Relocalizaciones (Aspectos Sociales).* Posadas: Entidad Binacional Yacyretá.

Epstein, Scarlett, and Akbar Ahmed. 1984. Development Anthropology in Project Implementation. In *Training Manual in Development Anthropology,* William Partridge, ed. pp. 31–41. Washington, D.C.: American Anthropological Association and Society for Applied Anthropology.

Escobar, Arturo. 1991. Anthropology and the Development Encounter. The Making and Marketing of Development Anthropology. *American Ethnologist* 18(4): 16–40.

———— 1995. *Encountering Development. The Making and Unmaking of the Third World.* Princeton, N.J.: Princeton University Press.

Escobar, Arturo, and Sonia Alvarez, eds. 1992. *The Making of Social Movements in Latin America. Identity, Strategy, and Democracy.* Boulder, CO: Westview Press.

Escolar, Marcelo, Silvina Quintero Palacios, and Carlos Reboratti. 1994. Geographical Identity and Patriotic Representation in Argentina. In *Geography and National Identity,* David Hooson, ed. pp. 346–366. Cambridge: Blackwell.

Esteva, Gustavo. 1987. Regenerating People's Space. *Alternatives* 12(1): 125–152.

Fahim, Hussein. 1981. Indigenous Anthropologists and Development-Oriented Research. In *Indigenous Anthropology in Non-Western Countries,* Hussein Fahim, ed. pp. 121–137. Durham, N.C.: North Carolina Academic Press.

———— 1983. *Egyptian Nubians: Resettlement and Years of Coping.* Salt Lake City, UT: University of Utah Press.

Fals Borda, Osvaldo. 1969. *Subversion and Social Change in Colombia.* New York: Columbia University Press.

Fardon, Richard. 1985. *Power and Knowledge: Anthropological and Sociological Approaches.* Proceedings of a Conference Held at the University of St. Andrews, December 1982. Edinburgh: Scottish Academic Press.

———— 1995. Introduction: Counterworks. In *Counterworks.* Richard Fardon, ed. pp. 1–22. New York: Routledge.

Faye, Jean Pierre. 1972. *Théorie du Récit.* Paris: Hermann.

Feldman, Steven. 1988. Secrecy, Information and Politics: An Essay on Organizational Decision Making. *Human Relations* 41(1): 73–90.

Ferguson, James. 1990. *The Anti-Politics Machine. "Development," Depoliticization, and Bureaucratic Power in Lesotho.* Cambridge: Cambridge University Press.

Fernández Ramos, Raimundo. 1931. *Misiones a Través del Primer Cincuentenario de su Federalización. 1881-Dic.20-1931.* Madrid: Talleres de Espasa Calpe.

Fernea, Robert, and John G. Kennedy. 1966. Initial Adaptations to Resettlement: A New Life for Egyptian Nubians. *Current Anthropology* 7: 349–354.

Ferradás, Carmen. 1986. Populism and Rural Movements. A Comparative Overview: Agrarian Leagues from Northeast Argentina and the Peasant Leagues from Northeast Brazil. Unpublished Manuscript.

———— 1996. El Interjuego de lo Global y lo Local en la Represa Yacyretá. In *América Latina en Tiempos de Globalización: Procesos Culturales y Transformaciones Sociopolíticas.* Daniel Mato, Maritza Montero, and Emanuele Amodio, eds. pp. 83–95. Caracas: UNESCO, U.C.V., ALAS.

———— 1997. From Vegetable Gardens to Flower Gardens: The Symbolic Construction of Social Mobility in a Development Project. *Human Organization* 56(4): 450–461

Ferradás, Carmen, Carlos González Villar, Yolanda Urquiza, and Lila Sintes. 1988. Las Políticas Culturales en una Realidad Multiétnica. Paper read at Simposio de Políticas Culturales. Secretaría de Cultura de la Nación, Dirección Nacional de Antropología y Folklore.

Foeint Link 77. 1997. *Green Light for Yacyretá Inspection Panel. Comments on the Request Filled by Sobrevivencia. (http:/www.x54.nl/rfoeint/077/220htrt).*

Foucault, Michel. 1972. The Archaeology of Knowledge. New York: Pantheon Books.

———— 1980. Truth and Power; Power and and Strategies. In *Power/Knowledge. Selected Interviews and Other Writings. 1972–1977,* Colin Gordon, ed. pp. 109–145. New York: Pantheon Books.

———— 1988. On Power. In *Michel Foucault. Politics, Philosophy, Culture.* Lawrence D. Kritzman, ed. New York and London: Routledge.

————1991a. Politics and the Study of Discourse. In *The Foucault Effect. Studies in Governmentality,* Graham Burchell, Colin Gordon and Peter Miller, eds. pp. 53–72. Chicago: The University of Chicago Press.

———— 1991b. Governamentatility. In *The Foucault Effect. Studies in Governmentality,* Graham Burchell, Colin Gordon and Peter Miller, eds. pp. 87–110. Chicago: The University of Chicago Press.

Franco, José. 1988. *Intercambio Comerical Paraguayo-Brasileño. Análisis de su Incidencia en la Economía Paraguaya.* Asunción: Centro Paraguayo de Estudios Sociológicos.

Frank, Andre Gunder. 1968. On Responsibility in Anthropology. *Current Anthropology* 9(5): 412–414.

———— 1975. Anthropology=Ideology, Applied Anthropology=Politics. *Race and Class* 17(1): 56–68.

Fraser, Nancy. 1988. Talking about Needs. *Public Culture* 1(1): 39–51.

Friedman, Jonathan. 1992. The Past in the Future: History and the Politics of Identity, *American Anthropologist* 94(4): 837–859.

—— 1996. The Politics of De-Authentification: Escaping from Identity, A Response to "Beyond Authenticity" by Mark Rogers. *Identities* 3(1-2): 127–136.

Furlong, Guillermo. 1978. *Misiones y sus Pueblos Guaraníes*. Posadas: Talleres Gráficos Lumicop.

García Canclini, Néstor. 1990. *Culturas Híbridas: Estrategias para Entrar y Salir de la Modernidad*. Mexico: Grijalbo.

Gardner, Katy, and David Lewis. 1996. *Anthropology, Development and the Post-Modern Challenge*. Chicago: Pluto Press.

Gates, Marilyn. 1988. Lessons from the Uxpanapa Resettlement Project, Mexico. *Cultural Survival Quarterly* 12(3):18–22.

Geertz, Clifford. 1973. *The Interpretation of Cultures*. New York: Basic Books.

Giarraca, Norma, and Miguel Teubal. 1995. Los Pequeños Productores Cañeros y la Integración Económica con el Brasil. In *Integración y Sociedad en el Cono Sur. Las Relaciones con el Mercosur y Chile*, Marta Bekerman, and Alejandro Rofman, eds. pp. 56–84. Buenos Aires: Espacio Social.

Giddens, Anthony. 1994. *The Constitution of Society: Outline of the Theory of Structuration*. Berkeley, CA: University of California Press.

—— 1994. *Beyond Left and Right. The Future of Radical Politics*. Stanford, CA: Stanford University Press.

—— 1996. Modernidad y Autoidentidad. In *Las Consecuencias Perversas de la Modernidad*, Josetxo Berian, ed. pp. 33–71. Barcelona: Anthropos.

Gledhill, John. 1995. *Neoliberalism, Transnationalization and Rural Poverty. A Case Study of Michoacán, Mexico*. Boulder, CO: Westview Press.

Goffman, Erving. 1959. *The Presentation of Self in Everyday Life*. New York: Doubleday.

Goldsmith, Edward, and Nicholas Hildyard. 1984. *The Social and Environmental Effects of Large Dams*. San Francisco: Sierra Club Books.

Gómez, Carlos. 1980[1869]. Cartas Polémicas Sobre la Guerra del Paraguay. In *Proyecto y Construcción de una Nación (Argentina 1846–1880)*, Tulio Halperín Donghi, ed. pp. 203–213. Caracas: Biblioteca Ayacucho.

Gottdiener, M. 1985. *The Social Production of Urban Space*. Austin, TX: University of Texas.

Gouldner, Alvin. 1954. *Patterns of Industrial Bureaucracy*. Toronto: Free Press of Glencoe.

Gow, David. 1993. Doubly Damned. Dealing with Power and Praxis in Development Anthropology. *Human Organization* 52(4): 380–397.

Gramsci, Antonio. 1953. *Note sul Machiavelli sulla Politica e sullo Stato Moderno*. Turin: Giulio Einaudi Editore.

Greenhouse, Carol A. 1985. Mediation: A Comparative Approach. *Man* 20(1): 90–113

Gregory, Derek. 1994. *Geographical Imaginations*. Cambridge and Oxford: Blackwell.

Greimas, A. J. 1983. *Du Sens II: Essais Sémiotiques*. Paris: Éditions du Seuil.

Grillo, Ralph, and Alan Rew. 1985. *Social Anthropology and Development Policy*. ASA Monographs 23. London: Tavistock Publications.

Grünwald, Guillermo Kaul. 1982. *Misiones, Clave de la Cuenca del Plata (Brasil, Fronteras en Marcha)*. Posadas: Copilandia (CEIM).

Gupta, Akhil, and James Ferguson. 1992. Beyond Culture: Space, Identity, and the Politics of Difference. *Cultural Anthropology* 7: 6–23.

Habermas, Jürgen. 1975. *Legitimation Crisis*. Boston: Beacon Press.

—— 1979. *Communication and the Evolution of Society*. Boston: Beacon Press.

—— 1984. *The Theory of Communicative Action*, Vol. 1. Boston: Beacon Press.

Hall, Richard. 1982. *Organizations, Structure and Process*. Englewood Cliffs, N.J.: Prentice Hall.

Halperin Donghi, Tulio. 1980. Una Nación para el Desierto Argentino. In *Proyecto y Construcción de una Nación (Argentina 1846–1880)*, Tulio Halperín Donghi, ed. pp. XI–CI. Caracas: Biblioteca Ayacucho.

Harvey, David. 1989. *The Condition of Postmodernity*. Cambridge, MA: Blackwell.

——— 1996. *Justice, Nature, and the Geography of Difference*. Cambridge, MA: Blackwell.

Havelange, Françoise. 1991. *Liberer la Parole Paysanne au Sahel*. Paris: L'Harmattan.

Hermitte, Esther, and Mauricio Boivin. 1985. Erradicación de Villas Miseria y las Respuestas Organizativas de sus Pobladores. In *Relocalizados: Antropología Social de las Poblaciones Desplazadas*, Leopoldo Bartolomé, ed. pp. 119–143. Buenos Aires: Instituto de Desarrollo Económico y Social.

Hernández, José. 1980[1870]. El Paraguay, El Comercio y la Alianza. In *Proyecto y Construcción de una Nación, Argentina (1846–1880)* Halperín Donghi, ed. pp. 284–288. Caracas: Biblioteca Ayacucho.

Hernández, Rafael. 1973[1887]. *Cartas Misioneras*. Buenos Aires: Editorial Universitaria de Buenos Aires.

Hettne, Bjorn. 1982. *Development Theory and Third World*. Stockhom: Sarec.

Hinshaw, Robert E. 1980. Anthropology, Administration and Public Policy. *Annual Review of Anthropology* 9: 497–522.

Hobart, Mark, ed. 1993. *An Anthropological Critique of Development. The Growth of Ignorance*. New York: Routledge.

Hoben, Allan. 1982. Anthropologists and Development. *Annual Review of Anthropology* 11: 349–375.

——— 1984. The Role of the Anthropologist in Development Work: An Overview. In *Training Manual in Development Anthropology*, William Partridge, ed. pp. 9–17. Washington, D.C.: American Anthropological Association and Society for Applied Anthropology.

Hopenhayn, Martín. 1994. *Ni Apocalípticos ni Integrados. Aventuras de la Modernidad en América Latina*. Santiago, Chile: Fondo de Cultura Económica.

Horowitz, Michael. 1996. Thoughts on Development Anthropology after Twenty Years. In *Transforming Societies, Transforming Anthropology*, Emilio Moran, ed. pp. 325–351. Ann Arbor, MI: The University of Michigan Press.

——— 1997. On Not Offending the Borrower: (Self?)-Ghettoization of Anthropology at the World Bank. *Development Anthropologist* 14(1 and 2): 1–12.

Hymes, Dell. 1974[1969]. *Reinventing Anthropology*. New York: Pantheon Books.

Jackson, Bernard. 1985. *Semiotics and Legal Theory*. London: Routledge and Kegan Paul.

Jackson, Jean. 1995. Culture, Genuine and Spurious. The Politics of Indiannes in the Vaupés, Colombia. *American Ethnologist* 22(1): 3–27.

Jakobson, Roman. 1964. Closing Statement: Linguistics and Poetics. In *Style in Language*, T. Sebeok, ed. pp. 350–377. Cambridge, MA: MIT Press.

Jaume, Fernando, and Marta Rombo de Jaume. 1984. *Comunidades Marginales del Departamento Capital*. Posadas: Universidad Nacional de Misiones, Facultad de Humanidades y Ciencias Sociales.

Johnston, R. J., Peter J. Taylor, and Michael J. Watts. 1995. *Geographies of Global Change. Remapping the World in the Late Twentieth Century*. Cambridge, MA: Blackwell.

Jones, Delmos. 1970. Towards a Native Anthropology. *Human Organization* 29(4): 251.

References   211

———— 1976. Applied Anthropology and the Application of Anthropological Knowledge. *Human Organization* 35(3): 221–229.

Kearney, Michael. 1991. Borders and Boundaries of State and Self at the End of Empire. *Journal of Historical Sociology* 4(2): 52–74.

———— 1995. The Local and the Global: The Anthropology of Globalization and Transnationalism. *Annual Review of Anthropology* 24:547–65.

———— 1996. *Reconceptualizing the Peasantry. Anthropology in Global Perspective.* Boulder, CO, and Oxford: Westview Press.

Kitching, G. 1982. *Development and Underdevelopment in Historical Perspective. Populism, Nationalism, and Industrialization.* New York: Methuen.

Knippers Black, Jan. 1991. *Development in Theory and Practice: Bridging the Gap.* Boulder, CO: Westview Press.

Kothari, Rajni. 1989. *Rethinking Development.* New York: New Horizon Press.

———— 1993. Masses, Classes, and the State. In *New Social Movements in the South*, Ponna Wignaraja, ed. pp. 59–75. New Delhi: Sage.

Laclau, Ernesto. 1979. *Politics and Ideology in Marxist Theory.* London: Verso.

———— 1985. New Social Movements and the Plurality of the Social. In *New Social Movements and the State in Latin America.* David Slater, ed. pp. 27–42 Amsterdam: CEDLA.

Laclau, Ernesto and Chantal Mouffe. 1992. *Hegemony and Socialist Strategy.* New York: Verso.

Laplanche, Jean and J. B. Pontalis. 1976. *Vocabulaire de la Psychanalyse.* Paris: Presses Universitaires de France.

Larrain, Jorge. 1983. *Marxism and Ideology.* London: Macmillan Press.

Latouche, Serge. 1989. *L'Occidentalisation du Monde.* Paris: Editions La Découverte.

———— 1993. *In the Wake of the Affluent Society. An Exploration of Post-Development.* Atlantic Highlands, N.J.: Zed Books.

Latour, Bruno, and Steve Woolgar. 1986. *Laboratory Life. The Construction of Scientific Facts.* Princeton: Princeton University Press.

Laurelli, Elsa. 1988. *Los Grandes Proyectos: Las Políticas del Estado y la Respuesta Local en la Transformación del Territorio, una Aproximación Metodológica.* Buenos Aires: Centro de Estudios Urbanos y Regionales.

Lawson, Michael. 1982. *Damned Indians: The Pick-Sloan Plan and the Missouri River Sioux, 1944–1980.* Norman, OK: University of Oklahoma Press.

Lechner, Norbert. 1986a. *La Conflictiva y Nunca Acabada Construcción del Orden Deseado.* Madrid: Centro de Investigaciones Sociológicas–Siglo XXI de España Editores.

———— 1986b. *Estado y Política en América Latina.* México: Siglo XXI.

Leistritz, Larry, and Steven H. Murdock. 1981. *The Socioeconomic Impact of Resource Development.* Boulder, CO: Westview Press.

Linkenbach, Antje. 1994. Ecological Movements and the Critique of Development: Agents and Interpreters. *Thesis Eleven* 39: 63–85.

Linnekin, Jocelyn. 1991. Cultural Invention and the Dilemma of Authenticity. *American Anthropologist* 93(2): 446–449.

Lista, Ramón. 1883. *El Territorio de las Misiones.* Buenos Aires: Imprenta La Universidad.

Little, Peter and Michael Painter. 1995. Discourse, Politics, and the Development Process: Reflections on Escobar's "Anthropology and the Development Encounter." *American Ethnologist* 22(3): 602–607.

Lomnitz, Larissa. 1979. Anthropology and Development in Latin America. *Human Organization* 38(3): 313–317.

Long, Norman and Ann Long. 1992. *The Battlefields of Knowledge: The Interlocking of Theory and Practice in Social Research and Development*. New York: Routledge.

Loomis, Charles. 1960. *Social Systems. Essays on their Persistence and Change*. Princeton, N.J.: Van Nostrand.

Lugones, Leopoldo. 1981[1904]. *El Imperio Jesuítico*. Buenos Aires: Editorial de Belgrano.

Lukes, Steven, ed. 1986. *Power*. New York: New York University Press.

Lyotard, Jean-François. 1974. *Discours, Figure*. Paris: Éditions Klincksieck.

Machiavelli, Niccolo. 1953[1532]. The Prince. In *Three Rennaissance Classics*, pp. 3–101 New York: Charles Scribner's Sons.

Manzi, Francisco. 1910. *Impresiones de Viaje. Breves Apuntes sobre el Territorio de Misiones*. Corrientes, Argentina: La Popular.

Marchand, Marianne H., and Jane L. Parpart, eds. 1995. *Feminism/ Postmodernism/Development*. New York: Routledge.

Marcus, George, and Fischer, Michael. 1986. Anthropology as Cultural Critique. An Experimental Moment in the Human Sciences. Chicago: University of Chicago Press.

Marqués, Norma, and Alejandro Rofman. 1995. Economías Regionales e Integración económica con el Brasil. In *Integración y Sociedad en el Cono Sur. Las Relaciones con el Mercosur y Chile*, Marta Bekerman and Alejandro Rofman, eds. pp. 87–142. Buenos Aires: Espacio Editorial.

Marx, Karl. 1964. *Early Writings*. New York: Mc Graw Hill Book Company.

———— 1987. *Capital* Vol. 1. New York: International Publishers.

Mato, Daniel. 1994. *Teoría de la Construcción de Identidades y Diferencias en América Latina y el Caribe*. Caracas: UNESCO, Nueva Sociedad.

———— 1996. On the Theory, Epistemology, and Politics of the Social Construction of "Cultural Identities" in the Age of Globalization: Introductory Remarks to Ongoing Debates. *Identities* 3(1–2): 61–62.

Mayntz, Renate. 1978. *Sociología de la Administración Pública*. Madrid: Alianza Editorial.

Melkote, Srinivas R. 1991. *Communication for Development in the Third World. Theory and Practice*.Newbury Park, CA: Sage Publications.

Melucci, Alberto. 1996. *Challenging Codes. Collective Action in the Information Age*. New York: Cambridge University Press.

Merquior, J. Q. 1979. *The Veil and the Mask: Essays on Culture and Ideology*. London: Routledge and Kegan Paul.

Messer-Davidow, Ellen, David R. Shumway, and David J. Sylvan, eds. 1993. Introduction: Disciplinary Ways of Knowing. In *Knowledges: Historical and Critical Studies in Disciplinarity*. Charlottsville: University Press of Virginia.

Messerschmidt, Donald A. 1981. *Anthropologists at Home in North America. Methods and Issues in the Study of One's Own Society*. New York: Cambridge University Press.

Mitre, Bartolomé. 1980. Cartas a Juan Carlos Gómez. In *Proyecto y Construcción de una Nación (Argentina 1846–1880)*, Tulio Halperín Donghi, ed. pp. 208–218. Caracas: Biblioteca Ayacucho.

Miyoshi, Maseo. 1993. A Borderless World? From Colonialism to Transnationalism and the Decline of the Nation-State. *Critical Inquiry* 19(4): 727–751.

Moemeka, Andrew A. 1994. *Communicating for Development. A New Pan-Disciplinary Perspective*. Albany, N.Y.: State University of New York Press.

Moran, Emilio. 1996. An Agenda for Anthropology. In *Transforming Societies, Transforming Anthropology*. Emilio Moran, ed. pp. 1–24. Ann Arbor, MI: The University of Michigan Press.

Moore, Henrietta. 1994. *A Passion for Difference*. Indianapolis: Indiana University Press.

Morse, Richard. 1965. *The Bandeirantes: The Historical Role of the Brazilian Pathfinders.* New York: Knopf.

——1972. A Prolegomenon to Latin American Urban History. *Hispanic American Historical Review* 52(3): 359–394.

Mouzelis, Nicos. 1967. *Organization and Bureaucracy: An Analysis of Modern Theories.* Chicago: Aldine Publishing Company.

Murphy, Kathleen. 1983. *Macroproject Development in the Third World: An Analysis of Transnational Partnerships.* Boulder, CO: Westview Press.

Nandy, Ashis. 1994. Culture, Voice and Development: A Primer for the Unsuspecting. *Thesis Eleven* 39:1–18.

Nash, June. 1997. When Isms become Wasms. Structural Functionalism, Marxism, Feminism, and Postmodernism. *Critique of Anthropology* 17(1): 11–32.

Nun, José. 1969. Superpoblación Relativa, Ejército de Reserva y Masa Marginal. *Revista Latinoamericana de Sociología* 5(2): 178–235.

——1987. La Teoría Política y la Transición Democrática. In *Ensayos sobre la Transición Democrática en la Argentina,* José Nun and Juan Carlos Portantiero, eds. pp. 15–56. Buenos Aires: Puntosur.

Offe, Claus. 1985. *Disorganized Capitalism: Contemporary Transformations of Work and Politics.* Cambridge, MA: MIT Press.

Ortner, Sherry. 1984. Theory in Anthropology Since the Sixties. *Comparative Studies in Society and History* 26: 126–166.

Palomares, Marta. 1975. *Estructura Agraria de Misiones, Parte I: Evolución de la Pequeña Propiedad Rural y la Tenencia de la Tierra en Misiones.* Posadas: Universidad Nacional de Misiones, Centro de Investigaciones Sociales.

Parajuli, Pramod. 1996. Ecological Ethnicity in the Making: Developmentalist Hegemonies and Emergent Identities in India. *Identities* 3(1–20): 15–59.

Parkin, David. 1985. Controlling the U-Turn of Knowledge. In *Power and Knowledge: Anthropological and Sociological Approaches.* Proceedings of a Conference Held at the University of St. Andrews, December 1982, Richard Fardon, ed. pp. 49–60. Edinburgh: Scottish Academic Press.

Partridge, William. 1985. Reasentamiento de Comunidades: Los Roles de los Grupos Corporativos en las Relocalizaciones Urbanas. In *Relocalizados,* Leopoldo Bartolomé, ed. pp. 52–66. Buenos Aires: Instituto de Desarrollo Económico y Social.

——, ed. 1984. *Training Manual in Development Anthropology.* Washington, D.C.: American Anthropological Association and Society for Applied Anthropology.

Peattie, Lisa. 1981. Thinking about Development. New York: Plenum Press.

Pecheux, Michel. 1975. *Les Vérités de la Palice.* Paris: Maspero.

Peet, Richard, and Michael Watts. 1996. Liberation Ecology. In *Liberation Ecologies. Environment, Development, Social Movements.* Richard Peet and Michael Watts, eds. pp. 1–45. New York: Routledge.

Peyret, Alexis. 1889. *Une Visite aux Colonies de la Republique Argentine.* Paris: Société Anonyme de Publications Périodiques.

Pfaffenberger, Bryan. 1988. Fetishised Objects and Humanized Nature: Towards an Anthropology of Technology. *Man* 23(2): 236–252.

Pickering, Andrew. 1996. *The Mangle of Practice. Time, Agency and Science.* Chicago: University of Chicago Press.

Pitt, David, ed. 1976. *Development from Below. Anthropologists and Development Situations.* The Hague: Mouton Publishers.

Pomer, León. 1968. *La Guerra del Paraguay. Gran Negocio!* Buenos Aires: Ediciones Caldén.

Pred, Allan, and Michael John Watts. 1992. *Reworking Modernity. Capitalisms and Symbolic Discontent*. New Brunswick, N.J.: Rutgers University Press.

Prigogine, Ilya. 1980. *From Being to Becoming. Time and Complexity in the Physical Sciences*. New York: W.H. Freeman and Co.

————1984. *Order out of Chaos: Man's New Dialogue with Nature*. New York: Bantam Books.

Prigogine, Ilya, and Isabelle Stengers. 1988. *Entre le Temps et l'Éternité*. France: Fayard.

Provincia de Misiones. 1988. Boletín Oficial 7294, May 4.

Puiggrós, Rodolfo. 1969. *De la Colonia a la Revolución*. Buenos Aires: Carlos Pérez Editor.

Radcliffe, Sarah and Sallie Westwood. 1996. *Remaking the Nation. Place, Identity, and Politics in Latin America*. London and New York: Routledge.

Rahnema, M. 1992. Participation. In *The Development Dictionary. A Guide to Knowledge as Power*, Sachs, W., ed. pp. 116–132. London: Zed Books.

Refslund Sorensen, Birgitte. 1997. The Expereince of Displacemente: Reconstructing Places and Identities in Sri Lanka. In *Siting Culture. The Shifting Anthropological Object*, Karen Fog Olwig and Kirsten Hastrup, ed. pp. 142–164. London and New York: Routledge.

República Argentina. 1914a. *Boletín del Departamento Nacional del Trabajo. No. 26.* Buenos Aires: Imprenta Alsina.

———— 1914b. *Censo de Población de los Territorios Nacionales. República Argentina, 1912.* Buenos Aires: Dirección General de Territorios Nacionales.

————1982. *Censo Nacional de Población y Viviendas 1980, Serie B. Características Generales: Provincia de Misiones*. Buenos Aires: Instituto Nacional de Estadísticas y Censos, Ministerio de Economía.

Rew, Alan. 1985. The Organizational Connection: Multidisciplinary Practice and Anthropological Theory. In *Social Anthropology and Development Policy*, Ralph Grillo and Alan Rew, eds. pp. 185–197. London and New York: Tavistock Publications.

Ribeiro, Gustavo. 1985. Proyectos de Gran Escala: Hacia un Marco Conceptual para el Análisis de una Forma de Producción Temporaria. In *Relocalizados*, Leopoldo Bartolomé, ed. pp. 23–47. Buenos Aires: Instituto de Desarrollo Económico y Social.

————1994. *Transnational Capitalism and Hydropolitics in Argentina. The Yacyretá High Dam*. Gainesville, FL: University Press of Florida.

Ricardo, Cassiano. 1956. *La Marcha Hacia el Oeste*. Mexico: Fondo de Cultura Económica. Tierra Firme.

Robertson, A. F. 1984. *People and the State. An Anthropology of Planned Development*. Cambridge: Cambridge University Press.

Rock, David. 1993. Antecedents of the Argentine Right. In *The Argentine Right. Its History and Intellectual Origins*, 1910 to the Present. Sandra McGee Deutsch and Ronald H. Dolkart, eds. pp. 1–34. Wilmington, DE: SR Books.

Rofman, Alejandro. 1983. *Monetarismo y Crisis en el Nordeste*. Buenos Aires: Ediciones CEUR.

————1984. *Evaluación Comparativa de las Metodologías Aplicadas en los Estudios de Grandes Represas*. Posadas: Universidad Nacional de Misiones and Entidad Binacional Yacyretá.

Rofman, Alejandro, Fernando Brunstein, Elsa Laurelli, and Alicia Vidal, eds. 1987. *Los Grandes Proyectos y el Espacio Regional. Presas Hidroeléctricas y el Sistema Decisional*. Cuadernos del CEUR 19. Buenos Aires: Centro de Estudios Urbanos y Regionales.

Rogers, Mark. 1996. Beyond Authenticity: Conservation, Tourism, and the Politics of Representation in the Ecuadorian Amazon. *Identities* 3(1-2): 73–125.

Rojas, Isaac Francisco. 1979. *La Ofensiva Geopolítica Brasileña en la Cuenca del Plata*. Buenos Aires: Nemont Ediciones.
————1980. *Una Geopolítica Nacional Desintegrante*. Buenos Aires: Nemont Ediciones.
Romero, José Luis. 1979. *Breve Historia de la Argentina*. Buenos Aires: Huemul.
————1986. *Situaciones e Ideologías en Latinoamérica*. Buenos Aires: Editorial Sudamericana.
Rossi Landi, Ferruccio. 1970. *El Lenguaje como Trabajo y como Mercado*. Venezuela: Monte Avila.
Rostow, W. 1960. *The Stages of Economic Growth, A Non-Communist Manifesto*. Cambridge: Cambridge University Press.
Routledge, Paul. 1993. *Terrains of Resistance. Nonviolent Social Movements and the Contestation of Place in India*. Westport, CT: Praeger.
Rozitchner, León. 1992. El Terror de los Desencantados. In *Rebeldes y Domesticados. Los Intelectuales Frente al Poder*. Raquel Angel, ed. pp. 38–48. Buenos Aires: Ediciones el Cielo por Asalto.
Sábato, Jorge F. 1988. *La Clase Dominante en la Argentina Moderna*. Buenos Aires: CISEA. Grupo Editor Latinoamericano.
Salisbury, Richard. 1976. The Anthropologist as Societal Ombudsman. In *Development from Below*, David Pitt, ed. pp. 255–265. The Hague: Mouton Publishers.
————1986. *A Homeland for the Cree. Regional Development in James Bay, 1971–1981*. Montreal: Mc Gill Queens's University Press.
Santos, Leinard Ayer, and Lúcia M. M. de Andrade. 1989. *As Hidreletricas do Xingu e os Povos Indigenas*. Sao Paulo: Comissao Pró-Indio de Sao Paulo.
Sarmiento, Domingo Faustino. 1961[1845]. *Life in the Argentine Republic in the Days of the Tyrants or, Civilization and Barbarism*. New York: Collier Books. (In Spanish, *Facundo: Civilización y Barbarie*. Buenos Aires: Kapelusz, 1971).
Schamber, Hugo R. 1984. *Perspectivas del Trabajo Social en Programas de Relocalización de Población Afectada por la Construcción de Represas Hidroeléctricas*. Posadas: Entidad Binacional Yacyretá.
Schilling, Paulo. 1978. *El Expansionismo Brasileño*. Buenos Aires: El Cid Editor.
Schneider, Cathy. 1995. Radical Opposition Parties and Squatters Movements in Pinochet's Chile. In *The Making of Social Movements in Latin America. Identity, Strategy, and Democracy*. Arturo Escobar and Sonia Alvarez, eds. pp. 260–275. Boulder, CO: Westview Press.
Scholte, Bob. 1974[1969]. Toward a Reflexive and Critical Anthropology. In *Reinventing Anthropology*, Dell Hymes, ed. pp. 430–457. New York: Vintage Books.
Schwartzman, Helen B. 1980. The Bureaucratic Context of a Community Mental Health Center: The View from "Up." In *Hierarchy and Society. Anthropological Perspectives on Bureaucracy*, Gerald Brittan and Ronald Cohen, eds. pp. 45–58. Philadelphia, PA: Institute for the Study of Human Issues (ISHI).
Scoones, I., and J. Thompson. 1994. *Beyond Farmer First: Rural People's Knowledge, Agricultural Research Extension Practice*. London: Intermediate Technology Publications.
Scudder, Thayer, and Elizabeth Colson. 1987[1972]. The Kariba Dam Project. Resettlement and Local Initiative. In *Technology and Social Change*, R. Bernard and P. Pelto, ed. pp. 41–71. New York: Macmillan.
————1982. From Welfare to Development: A Conceptual Framework for the Analysis of Dislocated People. In *Involuntary Migration and Resettlement*, A. Hansen and Oliver Smith, eds. pp. 267–287. Boulder, CO: Westview Press.
Searle, J. R. 1974. *The Philosophy of Language*. London: Oxford University Press.

Selznick, P. 1966[1949]. *TVA and the Grass Roots*. Berkeley, CA: University of California Press.

Serber, David. 1981. The Masking of Social Reality. In *Anthropologists at home in North America. Methods and Issues in the Study of One's Own Society*, Donald Messerschmidt, ed. pp. 77–87. New York: Cambridge University Press.

Shumway, Nicolas. 1991. *The Invention of Argentina*. Berkeley, CA: University of California Press.

Sikkink, Kathryn. 1991. *Ideas and Institutions. Developmentalism in Brazil and Argentina*. Ithaca, N.Y.: Cornell University Press.

Silverstein, Michael. 1976. Shifters, Linguistic Categories, and Cultural Description. In *Meaning in Anthropology*, Keith Basso and Henry Selby, eds. pp. 11–55. Albuquerque, NM: University of New Mexico Press.

Slater, David. 1985. Social Movements and a Recasting of the Political. In *New Social Movements and the State in Latin America*, David Slater, ed. Amsterdam: CEDLA.

———1995. Trajectories of Development Theory: Capitalism, Socialism and Beyond. In *Geographies of Global Change. Remapping the World in the Late Twentieth Century*. R. J. Johnston, Peter J. Taylor, and Michael Watts, eds. pp. 63–76. Oxford: Blackwell.

Smith, Carol A. 1996. Development and the State. In *Transforming Societies, Transforming Anthropology*, Emilio Moran, ed. pp. 25–56. Ann Arbor, MI: The University of Michigan Press.

Smith, Dorothy. 1990. *The Conceptual Practices of Power: A Feminist Scociology of Knowledge*. Boston: Northeastern University Press.

Smith, Neil. 1984. *Uneven Development. Nature, Capital, and the Production of Space*. New York: Blackwell.

Smith, Paul. 1988. *Discerning the Subject*. Minneapolis, MN: University of Minnesota Press.

Spegazzini, Carlos. 1914. *Al Través de Misiones*. La Plata: Talleres de Joaquín Sese.

Spivak, Gayatri. 1988. Can the Subaltern Speak? In *Marxism and the Interpretation of Culture*. Cary Nelson and Lawrence Grossberg, eds. pp. 271–313. Urbana: University of Illinois Press.

Stavenhagen, Rodolfo. 1971. Decolonizing Applied Social Sciences. *Human Organization* 30(4): 333–357.

Strathern, Marylin. 1985. Knowing Power and Being Equivocal: Three Melanesian Contexts. In *Power and Knowledge*, Richard Fardon, ed. pp. 61–81. Edinburgh: Scottish Academic Press.

Suárez, Francisco, Rolando Franco, Ernesto Cohen, eds. 1983. *Lo Social en las Grandes Represas: Elementos para una Estrategia*. Buenos Aires: OEA-CEPAL-ILPES. (Mimeog.)

Tambiah, Stanley Jeyarana. 1985. *Culture, Thought and Social Action: An Anthropological Perspective*. Cambridge, MA: Harvard University Press.

Taylor, Peter. 1989. *Political Geography. World-Economy, Nation-State and Locality*. New York: John Wiley and Sons.

Therborn, Göran. 1980. *The Ideology of Power and the Power of Ideology*. London: Verso.

Thompson, John B. 1984. *Studies in the Theory of Ideology*. Berkeley, CA: University of California Press.

Todorov, Tzvetan. 1984. *Mikhail Bakhtin: The Dialogical Principle*. Minneapolis, MN: University of Minnesota Press.

Turner, Víctor. 1967. *The Forest of Symbols*. Ithaca, New York: Cornell University Press.

Universidad Nacional de Misiones. 1982. *Estudio Sobre los Medios de Subsistencia y la*

Capacidad de Pago de la Población No-Propietaria de la Etapa I. Posadas: Instituto de Investigación. Facultad de Humanidades y Ciencias Sociales.

———1988. *Informe Sobre el Programa Pobreza Urbana en la Ciudad de Posadas.* Posadas: Instituto de Investigación, Facultad de Humanidades y Ciencias Sociales.

Van Gennep, Arnold. 1960[1908]. *The Rites of Passage.* London: Routledge and Kegan Paul.

Van Ufford, D. Q., and T. Downing, eds. 1988. *The Hidden Crisis in Development: Development Bureaucracies.* Amsterdam: Free University Press and United Nations Press.

Van Willigen, John. 1984. Truth and Effectiveness: An Essay on the Relationships Between Information, Policy and Action in Applied Anthropology. *Human Organization* 43(3): 277–282.

Verón, Eliseo. 1971. Condiciones de Producción, Modelos Generativos y Manifestación Ideológica. In *El Proceso Ideológico*, Eliseo Verón, ed. pp. 251–292. Buenos Aires: Editorial Tiempo Contemporáneo.

———1980. *La Semiosis Social.* Mexico: Universidad Autónoma de México y Editorial Nueva Imagen.

———1984. Semiosis de lo Ideológico y del Poder. *Espacios* 1: 43–51.

Viladrich Morera, Alberto. 1972. *América Latina. La Planificación Hidráulica y los Planificadores.* Santiago de Chile. Editorial Universitaria.

Viñas, David. 1992. Las Astucias de la Servidumbre. In *Rebeldes y Domesticados. Los Intelectuales Frente al Poder.* Raquel Angel, ed. pp. 49–66. Buenos Aires: Ediciones El Cielo por Asalto.

Voloshinov, V. 1973. *Marxism and the Philosophy of Language.* London: Academic Press.

Von Clausewitz, Karl. 1968. *On War.* Vol. 1. London: Routledge and Kegan.

Wali, Alaka. 1982. *Panamá's Dams: Consequences for the Indian People. Hydroelectrics in Central and South America.* Bulletin 11. Boston: Anthropology Resource Center.

———1989. *Kilowatts and Crisis: A Study of Development and Social Change in Panama.* Boulder, CO: Westview Press.

Wallace, Anthony. 1956. Mazeway Desintegration. The Individual's Perception of Socio-Cultural Disorganization. *Human Organization* 16(2): 23–27.

Watts, Michael. 1996. Mapping Identities. Place, and Community in an African City. In *The Geography of Identity.* Patricia Yaeger, ed. pp. 59–97. Ann Arbor, MI: University of Michigan Press.

Weaver, Thomas. 1985. Anthropology as a Policy Science: Part II, Development and Training. *Human Organization* 44 (2): 97–105.

Weber, Max. 1968. *Economy and Society.* New York: Bedminister Press.

Wignaraja, Ponna. 1993. Rethinking Development and Democracy. In *New Social Movements in the South*, Ponna Wignaraja, ed. pp. 5–35. New Delhi: Sage Publications.

Williams, Raymond. 1973. *The Country and the City.* New York: Oxford University Press.

Wolf, Eric. 1982. *Europe and the People Without History.* Berkeley, CA: University of California Press.

———1991. Distinguished Lecture: Facing Power—Old Insights, New Questions. *American Anthropologist* 92 (3): 586–596.

World Bank. 1990. *Operational Directive. O.D. 4.30.* Washington, D.C.: The World Bank.

———1996. *Social Development and Results on the Ground. Task Group Report.* October 15. Washington, D.C.: The World Bank.

———1997. *Resettlement Planning Guidance.* #783. Washington D.C.: The World Bank.

Yamamoto, Yoshinobi. 1996. Regionalizaton in Contemporary International Relations. In *Regionalization in the World Economy. Nafta, The Americas and Asia Pacific.* Van R. Whiting Jr., ed. pp. 19–42. New Delhi: Macmillan India Ltd.

Zeballos, Estanislao. 1893. Arbitration Upon a Part of the National History of Misiones Disputed by the United States of Brazil. Argentine Evidence.

Zinny, Antonio. 1975. *Bibliografía Histórica del Paraguay y de Misiones*. Buenos Aires: Editorial Monserrat.

Zizek, Slavoj. 1989. *The Sublime Object of Ideology*. New York: Verso.

————1994. *Tarrying with the Negative. Kant, Hegel, and the Critique of Ideology*. Durham, NC: Duke University Press.

Index

About the Author

CARMEN A. FERRADÁS is Assistant Professor of Anthropology at Binghamton University, State University of New York. She has taught at the Universidad Nacional de Buenos Aires and at the Universidad Nacional de Misiones, Argentina.

ISBN 0-89789-560-6

EAN

9 780897 895606

HARDCOVER BAR CODE

DATE DUE

GAYLORD

PRINTED IN U.S.A.